second edition

APPRENTICESHIP IN LITERACY

second edition

APPRENTICESHIP IN LITERACY

Transitions Across Reading and Writing, K–4

Linda J. Dorn
and Tammy Jones

Stenhouse Publishers
Portland, Maine

Stenhouse Publishers
www.stenhouse.com

Credits
Page 15: Excerpted lines from *Nighttime* by Joy Cowley. Copyright © 1990. Reprinted with permission of McGraw-Hill Education.
Page 32: Excerpted lines from *Pumpkin, Pumpkin* by Jeanne Titherington. Copyright © 1986 by Jeanne Titherington. Used by permission of HarperCollins Publishers.
Page 32: Excerpted lines from *The Doorbell Rang* by Pat Hutchins. Copyright © 1986 by Pat Hutchins. Used by permission of HarperCollins Publishers.

Library of Congress Cataloging-in-Publication Data
Dorn, Linda J.
  Apprenticeship in literacy : transitions across reading and writing, K-4 / Linda J. Dorn and Tammy Jones. -- 2nd ed.
      p. cm.
  Includes bibliographical references and index.
  ISBN 978-1-57110-966-8 (pbk. : alk. paper) -- ISBN 978-1-57110-971-2 (ebook) 1. Language arts (Early childhood)--United States. 2. Reading (Early childhood)--United States. 3. English language--Composition and exercises--Study and teaching (Early childhood)--United States. I. Jones, Tammy (Tammy P.) II. Title.
  LB1139.5.L35D67 2012
  372.6--dc23
                                                                                            2012013881

Cover design, interior design, and typesetting by designboy Creative Group

Manufactured in the United States of America

PRINTED ON 30% PCW
RECYCLED PAPER

18 17 16 15 14   9 8 7 6 5 4 3

To all the extraordinary literacy teachers and coaches who have allowed us to learn from you. These experiences are the heartbeat of this book. Also, to the memory of Marie Clay, one of the most influential educators in literacy history. We will always be humbled by the opportunity to have learned from you.

CONTENTS

ACKNOWLEDGMENTS

It's been almost fifteen years since the first edition of *Apprenticeship in Literacy* (1998), and a lot has happened since then. In 1998, Linda was a Reading Recovery trainer at the University of Arkansas at Little Rock (UALR), Tammy and Cathy (coauthors of the first edition) were Reading Recovery teacher leaders, and Carla (one of the spotlighted teachers in the book) was a Reading Recovery teacher.

Now, in 2012, Linda remains at the university, where she is a professor of reading education and director of the UALR Center for Literacy. Tammy went on to become the vice president for professional development for Benchmark Education; Cathy returned to teaching in the public school system; and Carla moved to the university, where she and Linda have collaborated on numerous literacy projects, including coauthoring four books. Although we, Linda and Tammy, are the coauthors of this new edition, we are cognizant of the contributions of Cathy and Carla, our colleagues and friends, in its pages.

Cathy, thank you for all you did to make the first edition a success. You were always in the schools, working alongside the teachers while also providing interventions for struggling readers. You were the creative (and practical) mind behind the design considerations of the literacy centers in the first edition. And as you will notice, we kept most of the activities, because they are just as relevant today as they were fifteen years ago. As we worked on the new edition, we could feel your presence with us.

Carla, it is impossible to put into words how much we appreciate all you have done to support children and teachers. In writing the first edition, we were in your classroom as much as we were in our offices, observing your masterful teaching and collaborating on ways to accelerate the literacy development of struggling readers. We always had a video camera handy so we could capture the rich interactions between you and your children and then rush back to the office to transcribe these into stories for the chapters. You'll notice that we kept your stories in the new edition, because they are just as timeless today as they were fif-

teen years ago. And over the years, you and I (Linda) have become partners in numerous publications and literacy projects, including the development of the Comprehensive Intervention Model and the Partnerships in Comprehensive Literacy model. Your literacy voice is evident in the pages of this new edition.

In writing this book, we apprenticed ourselves to many people who have supported us with their insights, knowledge, and genuine understanding of teaching and learning. The list is so long that we are worried we might forget someone. If we do, please accept our sincere apology and know that we appreciate all of you!

Special Thanks

In the book, you will meet a number of teachers who apply the theories of apprenticeship learning to their daily interactions with children. As you read, you will also spend time in their classrooms. They play a very important role, and are inspiring professionals who are committed to ensuring that all their children are successful readers. Their dedication makes a difference in the lives of children. Their classrooms contain active learners who are always on the cutting edge of development. They truly listen to their students and observe the processes they engage in as they read and write. They continually formulate their theories as they interact with their students and in turn plan their instructional interactions based on these theories.

Simply put, this book would not have been possible without the teachers who are on the ground, working daily to ensure their children's literacy success. Whenever we have needed student work, classroom pictures, schedules, rubrics, or videotapes of teaching and learning, you have always been there for us. Your willingness to share your knowledge with other teachers has been constant—a characteristic of your professionalism. Each of you has contributed substantially to our work and has made a real difference in the lives of many children. We offer our sincere appreciation to these teachers: Michelle Amend, Vicki Atland, Dana Autry, Barbara Andrews, Leanne Bongers, Jennifer Boyle, Claudia Crespo, Brittany Howard, Nancy Garrett, Annyce Kuykendall, Kimberli Kern, Jennifer Kays, Jackie Long, Angela Owen, Harriet Pool, Judy Reed, Donnie Skinner, and Esther Watson.

We owe our sincere thanks to Penny Antell, literacy coach in D.C. Everest School in Weston, Wisconsin, and Jennifer Kimbrell, literacy coach in the North Little Rock School District in Arkansas, who supplied many of the photographs in Chapter 8. And we appreciate Brian Reindl, literacy coach, and the teachers at Washington School for Comprehensive Literacy in Sheboygan, Wisconsin, for sharing photographs of students' logs, anchor charts, and writing rubrics. We also appreciate the contributions of all the literacy coaches who are part of the Partnerships in Comprehensive Literacy network through the University of Arkansas at Little Rock. Your teaching is visible in the stories and examples we share throughout the book.

We extend special recognition to the literacy coaches, teachers, and administrators in the Council Bluffs Community School District in Council Bluffs, Iowa, for their contributions to Chapter 11. This talented staff includes Kim Kazmierczak, principal, and Jane Burgett, literacy coach, at Carter Lake Elementary School; Lori Swanson, principal, and Amy Murray, literacy coach, at Franklin Elementary; Darrin Praska, principal, and Gjoa King, literacy coach, at Edison Elementary; and Mark Schuldt, principal, and Amy Anderson, literacy coach, at Roosevelt Elementary. We also are grateful to the teacher researchers, Jennifer Kimbrell, Linda Holman, and Dianne Presley, whose work provides us with a model of what it means to be a classroom researcher.

We offer special thanks to Julie Eckberg, literacy consultant, and the staff at LeRoy Elementary in LeRoy, Illinois, for sharing your story in Chapter 11. Your journey brings life to what is discussed within books such as this, and as a result, it brings understanding. Through you, other educators are learning, and for that, we thank you. At LeRoy Elementary, thank you to Erin Conn, principal; Jill Morrison, special education teacher; Tricia Larkin, speech-language pathologist; Angie Clark, first-grade teacher, Julie Schopp, second-grade teacher; Kim Wohlwend, teacher assistant; and Linda MacLaughlin, kindergarten teacher. We appreciate your willingness to share the Common Core State Standards checklists and rubrics that you created during your team meetings. And a special thanks to Julie, for designing these forms, plus numerous other documents, that are in the appendices.

Finally, we understand that writing a book requires scaffolding from many others in our lives. Linda gives special appreciation to her UALR Reading Recovery colleagues, Janet Behrend, Barbara Schubert, Stephanie Copes, Patsy Conner, and Carla Soffos, for the many stimulating conversations we've had about literacy. Tammy offers special thanks to Tom and Sera Reycraft, the CEOs of Benchmark Education Company; and to Carrie Smith and Margie Burton for their unrelenting support and their extraordinary expertise in helping her stay focused on the importance of high-quality instruction and professional development for teachers.

In writing this book, we have sounded the theme of apprenticeship learning—a theory of helping others achieve their highest potential. We owe special appreciation to Philippa Stratton, our editor, without whose help and guidance this book would not be in your hands now. More than fifteen years ago, Philippa believed in our work and encouraged us to write our first book. Now with the second edition, she remains by our side with her gentle nudges and masterful comments. Thank you, Philippa, for allowing us to serve our apprenticeship in writing with you. We also owe thanks to Pat Johnson for her insightful comments on our manuscript, and we thank the entire Stenhouse team for their ongoing support of our work. Your commitment to teachers is evident in all you do, and we feel fortunate to be associated with you.

INTRODUCTION

What will it take to change the way students are taught? What will it take to close the learning gap? We don't need to overwhelm teachers with a long list of new methods to try. Rather we believe what is needed is a *theoretical model* that explicates the *teaching and learning process*; a model that will allow the integration of multiple teaching methods, and that will challenge educators to rethink their efforts.

—*Meichenbaum and Biemiller (1998)*

This quote from Meichenbaum and Biemiller seems an appropriate way to introduce the new edition of *Apprenticeship in Literacy*. Our purpose is to explain how a theory-based model of teaching and learning looks in an elementary classroom. We use Vygotskian theory to illustrate how children acquire higher-level understandings during assisted activities with a more knowledgeable person. This theory emphasizes the importance of the teacher as one who understands what the child brings to the learning task, but also understands how to help the child use his knowledge as a foundation for learning something new. We believe that teaching and learning occur in apprenticeship-type settings and that teachers use language and scaffolding techniques within meaningful contexts to engage children's minds in noticing, acquiring, and consolidating new knowledge. Throughout the book, we provide a myriad of authentic examples that illustrate how teachers apply apprenticeship theories to their instructional interactions with their students.

When we were approached about writing a second edition of this book, our first step was to determine what would remain in the text, what should be revised, and what new information should be included. During the past decade, schools have been bombarded with new initiatives (No Child Left Behind, Race to the Top, Response to Intervention, Common Core State Standards), which have increased the accountability for teacher performance (higher standards, high-stakes testing, teacher evaluations). Consequently, many schools have become vulnerable to the quick fixes that are associated with many programs and methods. This reality makes it even more critical for teachers to possess a strong theory of teaching and learning, as this theory will certainly in-fluence their perceptions and instructional practices. We believe that a strong theory, along with keen observation skills and high-quality resources, provides teachers with the data for making evidence-based decisions about student learning. In these pages, we demonstrate how teachers apply a theoretical model of teaching and learning to their everyday practices with their students. In the next section, we provide a brief overview of each chapter.

A Preview of the Chapters

Apprenticeship in Literacy is designed to help elementary teachers meet the needs of all students through differentiation and scaffolding techniques within a balanced literacy approach. We encourage teachers to begin with Chapter 1 and proceed through each chapter in order. After the first reading, the chapters should be revisited for more in-depth application and support.

In Chapter 1, we emphasize the importance of early reading success, including recent research on the relationship of third-grade reading proficiency to high school graduation, as well as other social and economic advantages. We stress the need for teachers to align their instructional goals across supplemental programs to promote self-regulation and transfer. The theme of early reading is carried over to the role of background knowledge and its relationship to self-regulated activity. The chapter includes information on the reflective learning cycle and how the brain works in constructing new knowledge, including the importance of motivation in the decision-making process. As with the first edition, the chapter is grounded in an apprenticeship theory where the teacher creates the conditions to mediate the students' learning.

In Chapter 2, the seven principles of apprenticeship learning are just as relevant today as they were in 1998, when the first edition of this book was published. The chapter elaborates on scaffolding principles and provides new examples of language prompts that teachers can use to assist students' learning. A critical aspect of self-regulated learning is the student's ability to initiate problem-solving strategies in the absence of the teacher. Therefore, we have included a new section on the use of nonverbal scaffolds as tools that promote students' independent learning. We believe this chapter is the heartbeat of the book, as it emphasizes the relationship between language, action, and the construction of literate knowledge.

In Chapter 3, we begin by discussing the cognitive and social processes of learning to read, and the teacher's role in creating the conditions for shaping children's literacy development. The teacher must understand how to interpret children's reading behaviors and how to design instruction that is based on their strengths and needs. A balanced literacy curriculum includes a range of literacy activities, carefully selected materials for each activity, and a responsive teacher who knows how to structure literacy interactions that move children to higher levels of understanding. The chapter maintains many of the examples from the first edition, but also includes new examples that illustrate how teachers are using a balanced literacy curriculum and incorporating informational texts in an apprenticeship approach.

Chapter 4 focuses on the implementation of a guided reading program within a balanced literacy framework. We include specific details, such as selecting the book, introducing the book, prompting during the first reading, and activities for subsequent readings, plus a new section on silent guided reading. As with the first edition, the reciprocity between reading and writing remains a focus. However, the new edition includes refinements to the transitional level, the addition of the fluent level, and an alignment of all behaviors (emergent to fluent) to the Common Core State Standards.

In Chapter 5, we describe two types of assisted writing: interactive writing and writing aloud. We provide details for implementing each type, including materials needed, the purpose of each type, procedural steps, and examples of rich interactions between teachers and children as they participate in assisted writing experiences. This new edition includes a section on self-help resources: writing checklists and writing guides. The goal of assisted writing is achieved when the children are able to transfer their knowledge to independent writing.

Chapter 6 emphasizes the independent-writing component of assisted writing. We focus on the transfer principle, and we encourage teachers to reflect on the effect of assisted performance on the students' independent performance. This second edition places a greater emphasis on the writing process, including the writing continuum of emergent to fluent writing behaviors that aligns with the Common Core State Standards, and several new examples of teacher/student writing conferences.

In Chapter 7, we share significant revisions and additions, including more details for assessing students' orthographic and phonological knowledge with implications for planning word study lessons. We kept many of the examples from the first edition; however, we expanded the word study section to include more activities at the transitional and fluent levels.

Chapter 8 focuses on organizing the environment for learning. We share how teachers can implement a workshop framework for differentiating instruction, including whole-group, small-group, and independent opportunities. In well-organized classrooms, children learn self-management techniques for regulating their learning across multiple contexts. In this chapter, we present details, including photographs and design considerations, of how teachers can create meaningful literacy centers that align with the classroom curriculum.

In Chapter 9, we emphasize the importance of high-quality classroom instruction for all children, while recognizing that some children will need additional support. We illustrate how a workshop framework provides a structure for integrating the curriculum while also differentiating instruction to meet student needs.

In Chapter 10, we emphasize that supplemental instruction must be aligned with classroom instruction, and that children must be able to transfer their knowledge, skills, and strategies across multiple contexts. In this chapter, we share details for implementing a small-group reading intervention.

The final chapter places the focus on teachers as reflective practitioners. Through reflective practice, teachers become more empowered decision makers, and they take more responsibility for their actions. We believe that learning to teach is an ongoing journey, and that teachers refine their craft of teaching through on-the-job professional learning experiences with other teachers. Teacher collaboration is essential to produce student learning, and the school is a natural learning lab for increasing teacher expertise. Within this context, teachers develop and test their theories of teaching and learning. They view themselves as classroom researchers—observing behavior, collecting evidence, collaborating with peers, constructing new knowledge, and sharing results. In this chapter, we share the stories from many teachers who are applying the principles of apprenticeship learning to their profession.

Closing Thoughts

We have been in education for more than half of our lives, and our experiences are reflected in the pages of this book. We began our careers as classroom teachers; then we became Reading Recovery educators; and for the past twenty years, we have been working directly with teachers, literacy coaches, and intervention specialists within their schools. The teachers keep us grounded in the realities of school, and we always learn a lot from being in their classrooms. This new edition of *Apprenticeship in Literacy* is full of photos, children's writing, and stories from real classrooms, and we hope you, our readers, enjoy reading the book as much as we have enjoyed writing it.

chapter one

THE RIGHT TO LITERACY

Since the first edition of *Apprenticeship in Literacy* (1998), education has been influenced by years of federal and state initiatives focused on teaching the struggling reader. As a result, instruction has been affected by the No Child Left Behind Act, Reading First, and, more recently, Response to Intervention and the Common Core State Standards. Throughout, we have maintained our belief that schools should invest in teachers' learning—in contrast to programs—for meeting the needs of all children, including those with reading difficulties. Rather than overwhelm teachers with an itemized list of standards and methods, we believe that teachers need a theory of teaching and learning—a theory that is grounded in responsive teaching and scaffolding techniques for ensuring their students' success.

In this second edition, we continue the themes of assisted performance and transitions in literacy learning. We discuss how learning theory and research-based practices provide an apprenticeship framework for scaffolding young learners. In this chapter, we argue that reading proficiency in the early grades is essential for future success, and we present a theory of interactive learning within social contexts. Why should schools invest so heavily in early reading? And why does a teacher's theory of teaching and learning matter?

Urgency of Early Reading Success

The urgency is real: if children do not become successful readers by the end of third grade, it is difficult for them to catch up with their peers in later years (Juel 1988; Snow, Burns, and Griffin 1998; National Research Council 1998). As a result, many groups have joined together to support a national agenda for early reading proficiency (see, for example, Annie E. Casey Foundation 2010).

Everyone agrees that the future of our nation depends on a literate society, and that the basic right for all people would be a high school education. Yet, in 2007 nearly 6.2 million young people did not earn this minimum degree (Center for Labor Market Studies 2009). The relationship between early reading proficiency and high school graduation is well documented. In fact, a longitudinal study of nearly four thousand students found that one in six children who were not reading proficiently by the end of third grade failed to graduate from high school on time, a rate that was four times greater than that of proficient readers (Hernandez 2011; Lesnick et al. 2010). This is an alarming statistic, which is further compounded by the fact that poor readers in the early grades are at risk of becoming adults with limited workforce opportunities. Indeed, the negative consequences of poor reading are far-reaching, impacting one's social, economic, and educational status in tomorrow's world.

The good news is that a teacher can prevent or reverse students' reading failure. Research shows that the teacher—not methods or programs—is the most important factor in a student's reading success (Allington 2002b). Teachers who know a lot about teaching and learning and who work in school environments that allow them to know their students well are the elements most critical to student achievement (Darling-Hammond and McLaughlin 1999). Many researchers have documented the relationship between high-quality classroom instruction and the success of at-risk readers. Yet we all know that simply immersing children in literacy-rich environments is not enough to offset the difficulties of struggling readers. For children to become successful learners, they need their teachers to be knowledgeable about the literacy process and to provide them with constructive reading and writing opportunities that guarantee their right to literacy.

Sociocognitive Theory in Teaching and Learning

Literacy is no longer regarded as simply a cognitive skill to be learned. Rather, it is viewed as a complex interactive and interpretive process whose development is determined by social and cultural context. As adults and children engage in interactive oral discussions about written language, children acquire important tools for the mind. During these literacy events, the adult as the more knowledgeable person carefully monitors the child's interpretation of the situation and provides timely support that enables the child to achieve the highest levels of understanding.

From a Vygotskian perspective, cognitive development and social interaction are perceived as complementary processes that work together to promote the child's intellectual growth. Therefore an influential force in the child's learning is the teaching that occurs around the literacy event. According to Vygotsky, mental development, teaching, and learning share reciprocal relationships that cannot be discussed separately. We believe that to promote higher-level literacy development in young children, teachers must

- carefully observe young children in the process of learning;
- design instructional interactions that involve children in using their personal knowledge as a foundation for constructing new learning;
- monitor children's progress in the new situation and be prepared to make spontaneous adjustments in their levels of support to ensure that children continue to learn; and
- use their observations of children's learning to evaluate and plan new instructional interactions that validate old knowledge and activate new learning.

The complementary actions of validation and activation lead the child to a higher level of cognitive development: (a) the teacher praises (acknowledges) what the child knows and (b) the teacher uses the known information as a bridge to activate new problem solving. From research on brain theory, we have learned the importance of connecting individual sources of knowledge to a larger network of information. When we ask young learners to use something they know to learn something new, they make an important discovery: their knowledge can be generalized. This is a lesson that many at-risk readers have not yet learned; instead, they view each learning experience as a new experience. These children need us, as their teachers, to structure literacy events and informative dialogues that emphasize the constructive and generative value of their own learning.

Observation and responsive teaching play critical roles in the literacy development of young children. Wells and Chang-Wells (1992) describe this process as "leading from behind," which implies that teachers must have a good understanding of what children know in order to guide them toward higher levels of development. During shared experiences, the teacher listens carefully to the child and is prepared to make spontaneous adjustments in her contributions that reflect the child's current ability. Language is a powerful tool with which to negotiate and regulate responsibility for completing the task at hand. In the following example, the balance of control shifts between the teacher and the child as they both use language to negotiate an appropriate ending for the story:

> Allen and Janie, his teacher, are completing the writing of a story based on eating M&M candies. Janie asks, "Now what are we going to call this book?"
>
> Allen turns to a blank page at the end of the book and remarks, "Hey, we got one more!"
>
> Janie responds, "Oh, yeah, we need to put something on that last page." Then Janie attempts to link Allen's story to a similar story titled *The Chocolate Cake* (Melser 1990), which has a repeated pattern of "mmm" on each page. She asks, "What do we say when something tastes really good? Do we say 'mmm'?"
>
> In response, Allen expands on Janie's intentions and initiates his own ending: "We can write 'It's all gone.'" Janie acknowledges Allen's contribution as an appropriate ending for the story as she exclaims, "It's all gone! That's a great way to end your story!" (Dorn 1996, 31–32)

These ideas are supported by the work of Rogoff (1990), who emphasizes the importance of social interaction for stimulating children's cognitive growth through guided participation in structured literacy activities. Rogoff views children as apprentices in learning who acquire a diverse collection of skills and knowledge under the guidance and support of more knowledgeable people. In the beginning, the adult assumes responsibility for structuring the learning task and guiding the interaction, but as the child acquires higher-level understanding, there is a noticeable transfer of responsibility from the adult to the child.

During socially constructed events, language is used to communicate a useful (i.e., meaningful) message to another person. In an apprenticeship setting, adults model the significance of written language as an important tool for documenting and communicating information. For example, Cathy and her daughter Elizabeth are preparing to cook Thanksgiving dinner. As Cathy prepares the turkey, Elizabeth creates a recipe for cooking it (see Figure 1.1). During this social moment, Elizabeth learns an important lesson about the functional role of written language in planning and organizing information for everyday experiences. These literacy opportunities provide young children with a strong foundation for success in reading and writing.

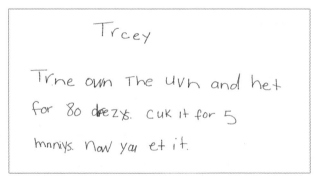

Figure 1.1 Elizabeth's turkey recipe: "Turn on the oven and heat for 80 degrees. Cook it for 5 minutes. Now you eat it."

Waterland applies apprenticeship to reading in the primary grades. She describes how the adult has three parts to play in helping the child learn to read:

- The adult chooses kinds of text that enable the child to learn about reading.
- The adult reads the parts of the story that the child is unable to read while hesitating at appropriate places to encourage the child to contribute the parts he or she knows.
- The adult ensures that the child will be successful by eliminating any negative or competitive aspects of the situation. (1985, 13–14)

Wood, Bruner, and Ross (1976) use the term *scaffolding* to describe a support system for helping children achieve success with a task that would be too difficult for them to accomplish on their own. In an apprenticeship approach, the teacher and child work together in constructing a meaningful interaction around a common literacy event. The teacher analyzes the child's level of independent functioning on the new task, discovers the child's intentions for solving the task, and supports the child with appropriate comments.

Scaffolding is portrayed in the following example. Judy (the teacher) and Nicholas have just finished reading a simple book about moms and their jobs. Judy asks Nicholas, "What does your mom do?"

Nicholas responds, "She works at Burger King." Then Judy asks Nicholas if he would like to write a story about his mom and her job. Nicholas picks up his marker and writes an *m* on his page. The balance of support changes with Nicholas's developing control for accomplishing the writing task:

Response	Analysis
Judy: That's great you knew *my* started with *m*.	Provides explicit feedback
Just let me put that *y* on the end of *my*.	Supplies unknown information
Now what is that word?	Increases word accessibility
Nicholas: *My*.	Accesses word information
Judy: What is your next word?	Prompts for new action
Nicholas: Mom *(Making no attempt to write it)*	
Judy: It starts like *my*. Say *my* and *mom*. What did your mouth do?	Increases letter-sound accessibility
Nicholas: M . . . m . . . m . . . It didn't open. M . . . m . . . y . . . m . . . m . . . o . . . m . . .	Accesses sensory information
Judy: Yes, did you feel your mouth close at the beginning and at the end of *mom*?	Provides informative feedback
Nicholas: *(Picks up the marker, writes* m, *skips a space, adds another* m *for* mom, *then hands the marker to Ms. Reed to add middle letter.)*	Initiates new action Seeks help

In this short episode, we see how Judy uses her observations of Nicholas to guide her levels of support. According to Wood (1988, 2002), the critical part of scaffolding is the adult's ability to determine the child's zone of proximal development, thus providing appropriate instructional strategies that create a shift in the child's level of cognitive functioning.

The Zone of Proximal Development

How do we help young children—particularly low-achieving children—learn faster? The answer lies in the zone of proximal development. Typically in education we have focused our attention on the child's actual development as indicated by summative assessments. From Vygotsky's perspective, advanced learning does not occur at the actual level of development; rather, it occurs in the zone of proximal development, "the distance between the actual developmental level as determined by individual problem-solving and the level of potential development as determined through problem-solving under adult guidance or in collaboration with more capable peers" (Vygotsky 1978, 86). Adults work within this zone to support and scaffold a child until he or she can function independently, thus enabling the child to move to a higher level in cognitive functioning. Basically, cognitive development occurs on two levels:

1. Zone of actual development (ZAD). This refers to the child's independent level of performance, what the child knows and can do alone.
2. Zone of proximal development (ZPD). This is the maximum level of development the child can reach with assistance. Varying degrees of partially assisted performance lie within the ZPD. Higher levels of understanding occur as a result of assisted performance in the zone of proximal development. What the child was able to accomplish with assistance yesterday becomes the independent level today, moving the child to a higher level of intellectual development.

According to Vygotsky (1978, 90), through adult-assisted performance, "learning awakens a variety of internal developmental processes that are able to operate only when the child is interacting with people in his environment and in cooperation with his peers." In a cognitive apprenticeship approach, a teacher considers the mediating influence of the social situation (i.e., the literacy event) when helping the child develop a conscious awareness of specific knowledge. This theory places an importance on explicit demonstrations and active engagements that are capable of awakening and guiding the child's literacy development to a higher level.

Let's apply this theory of assisted learning to two examples taken from a writing conference between Christy (the teacher) and Allison, a first grader. The first example illustrates how Christy uses language to help Allison construct a story based on a personal experience. In the second example, Christy uses language to direct Allison's attention to problem-solving strategies for helping herself during the actual writing.

Christy observes that Allison is having difficulty starting her story. She sits beside Allison and asks, "Did you do anything special this weekend?"

Allison responds, "I went to the zoo."

Christy smiles and says, "Well, that sounds like fun. I haven't been to the zoo in a long time. Can you tell me more about it?" As the conversation continues, Allison tells Christy about the monkey, the bear, and the elephant at the zoo. She concludes with a warning that "you can't feed the animals because it will make them sick."

After responding enthusiastically to Allison's story, Christy encourages her to rehearse the story for writing: "That is a great story. Let's put it all together, so we can listen to how it will sound to your readers." Christy's final statement has three intentions:

- to provide Allison with a verbal model of the story that Allison can use to monitor her written version
- to direct Allison's attention to the importance of reflection as a tool for evaluating her own work
- to emphasize that the reason for writing is to communicate a coherent and meaningful message to a particular audience

Next Christy uses language to direct Allison to productive strategies for helping herself write the story:

Teacher/Child Language	Intention of Language
Christy: How would you start to write *went?*	Prompts child to constructive activity.
Allison: I don't know.	Seeks help.
Christy: Say it slowly and listen to what you can hear. W—e—n—t.	Prompts the child to use slow articulation to hear sounds in sequence.
Allison: W—e—n—t. I hear a *t.*	Applies process of slow articulation and analyzes final sequence of sound.
Christy: There is a *t.* Where do you hear it?	Confirms child's knowledge and prompts for further analysis.
Allison: W—e—n—t. At the end.	Uses strategy in new problem-solving activity.
Christy: Yes, it is at the end. Say it again and listen to the beginning.	Confirms child's knowledge and prompts for further analysis.
Allison: W—e—n—t. I hear a *w.*	Analyzes beginning sound.
Christy: Yes, that's good listening. You heard the *w* at the beginning and the *t* at the end. I'll write the other letters for now. This is the way *went* looks in books. Use your checking finger to see if it looks right.	Provides explicit feedback and directs child's attention to new confirming activity.
Now reread your story and think of what would come next.	Prompts for rereading to anticipate text response.
Allison: I went to . . .	Rereads to anticipate the next word.
Christy: You can write *to.*	Activates old knowledge for application to a new situation.
Christy: Now you know some ways to help yourself. Say your words slowly and write what you can hear. Don't forget to reread each time to help yourself think of the next word in your story. I'll be back in a few minutes and you can show me what you've written.	Prompts child to use strategies for independent problem solving.

Christy uses the writing situation as an instructional tool to help Allison acquire important learning in several areas. Her teaching priorities are revealed in her closing comments:

- Words can be analyzed according to their sequence of sounds.
- Rereading helps a writer predict the next word.

The importance of the adult's role in helping children acquire higher-level knowledge cannot be overstated. Observant teachers collect important data for making informed decisions that keep children working at the cutting edge of their development (i.e., the zone of proximal development). Because new learning is both generative and recursive, the teacher must adjust his or her support in compliance with how the child is responding to the task at hand.

Progressing Through the Zone of Proximal Development

As children progress through the zone of proximal development, it is important that teachers value the ups and downs of new learning and be able to provide adjustable support that accommodates it. Tharp and Gallimore (1988) describe the learner's progression through the ZPD and the role of the adult in guiding the child to a higher level of cognitive activity. It may be helpful to apply this theory to the previous example with Allison and Christy, her teacher. We will begin with Stage 1 (i.e., Allison's present stage) and make predictions about her progression through the ZPD that reflect a movement from teacher-regulated activity to child-regulated activity.

In Stage 1 of the ZPD, Allison requires a great deal of support in accomplishing a particular task. The responsibility for regulating her participation in the task rests primarily with the teacher, who is constantly adjusting support to ensure that Allison is successful. For instance, Christy bases her teaching priorities on knowledge of the learning process (the role of phonology in reading and writing development) and her observations of Allison's current abilities (saying words slowly as a way to analyze sounds in words). Wells and Chang-Wells (1992) describe how instructional interactions must be based on the child's current ability and the adult's pedagogical intentions and how the adult must be prepared at any moment to modify the level of instructional support in light of feedback from the child. This suggests that clear models and guided participation are critical elements of a successful interaction that has the potential for supporting new learning. In an apprenticeship setting, Allison will learn how to use teacher-demonstrated models for guiding her own learning to a higher level.

During Stage 2, Allison will display the capacity to assist her own learning process. During the previous writing activity, Christy gave Allison an opportunity to learn how to use problem-solving strategies. As Christy left the writing conference, she reminded Allison of two important strategies that she must now use to help herself. At Stage 2, external prompts (for example, the teacher's language) are no longer needed because the child provides her own support system through self-directed speech. In the case of analyzing sounds in words, we expect Allison independently to initiate the action of slow articulation and use this strategy for matching sounds to letters. Through repeated practice, Allison's knowledge about letters and sounds will become more automatic.

In Stage 3, assistance from the adult or the self is no longer needed, because the behavior has been internalized. At this stage, Allison will be able to write words fluently and flexibly in different places and for varied purposes. The behavior (i.e., analyzing letters and sounds) places no new demands on the brain. The goal of instruction has been reached when Allison becomes a self-regulated learner with the capacity to use her knowledge for monitoring, guiding, and regulating her own learning activity.

During Stage 4, an internalized behavior can be temporarily disrupted by a variety of influences, such as environmental changes, new cognitive demands, or physical trauma. When this occurs, the goal of instruction is to guide the learner back through the ZPD, providing the necessary levels of support to regain automatization. For instance, there may be times when Allison will have to slow down and attend to certain features of print. Also, there may be times when Allison's writing will reflect a regressive behavior in regard to a known sound, and Christy will have to issue a gentle reminder about how to access this information. ("Say the word slowly and listen to the middle.") It is important to keep in mind that new learning is somewhat fragile and may be temporarily thrown off track when the brain becomes absorbed

with new problem-solving activity. With a little self-help or teacher help, the learner will regain automatic control of the behavior.

According to Vygotsky, instruction is a major contributor to children's growing consciousness and the regulation of their own cognitive processes. As children engage in literacy conversations with more knowledgeable people, basic cognitive processes, such as perception, attention, and memory, are transformed into higher intellectual functions, which are represented by intentional and reflective thinking. During instruction, children learn how to set goals, monitor their progress, adjust their thinking when a problem occurs, work toward the best solution, and accomplish these complex processes with deliberateness, consciousness, and efficiency. This higher-level thinking represents the child's ability to learn from others, including how to ask questions, respond to instruction, and access relevant information from the environment (while ignoring irrelevant information). Vygotsky describes how each intellectual function must appear two times: first on a social, external plane between two or more people, and next on a personal, internal plane within the child.

This theory is important for education because it emphasizes the interaction between teacher and student as integral to independent problem solving. Vygotskian theory maintains that children move from other-regulatory (external) to self-regulatory (internal) behavior through interactions with individuals in their environment. The child's ability to organize and monitor his or her own thinking occurs as a result of demonstrations during social exchanges with others. Mediated experiences with more literate individuals demonstrate the language needed to guide the child toward regulating his or her own thinking. The end point of teaching is a self-regulated learner who exhibits the potential to use his or her knowledge for varied purposes and in different situations (Diaz et al. 1990; Karpov 2003).

Promoting Conscious Awareness of Literate Knowledge

Children develop a conscious awareness of their own mental functions as they engage in literacy activities with their teacher. In her book *Children's Minds,* Donaldson (1978, 129) establishes the link between the growth of consciousness and the growth of the intellect: "If the intellectual powers are to develop, the child must gain a measure of control over his own thinking and he cannot control while he remains unaware of it." Consciousness is constructed through the child's interactions with the world. The more literate person represents the consciousness of the child, thus enabling the child to experience the behavior vicariously (Bruner 1986), but coming to control the behavior as self-awareness leads to internalization. In apprenticeship settings, language is used as a literacy tool for seeking help from others, generating solutions to problems, and reflecting on one's learning.

The research on metalinguistic awareness emphasizes the importance of helping young children acquire a conscious awareness of the structure and function of written language. This awareness does not develop as an isolated skill; instead, it is naturally woven into the literacy process. During interactive events, teachers use explicit language as an important tool to help children acquire higher-level understanding about literacy concepts (Dorn 1996):

- Language is used to activate the child's awareness of specific concepts about print. (For example, before the teacher reads one page, she remarks, "I'm going to use my finger to read this page because it helps me match my words.")
- Language is used to promote the child's self-reflective activity. (For example, the teacher invites the child to "show me on this page where you put your nicest space between your words.")
- Language is used to provide the child with explicit feedback that acknowledges his or her use of a particular concept about print. (For example, the child says a word slowly and the teacher remarks, "I like the way you are saying the word slowly. That helps you hear the sounds, doesn't it?")
- Language is used to help the child develop a more conscious awareness of the importance of a particular concept of print. (For example, after the child writes a capital letter at the beginning of the sentence, the teacher asks, "How did you know to write a capital letter there?")

In cognitive apprenticeship, the adult guides the child toward a meaningful interaction with her, making adjustments in her support based on constant feedback received from the child. Through these personal communications, the child begins to internalize the actions and the language of the adult and begins to use these tools as internal devices to guide and monitor his own processing behavior. Vygotskian theory proposes that once an externalized activity becomes an internalized function, the structure and the organization of the brain is changed, moving the child to a higher intellectual level (Diaz et al. 1990; Karpov 2003; Vygotsky 1978).

The Role of Integration

The processing of information occurs at three levels: input, integration, and output. The first step is for the brain to attend to the new information, and attention is determined by meaningfulness and relevance. Once information enters the brain, it must be integrated with other related information. This process triggers a series of coordinated movements that provide personal feedback for each other. For instance, when a child constructs a form (motor) for the sound he hears (auditory) and checks it with his eyes (visual), the child receives feedback from each sensory system. It is as though the brain is checking each sense against the other and confirming its identity. Sylwester (1995, 14) describes it this way: "When objects and events are registered by several senses (e.g., seeing, hearing, and touching), they can be stored in several interrelated memory networks. A memory stored in this way becomes more accessible and powerful than a memory stored in just one sensory area, because each sensory memory checks and extends the others." So there must be a smooth coordination of behavior if the child is to receive the maximum feedback from each sensory category.

Language and action work together to help children develop conscious awareness of their literacy. The following example illustrates how the teacher combines language and motor actions to focus the child's attention on the features of an unknown word from the story. Jeff is having difficulty with the word *here* in his new book. So that Jeff can finish the story with the meaning relatively intact, Esther, his teacher, tells him the word. Afterward she turns back to the difficult page and asks Jeff to locate the problem word. Without hesitation, Jeff locates the word *here*. Esther then uses the word *here* to help Jeff learn how to integrate multiple sources of sensory information:

Teacher Prompt	Sensory System	Literacy Tools
Check the word with your finger and see if it looks like *here*.	Motor, visual	Magnetic letters
Say the word as you check it.	Auditory, visual, motor	Magnetic letters
Write the word and say the word as you write it.	Motor, visual, auditory	Dry erase board, marker
Find the word in your story.	Visual	Text
Check to see if the word in your story looks like the word you just wrote.	Visual	Text, dry erase board, marker
Read that page again.	Visual	Text

In the early stages of development, the word is represented through external, concrete, and manipulative tools that eventually become internalized as mental tools that can exist without external support. For Jeff, the magnetic letters are manipulative tools for learning how to attend to the visual features of an unknown word in his story. This momentary scaffold gives Jeff a visual model that can be checked against other sources of information from the text. For example, when the teacher first asks Jeff to locate the word, he is able to do it based on the meaning and structural pattern of the story. Esther's final prompt brings Jeff back to the story so he can integrate and confirm all sources. The teacher's language plays an important role in guiding the child through the perceptual process. The goal of instruction is for Jeff to turn the external models into an internal model that can be used flexibly to monitor and plan his behavior

during various literacy events. The table below illustrates the continuum of teacher/child control in the development of self-regulated activity.

Teacher-Regulated Behavior *(External Tools)*	Child-Regulated Behavior *(Internal Tools)*
Clear and concrete demonstrations	Plan, assemble, monitor, and check information
Explicit and redundant language	Self-directed speech
Teacher control	Internal control

Constructing New Knowledge

Learning is a constructive process, in which existing knowledge is integrated with novel information, resulting in the creation of new knowledge. Keep in mind that bits and pieces of information are meaningless—these items must be networked with other related information and mobilized at a moment's notice to deal with a new problem. Networking is a complex process orchestrated by strategic activity, such as planning, cross-checking, hypothesizing, monitoring, linking, searching, confirming, and regulating actions. This neural activity is transformative: a systematic process for converting old knowledge into something new.

The mind is designed to learn from experience. The role of teaching is to create opportunities that lead to structural changes in the learner's brain. Here is a simplistic explanation of this complex process (see Figure 1.2):

1. The brain picks up sensory data from the environment and stores it as concrete experiences. ("This is what I already know.")
2. New information from the environment is observed and quickly linked to existing information, thus creating a temporary state of disequilibrium that results in questioning and reflecting. ("Uh-oh, this word doesn't look right.")
3. Self-reflecting is the basis for forming a hypothesis (an informed guess) and proposing a tentative solution to the problem. ("I can look all the way through the word to help me figure it out.")

4. The proposed solution is actively tested and adjustments and corrections are made, resulting in the production of new knowledge ("The strategy helped me to learn the word, and I can use this strategy on other words.")
5. New concrete experiences are created (based on Zull 2002, 2011).

The yearning to understand why things happen is a basic instinct of the human mind. As intellectual beings, we question, we ponder, and we seek, and although some things might not have clear answers, the human desire to create meaning is the very foundation on which knowledge is built. From this theoretical stance, the teacher creates a meaningful environment that engages children's minds in active decision making that leads to the production of new knowledge.

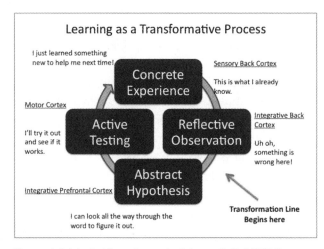

Figure 1.2 Adapted from the work of James E. Zull (2002).

A Decision-Making Process

Comprehension is the ultimate goal of reading, and the desire to make meaning is the driving force behind every reading act. The very act of comprehension is a systematic process that is regulated by the mind's desire to make meaning. These cognitive sequences are motor functions: planning actions that require the mind to assemble background information, integrate multiple sources, and apply strategies for gaining understanding. Good readers make deliberate choices, including decisions about particular strategies for solving words and the amount of time to spend on particular aspects of the comprehending process. This

implies that meaning making is not a random act, but rather a self-regulated process for achieving a particular literacy goal.

Developing Self-Regulated Learners

A self-regulated reader is one who uses his knowledge to advance his own learning. Self-regulation is defined as "the child's capacity to plan, guide, and monitor his or her behavior from within and flexibly according to changing circumstances" (Diaz et al. 1990, 130). This definition implies a network of strategies working together toward a common goal. During instructional interactions, students acquire strategies for remembering, comparing, searching, checking, and confirming relationships.

In *Becoming Literate*, Clay (1991) describes a reading system that comprises a network of interrelated strategies that work together to ensure that the reader will have a meaningful and self-extending experience. The characteristics of a self-extending system include the child's capacity to do the following:

- monitor reading and writing
- search for cues in word sequences, in meaning, in letter sequences
- discover new things
- cross-check one source of cues with another
- repeat to confirm reading or writing
- self-correct, assuming the initiative for making cues match or getting words right
- solve new words by flexible and varied means

The important point here is that no action exists in isolation from another action. These internal processes that the child engages in are interlocking systems that tap into each other, providing feedback and feed-forward assistance (Clay 1991) for making the reading process run smoothly and effortlessly. The learner grows intellectually as he uses his existing knowledge to regulate his own learning and guide it to a higher cognitive level. Cognitive behaviors such as generating, monitoring, confirming, linking, planning, reflecting, and guiding depend on the reader's ability to activate information beyond the initial response and to use this personal form of feedback for problem solving in the new situation. These problem-solving actions are organized into a complex system of internal activity that has one goal: to make sense of the incoming information.

Holdaway (1979, 170) describes the importance of establishing self-regulation in the learner. "There is no better system to control the complexities and intricacies of each person's learning than that person's own system operating with genuine motivation and self-determination." In other words, to feel in control—to feel that one is making progress—is a necessary condition of learning.

Motivation and Determination

Research by Dweck (2000, 2006) has tremendous implications for teaching and learning. Her work focuses on the conditions that contribute to a learner's self-perception (mindset) of his capacity to solve problems. According to Dweck, what matters most in terms of motivation is whether a learner views his ability as fixed (limited) or growth (limitless). Children with a fixed mindset will attempt only those tasks that they already know how to do, whereas children with a growth mindset are motivated to tackle challenging tasks. Furthermore, children with a growth mindset use self-monitoring language to regulate their planning actions; for instance, "I need to slow down and try to figure this out," or "I can go back and reread this part to help me understand what happened." The language is self-congratulatory, thus promoting task persistence and motivation. Here are a few examples:

- Well, that was a good try. I bet I can solve it next time.
- That problem was a little harder, but I think I know what I did wrong.
- I did a good job on that one. Do you have anything that is a little harder?
- I'm getting better at this every time.
- Uh-oh, I missed that one. That's okay. I know what to do next time.
- I can't wait to show someone how to do this.
- I'm proud of my hard work today.

In his book *Opening Minds*, Peter Johnston (2012) describes how teachers use language that shapes children's theories of learning. In apprenticeship settings, teachers create challenging opportunities that engage children's minds in asking questions, forming hypotheses, examining relationships, and constructing new knowledge. Teachers provide students with explicit feedback that focuses on the problem-solving attempts, such as, "Writing that word in parts helped you figure it out," in contrast to praise that emphasizes a particular outcome, such as, "You are really good at spelling words."

Processing Behavior Versus Items of Knowledge

The ability to solve a word provides the learner with an important tool for learning new words. Thus the emphasis needs to be placed on the problem-solving activity, rather than on the word. The teacher plays a critical role in shaping children's processing behavior, but for this to happen, teachers must understand the skills and strategies that good readers use. In addition, teachers must be able to

- observe the knowledge, skills, and strategies used by their students when they read and write;
- use supportive materials that enable their students to practice effective strategies across a range of reading and writing events;
- use language prompts that direct students' attention to the processing activity rather than to the accuracy of the word; and
- be willing to accept some errors that do not interfere with meaning.

Apprenticeship requires that the teacher accept that the child will make mistakes (in fact, must make mistakes) and will need time to sort them out and permission to ignore them if they do not matter. Teachers who emphasize accuracy are depriving their students of opportunities to learn how to generalize problem-solving and confirming strategies to new situations.

An emphasis on problem-solving activity is illustrated in the following example with Stephanie and Julie, her teacher. The previous day, Julie had introduced Stephanie to a simple little book titled *Nighttime* (Cowley 1990). During the introduction, she exposed Stephanie to two new words, *stable* and *sty*, as she related the pictures to the words. It is important to remember that Stephanie is a first-grade student from the city; these particular words had little meaning for her. Stephanie's running record on the following day provides an interesting analysis of the complexity of her problem-solving behavior:

√   √   √   √   √   <u>table</u>
The horse is in the stable.

√   √   √   √   √   <u>stable</u>
The pig is in the sty.

Examining Stephanie's responses, we can make several assumptions about her processing activity. First, since *stable* was an unfamiliar concept (in spite of her introduction to the word on the previous day), we can understand how she may have mentally linked it to a known word that sounded like it. We can also assume that she activated the sound pattern rather than the visual pattern. This seems logical since Stephanie is an emergent reader with limited knowledge about visual patterns at this time. However, as she reads the next line, notice how she attaches the memory trace of *table* to the *st* chunk (which she knows visually from her name) and responds with the word *stable* for *sty*. In the transcript that follows, Julie emphasizes the processing activity behind the second error. First, Julie rereads the line fluently and engages Stephanie in a brief dialogue about the "place where pigs live."

Julie: When you were reading that part of your story, you noticed something at the beginning of the word, didn't you? What did you notice?
Stephanie: *St.*
Julie: That's right. Do you know another word that starts like that?
Stephanie: My name. Stephanie.
Julie: Yes, *Stephanie* and *sty*. They do start the same, don't they? That's good that you were looking at the beginning of the word. That helps you when you're reading, doesn't it? Let's read that page together.

If Julie had chosen to go to the word *stable* or *sty* and insisted that Stephanie sound out the letters for the sake of the word, the teaching would have focused on accuracy. In contrast, the teacher chose to emphasize two important processing strategies: (1) using first-letter cues and (2) searching for known chunks of visual information. From this perspective, Stephanie acquired a tool that she can use to initiate new problem-solving activity on different texts.

We know that reading is a meaning-making process that is successful when a reader understands the author's intended message. When a story makes sense, the reader receives valuable feedback that confirms everything is proceeding reasonably and coherently. Confirmation feedback about meaning preserves the integrity of the story and enables the reader to anticipate the occurrence of new events almost before the next line is read or the page is turned.

If the reader misses the point of the story, the goal of reading (which is understanding) is jeopardized. In an apprenticeship approach, the teacher guides the child to apply checking and confirming strategies that are grounded in meaningful interactions with the text. Therefore, the teacher's role in responding to the child's error is critical to helping the child build effective processing systems that lead to more complex reading activity.

Let's look at an example. Blake is reading a story about a little boy who lost his teddy bear. The pictures illustrate that the boy is searching in several places for the lost bear. Yet when Blake reads the text, he substitutes the word *here* [is the teddy bear] for *where* [is the teddy bear]. Since *here* and *where* are visually similar words, we can assume that Blake's response was influenced by visual information. However, a serious problem arises when Blake does not notice the effect that his substitution has created on the story's development. In the following transcript, Carla, the teacher, focuses Blake's attention on checking for meaning:

Carla: You said, "Here is the teddy bear." Can you find the teddy bear in the picture?
Blake: He's not there.
Carla: No, he's not. So, does it make sense to say, "Here is the teddy bear"?
Blake: No.
Carla: Well, if the boy is still looking for the teddy bear, what do you think he would say?
Blake: "Where is the teddy bear?"
Carla: Read it and see if you are right.
Blake *(Reading)*: "Where is the teddy bear?"
Carla: Yes, you were thinking of what would make sense and look right.

The success of children's reading and writing endeavors is largely determined by the adult/child interaction during literacy events. The child is encouraged to be an active participant, with his or her interpretation of the text validated by the adult's acceptance (Wells and Chang-Wells 1992). As the adult supports the child at his or her present level of understanding, the child is gently pushed into thinking about literacy at a higher level.

Teaching for Transfer

Intellectual development is related to transfer. Campione, Shapiro, and Brown (1995, 39) provide the following definition of transfer: "Transfer means understanding; and understanding is indexed by the ability of learners to explain the resources (knowledge and processes) they are acquiring and to make flexible use of them in the service of new and continued learning." (See Figure 1.3.)

The definition of *self-regulation* implies that the learner is engaged in reflective and metacognitive processing. Thus we believe we cannot talk about self-regulatory learning without also discussing its relationship to other concepts:

- *Teaching for Transfer.* When a teacher teaches for transfer, she must be aware of what the child knows. Therefore, the teacher designs instructional interactions that provide the learner with opportunities to transfer existing skills, strategies, and knowledge to new problem-solving activity across changing and varied situations.
- *Teaching for Strategies.* When a teacher teaches for strategies, she is prompting the child toward processing activity based on the child's existing knowledge and the ability to apply problem-solving strategies while working with unknown information.
- *Processing Activity.* When a child engages in processing activity, he taps into his background knowledge, notices relationships, monitors his performance, and applies flexible strategies to construct meaning for the activity at hand.
- *Self-Regulation.* When a child becomes a self-regulated learner, he uses his current skills, strategies, and knowledge at a new level of cognitive activity; that is, he plans and guides new learning and uses existing knowledge for solving new problems in a variety of situations.

Figure 1.3 Important concepts related to self-regulation.

Let's apply this definition to the classroom. Can you recall a situation where a child successfully performed a task in one context, yet was unable to carry out the same task or use similar knowledge in a different setting? We see this a lot in our work with struggling readers. When this occurs, there are two possible influences: (1) the child has become dependent on the context; in other words, the cues from the environment are regulating the child's response; and/or (2) the child has developed a fixed mind-set and is unwilling to tackle new problems. It is important for us, as teachers, to understand that the child's difficulty with transfer is most likely an instructional problem, rather than a learning disability.

So how can teachers promote transfer? Simply put, the heart of transfer lies with the adult, who must create instructional activities that enable children to recognize the transferability of their knowledge and its potential for working out new problems in different places. Children depend on adults to observe what they know and to select appropriate materials and activities that help them realize that learning is generalizable (Lupart 1996). Language and other forms of nonverbal scaffolds (such as rubrics, text maps, and anchor charts) can foster generalization. As students learn to summarize, predict, and monitor their performance, the potential for transfer increases (Palincsar 1986).

We know from Tharp and Gallimore's recursive cycle that new learning is fragile and can be disrupted by new demands or changes in the environment. For that reason, the adult's role in scaffolding the child at points of difficulty (that is, in the ZPD) is critical to enabling the child to acquire knowledge that is both stable and flexible. Intellectual development occurs when the child recognizes the self-generative value of his own knowledge for monitoring his performance and creating new information. Therefore, an important lesson for children is that their knowledge is stable regardless of the changing situations in which it is used.

Shaping Literate Minds Through Teaching

In the introductory section, we posed this question: Why does a teacher's theory of teaching and learning matter? There is no doubt that a teacher's theory will impact the methods, practices, and language that she uses with her students. There is overwhelming evidence from social, cognitive, and educational research on the effects of instruction on student learning. Zull (2002, 5) describes the art of teaching as the art of changing the brain. He writes, "The role of teaching is to create experiences that lead to structural changes in the brain." Eisner (2002, 23) emphasizes the role of teaching in developing the learner's mind: "Brains are born, and minds are made; and one of the privileges of the teaching profession is to have an important part to play in the shaping of minds." What an incredible responsibility for teachers!

Some Closing Thoughts

In closing, here are some key concepts to share with other educators:

- Prevention of reading problems must begin in the early grades. If children are not reading on grade level by the end of third grade, their chance of success in later years is minimal. One characteristic of problem readers is their lack of literacy experiences during their preschool years. Schools must compensate by providing the children with rich literacy classroom programs and supplemental literacy services that focus on early intervention.

- Children acquire higher-level mental functions through social interactions with observant and responsive adults. Therefore, teachers should be trained in how to observe children's processing behavior and how to use this information when they respond to children.

- School instruction should be aimed at children's potential level of development (i.e., the zone of proximal development). Teachers should use information about children as a basis for designing instructional situations that allow them to use existing knowledge as a scaffold for new problem-solving activity.

- An apprenticeship approach to literacy emphasizes the role of the adult in supporting children's developing control of literacy knowledge. In this model, the teacher provides clear demonstrations, engages children appropriately, monitors their level of understanding, makes necessary accommodations to ensure that they are successful, and withdraws support as they exhibit greater control. A critical factor is the teacher's ability to remove the support in accordance with children's higher levels of understanding.

- Schools should provide children with multiple opportunities to make connections, establish relationships, and apply their knowledge across a wide range of literacy experiences.

- The goal of teaching is to develop self-regulated learners—children with the capacity to use their knowledge for guiding, monitoring, and planning new cognitive activity. During instructional interactions, teachers give children opportunities to tap into existing knowledge and to apply problem-solving strategies to novel information.

- Teachers structure literacy opportunities that promote the flexible transfer of knowledge, skills, and strategies to different situations. In the process, children learn the stability of knowledge and the power of strategies for integrating information and constructing new learning.

chapter two

A COGNITIVE APPRENTICESHIP APPROACH TO LITERACY

Cognitive apprenticeship implies that children acquire cognitive and metacognitive processes through assisted instruction with a sensitive and knowledgeable adult (Collins, Brown, and Newman 1989). The teacher carefully observes the knowledge and skills of young children and uses language to build bridges that enable children to use what they already know to acquire new and unknown information (Clay and Cazden 1990). Thus the teacher focuses on "arranging and structuring children's participation in activities, with dynamic shifts over development in children's responsibilities" (Rogoff 1990, 8). In other words, teachers must create transitions in both language and activities to reflect children's higher-level development. To that end, predictable routines and organizational structures that provide the children with expectations and standards for promoting independence are very important. The seven theoretical principles in Figure 2.1 provide an apprenticeship framework for accelerating the learning of all students.

The Role of Language in Promoting Literacy

From Vygotsky's point of view, instruction leads development; therefore, the role of teaching is strongly emphasized. We cannot discuss teaching without also examining the language of instruction (see, for example, Johnston 2004, 2012). During literacy activities, teachers use language as a tool for communicating specific knowledge, skills, and strategies to children. In Chapters 3–11, we include numerous examples of language interactions whereby teachers

- use language prompts that stimulate children's problem-solving processes across a wide range of literacy activities (see Figure 2.2); and
- provide immediate feedback that explicitly describes children's behavior, thus reinforcing the desirable response (see Figure 2.3).

1. **Observation and Responsive Teaching:** Teachers observe children's literacy behaviors and design instructional interactions based on children's strengths and needs.
2. **Modeling and Coaching:** Teachers use modeling and coaching techniques with memorable demonstrations and explicit language.
3. **Clear and Relevant Language for Problem Solving:** Teachers use language prompts that enable children to initiate planning, monitoring, and regulating actions for resolving problems with efficiency during literacy activities.
4. **Adjustable and Self-Destructing Scaffolds:** Teachers provide adjustable scaffolds that are removed when they are no longer needed.
5. **Structured Routines:** Teachers create predictable frameworks with organizational structures that promote children's independence.
6. **Assisted and Independent Work:** Teachers provide balanced opportunities for children to work at assisted and independent levels.
7. **Transfer:** Teachers teach for the transfer of knowledge, skills, and strategies across shifting circumstances and for varying purposes.

Figure 2.1 Seven principles of an apprenticeship approach to literacy.

In all cases the teacher's language is immediately related to a problem that has arisen from children's reading and writing and focuses on helping them apply appropriate strategies for resolving the conflict. However, for learning to occur, children must be able to

- understand the intent of the teacher's language for communicating a specific message, and
- perform successfully the action for which they are being prompted.

Teachers can monitor their language by asking two simple and important questions:

- Is your language meaningful to the child?
- Is your language relevant to the task at hand?

Using these questions as guides requires teachers to

- identify what the child brings to the task and
- identify what is important for accomplishing the task.

If a child is expected to apply information before he has the necessary background experience (or concept knowledge), the activity will be empty and meaningless. This means that the child must understand the relevance the teacher's language has for helping himself. The teacher is responsible for observing the child for signs of understanding and adjusting her language to ensure that the child will gain meaning from the interaction. Through recurring successful experiences, the child learns the significance of the teacher's prompts for planning and solving problems. The goal of instruction is achieved when the child learns how to plan and initiate appropriate actions for directing his own reading progress.

Language to Establish Learning Goal
- The goal of today's task is to learn how to write a summary.
- Today you will read to find out how the problem was solved.
- Today you will learn how authors use real photographs to help their readers understand the content.

Language to Activate Background Knowledge
- What do you already know about this topic?
- Where have you used this strategy before?
- What additional information do you need to know?

Language to Promote Cue Integration
- Does that make sense?
- Does that sound right?
- Does that look right?
- Does it look make sense, sound right, and look right?

Language to Promote Problem-Solving Actions
- What are you trying to figure out?
- What can you do to help yourself there?
- What strategy would work there?
- What's wrong?
- What did you notice?
- That was a good try, and you almost got it right. What else can you try?

Language to Promote Metacognition
- What advice would you have for someone who is stuck on this problem?
- Help me understand how you solved this problem.
- Can you explain what you are thinking?
- Why did you decide to try that? Is there anything else you could have tried?
- What can you do to help yourself understand this part?
- How are you doing? Do you need to do anything differently?

Language to Anticipate Potential Difficulties
- What tricky parts do you need to watch out for?
- What are some strategies you need to try when you run into problems?
- What don't you understand? What do you need help with?
- What is easy for you to do? How can you use that to help you with the hard parts?

Language to Promote Transfer
- When you learn how to do this, you will be able to use it to help you solve other problems.
- How can you use what you learned today in writing to help you with your reading?
- During your word study lesson, you learned how to use parts of words to help you solve an unknown word. How can you use this strategy to help yourself when you come to an unknown word in your reading?
- How is this like what we learned yesterday?
- Have you seen this type of problem before?
- Where have you used this before?

Figure 2.2 Examples of language prompts for assisting student performance.

> **Child:** *(The child hesitates when he comes to an unknown word, but makes no attempt to solve it.)*
>
> **Teacher:** That's good that you noticed that tricky word. Could the word be _____? Read it again and see if that works there.
>
> **Child:** *(The child initiates a good problem-solving attempt on an unknown word, but is unable to self-correct.)*
>
> **Teacher:** Good checking on that hard word. You almost got it right. Take a closer look at the ending.
>
> **Child:** *(The child rereads and self-corrects his error.)*
>
> **Teacher:** You went back and fixed that, didn't you? That was good problem solving there.
>
> **Child:** *(The child reads in a fluent and expressive manner.)*
>
> **Teacher:** You read that just like talking. That makes it interesting to listen to.

Figure 2.3 Examples of feedback language for describing appropriate literacy actions.

Teaching for Common Understanding

Does your language have meaning for the child? Consider a teacher who repeatedly prompts the child to reread a word of text and articulate the first letter. If the child consistently engages in this behavior but does not use it to initiate an appropriate response to the word, the child may not understand the relevance of the prompt. For the teacher's language to be meaningful to the child, the child must experience a productive attempt. It is only through these successful experiences that the true meaning of the teacher's language becomes evident.

This leads us to an important concept in apprenticeship learning: intersubjectivity (Rogoff 1990; Wertsch 1984, 1985). Simply put, this means that the teacher and children share a similar understanding of a particular task. Because of their limited experiences, young learners may be confused by the teacher's mature language. If a mismatch in communication occurs, the teacher must use language to negotiate understanding and reestablish a common link.

For example, during a shared writing experience (Dorn 1996), Judy, the teacher, invites George to write a "little" *d*. George misunderstands her intentions and writes a very small capital *D*. Judy realizes her language is creating confusion for George and at-

tempts to clarify her meaning. She picks up the marker and writes a lowercase *d* on the page. With a puzzled expression, George examines the size of Judy's *d* and comments, "I thought you said make it little." Judy then increases her level of support, writes the two forms, and directs George's attention to them. As she explicitly points to the two letters, she says, "You were making a capital *D*, and I was talking about this kind of *d*. That's a lowercase *d*—or a little *d*." Judy accepts responsibility for ensuring that George will gain meaning from the shared experience.

When a teacher is working in a child's zone of proximal development (ZPD), the child's definition of a situation will naturally be different from the teacher's definition (see Wertsch 1984), simply because the ZPD is an area in which the child needs our assistance. Because the development of new learning depends on the child's relevant interpretation of the situation, the teacher must keep in mind that the child is faced with two challenges (Phillips and Smith 1997):

- finding meaning in the teacher's words
- making an appropriate response to the teacher's words in a context that the child does not yet understand

Using Language to Learn About Literacy

During literacy events, the teacher prompts children to describe, explain, and justify what they are doing to help themselves. Language is used to build connections between past, present, and future learning. Meichenbaum and Biemiller (1998, 82–86) describe six regulatory functions of language for assisting a learner's task performance:

- Language is used as a problem-solving device, a tool for learning, and a solution generator.
- Language is used as a means for accessing and activating stored information and for enhancing conceptual understanding.
- Language is used as a process that facilitates transfer.
- Language is used as a way to seek and access assistance.
- Language is used as a tool for sharing and consulting with others, as well as with oneself.
- Language is used as a means to become a member of a community of learners.

Language Principles for Assisting Performance

Rogoff (1990, 39) characterizes apprenticeship learning as shared problem solving between an active learner and a more skilled partner. She identifies the following features of guided participation: "the importance of routine activities, tacit as well as explicit communication, supportive structuring of novices' efforts, and transfer of responsibility for handling skills to novices." This can be brought about through modeling, coaching, scaffolding, articulating, and reflecting (Collins et al. 1989).

Modeling

In modeling, the teacher demonstrates a literacy task, and the children observe the processes that are required to accomplish the task. Thus the children are provided with a conceptual model of the literacy task before they are asked to attempt to perform it independently. According to Collins et al. (1989, 456), a conceptual model gives the child

- an advanced "organizer" for planning and performing a complex skill;
- a structure for making sense of the teacher's feedback, hints, and corrections; and
- an internalized guide for supporting independent practice.

For example, during a writing-aloud session at the interactive whiteboard (see Chapter 5), Donna, the teacher, models for the children the process of problem solving words as she composes her message. She says, "When I come to a word I don't know, I can try it out on my practice board. First, I can think of some things I know about other words that can help me. Then I can write the word several ways to see which one looks right to me." Donna is aware of the relationship between language and action; thus she looks for productive examples to demonstrate the process of solving words. As she works on her practice board, she uses explicit language to describe her actions. During her demonstrations, she carefully observes how the children interpret her performance. From time to time, she offers particular prompts that focus their attention on her problem-solving solutions: "Help me check this. Does it look right to you? Did that help us with that tricky word?"

Being presented with simultaneous models of language and action enables children to observe the types of strategies and skills they need to apply as they problem-solve on their own. Without clear models, children may not be able to conceptualize the goal of instruction. That is, the task may be an abstraction for them, and as a result, they may develop an inappropriate definition of the task. Good models provide children with standards (or benchmarks) against which they can reflect and evaluate their own progress.

Coaching

Coaching involves guided participation, whereby the teacher observes the children during literacy events and offers hints, reminders, feedback, modeling, and other types of support to ensure successful performance (Collins et al. 1989; Meichenbaum and Biemiller 1998). Through language prompts, teachers assist children in integrating various sources of information and applying strategies for working out new solutions.

The following example illustrates the role of language and action in coaching a child to check the letters after making a meaningful substitution during guided reading. When Derrick comes to the word *fast,* he responds with the word *quick.* Jackie, his teacher, recognizes the importance of this meaningful response, but she wants Derrick to use first-letter cues more efficiently. She prompts him directly to the source of information he needs to attend to in order to accomplish the expected action: "*Quick* makes sense, but does that word look like *quick*? Read it again and think of a word that would make sense and starts with an *f.*" With this prompt, Derrick is able to integrate meaning and visual cues in a successful and fluent action. However, if Derrick were unable to accomplish the action, Jackie would need to be ready to coach him further with a higher level of support. For instance, she might say, "Try the word *fast* and see if it works there" and then prompt him to confirm the response and to apply the knowledge to a new situation: "Did that work? Did it make sense and start with the right letter? You should try that the next time you come to a word you don't know." The goal of coaching is to help the child understand a new concept, and understanding is derived from a meaningful and successful performance.

As children acquire more problem-solving strategies, the teacher relinquishes more control. For instance, in early learning, the teacher's language is much more explicit and direct; once children understand the significance of the behavior as a way to help them problem-solve, the teacher's language becomes more general: "Try that again," or "Something isn't quite right." As the child learns how to monitor his own reading, the teacher must be careful that her language does not find the error for the child, thus denying him an opportunity to problem-solve on his own. One question teachers might ask is, "Am I requiring the child to correct his mistake before he has found it?" If so, the teacher's language may be inhibiting the child's ability to develop effective searching and problem-solving behavior. In apprenticeship, the teacher's language is critical for guiding successful experiences that shape higher-level understanding.

During shared reading (see Chapter 3) and interactive writing (see Chapter 5), the teacher's language serves two purposes:

- to expose children to academic language and concepts that are used during literacy activities
- to help children understand how the concept label relates to the reading and writing experiences

Here are some examples of explicit language for teaching print concepts:

Print Concept	Example of Teacher's Language
Title	Who can show me the title of our new book?
Pictures	What's happening in this picture?
Directionality	Who can show us where to start reading? Where do we go next?
One-to-one match	Let's point to the words as we read.
Words	Who can find the word *me* on this page?
Letters	Who can find a word that starts with the letter *b*?
Capital letters	Who can find the word *The* with a capital letter?
Lowercase letters	Who can find the word *the* with a lowercase letter?
Sequence	Turn to the first page in our story. Turn to the last page in our story.
Punctuation	Let's read the punctuation.

Scaffolding

Assisting a child in the zone of proximal development is called scaffolding (Bruner 1986; Wood 2002). During guided instruction, teachers provide children with varying degrees of support that enable them to accomplish specific tasks. As children become more competent, the scaffolding is removed and the children take over more of the responsibility. Scaffolding is not simply a case of breaking learning segments down into scope and sequence. Instead, it is a complex interactive process whereby the teacher regulates levels of support according to how well the children understand the task at hand. An essential quality of a scaffold is that it be self-destructing. By that we mean that the child's behavior signals the teacher, I don't need your help anymore. I can do this all by myself.

During scaffolded instruction, levels of support are determined by what the child brings to the task. In the beginning, the teacher may use explicit language and corresponding actions that specifically direct the child to the source of information needed to solve the problem at hand. As the child develops competence, the teacher's support is adjusted to accommodate the child's increasing control. (See Figure 2.4.)

Consider, for example, how Harriet (the teacher) provides Tony with varying degrees of support for writing a known word. She first asks Tony to write the word *can,* and he writes the word *is.* Harriet realizes that Tony has activated the wrong visual pattern for two known words. She says, "Take a good look at that word. Is that word *can*?"

"No," Tony says, "that's *is.*"

Then Harriet prompts Tony to the source of information needed to activate the correct visual pattern: "Say *can.*" Tony repeats the word. The teacher says, "How would you start to write it?"

Tony responds, "*C.*"

Harriet confirms, "Yes, it starts with a *c.*"

Tony writes the letter *c* and exclaims, "Oh, I know how to do it!" Then he correctly writes the word.

The goal of scaffolding is to provide a temporary structure that enables the child to accomplish the action successfully. However, the scaffold must provide the minimum amount of support that the child needs at that particular time. In the previous example, Tony's regressive behavior may have been triggered by the interference of another known word (*is*) or by a new environmental context for writing the word. Whichever the case, Harriet provides just enough support to enable him to sort out the confusion and resolve the problem.

The degree of support will depend on how much the child brings to the task. To promote self-checking behavior, the teacher should ask the following questions:

1. What source of information does the child need to attend to?
2. What is the least amount of support I can give him to ensure that he will accomplish the task?

Level	Degree of Assistance	Example of Prompt
Level 1	General Verbal	Provides no assistance: "You try it."
Level 2	Specific Verbal	Directs child's attention to needed source of information: "Read it again and see what would make sense there."
Level 3	Specific Verbal Plus	Directs child's attention to needed source of information by using verbal prompt—"Search through the word to the ending"—plus uses a sliding card to uncover word's ending.
Level 4	Prepares for Next Action	Supplies correct word and asks child to confirm, "Could that word be *take*? Try it and see if it fits."
Level 5	Demonstrates Next Action	Models the action: "I'll add an *e* on the end of the word to make it look right."

Based on D. Wood (2002).

Figure 2.4 Degrees of teacher scaffolding during assisted performance.

A Few Words About Nonverbal Scaffolds

Nonverbal scaffolds are resources that children use to help their performance on particular literacy tasks. For a nonverbal scaffold to be effective, teachers introduce the resource in an assisted situation, including an explicit demonstration of how to use the resource as a self-help tool. It is essential that children understand the purpose of the scaffold in enabling them to accomplish a literacy task without teacher assistance. Here are five examples of nonverbal scaffolds:

- Knowledge Binder. This is a personal binder (or folder) that holds resources for helping the student during reading and writing activities. At the emergent and early levels, knowledge binders can hold resources such as an alphabet chart, names of classmates, color words, and high-frequency words (see Figure 2.5). At the upper levels, knowledge binders might include resources such as text maps, writing checklists, lists of academic words, Internet sites, and other useful sources for literacy activities.

- Reading Log. The reading log is a hardcover composition notebook that is organized according to relevant topics. A typical reading log might include four sections: my thinking (comprehension responses), reading strategies, powerful words/phrases, and text maps (see Figure 2.6; also see Dorn and Soffos 2011, 2005). The student uses the reading log as a resource during and after reading events.

- Writing Portfolio. The writing portfolio is a folder with several pockets for housing writing resources, such as lists of verbs, adverbs, adjectives, transitional words, interesting vocabulary, figurative language, and good beginnings and endings. The children use these resources to help them craft their writing during writing workshop. (See Figure 2.7; also see Dorn and Soffos 2001a.)

- Rubrics and Checklists. Children use rubrics and checklists to plan and reflect on their literacy performance. Examples of these resources include revising and editing checklists and rubrics for particular modes of writing. (See Figures 2.8a and 2.8b for an example of kindergarten and first-grade writing checklists.)

- Anchor Charts. An anchor chart is a visual display of specific information that was discussed and recorded during a teaching demonstration. Anchor charts can include procedures, text features, discussion guidelines, and a variety of grade-level concepts. The students use anchor charts as a scaffold when the teacher is not available (see Figures 2.9a and 2.9b).

Figure 2.5

Figure 2.7

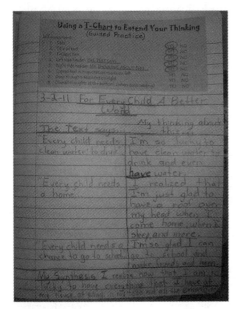

Figure 2.6a

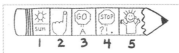

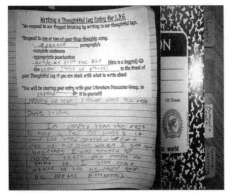

Figure 2.6b

1. Does your picture match the text for meaning?

2. Did you use finger spaces between words?

3. Did you begin the sentence with a capital letter?

4. Did you end the sentence with a period, question, or exclamation mark?

5. Did you stretch out words you don't know or use words that you do know?

Figure 2.8a

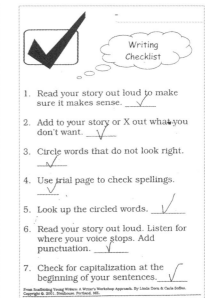

Writing Checklist

1. Read your story out loud to make sure it makes sense. ✓

2. Add to your story or X out what you don't want. ✓

3. Circle words that do not look right. ✓

4. Use trial page to check spellings. ✓

5. Look up the circled words. ✓

6. Read your story out loud. Listen for where your voice stops. Add punctuation. ✓

7. Check for capitalization at the beginning of your sentences. ✓

From Scaffolding Young Writers: A Writer's Workshop Approach. By Linda Dorn & Carla Soffos. Copyright © 2001. Stenhouse. Portland, ME.

Figure 2.8b

Figure 2.9a

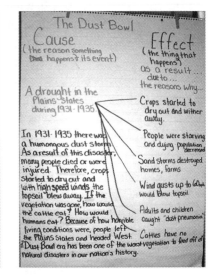

Figure 2.9b

Articulation

Articulation is any language prompt that encourages children to articulate their knowledge or problem-solving strategies during a particular task. The purpose of articulation is to make the child more metacognitive of his own cognitive processes. Here are some examples of language prompts that promote articulation:

- How did you know?
- What can you try?
- What did you notice?
- What are you thinking?
- What is your plan?

For example, Judy, the teacher, suspects that Sean, an emergent reader, is reading the four-word recurring pattern (I see a _____) based on his memory of the text. She coaches Sean to locate and confirm first-letter cues. She uses language to help him notice the initial similarity between his name and an unknown word: "Can you find a word on this page that starts like your name?" After Sean successfully locates the word *see,* Judy prompts him to articulate the reasoning behind his response: "How is it like your name?"

Sean responds, "They both start with an *s.*"

Another way that teachers use articulation is to help children learn how to plan, organize, and reflect on their literacy performances. In this case, articulation is difficult to separate from models and reflection. For instance, before students edit their writing, the teacher says, "Now, what are some important things you need to do when you edit your story?" Or, after a guided reading group, the teacher prompts the children by saying, "Tell me some strategies you used to help yourself when you were reading." In each case, the children must use language to describe good reading and writing practices. Articulation gives children a tool for guiding their own performance. However, for articulation to be effective, the children must know the meaning of the language as it describes a way to help them accomplish the goals of the literacy task.

There is a point when the teacher discourages articulation. For instance, in Chapter 1, we discussed how an external behavior (speech) becomes an internal behavior (thought) after successful and prolonged practice. If internal speech is the goal, the teacher who insists on a child's verbalization of well-known information may actually be inhibiting the child from developing automatic responses. At this point, it is more productive to increase the challenge within the child's zone of proximal development than to spend unnecessary time on something the child no longer needs.

Reflection

When children become reflective learners, they acquire an important skill that enables them to judge their performance in terms of external standards. This means that children should be taught how to analyze and reflect on their own progress. Here are some prompts that encourage such reflection:

- How do you think you did on that?
- Where do you think you did your best work?
- Can you find a part that you would like to spend more time on?
- Did you have any problems with this part?
- Show me the hardest part.
- As you look back at your work, what changes do you see?
- How has your writing changed since the beginning of the year?

Teachers promote reflection through questions that focus on personal accomplishments. For instance, during a conference with an emergent writer, the teacher might ask the child, "Show me your best letter" or "Show me a good space." The child thus develops a personal model that can be used as a standard for future comparisons. After these prompts, the teacher might encourage the child to articulate his reasons to promote a more conscious awareness of the concept.

While writing aloud (see Chapter 5), the teacher can also model reflective language. For example, she might pause at a particular sentence and comment, "Does that sentence sound right to say it that way?" Or she might reflect on her story by rereading and evaluating it for clarity: "I need to hear my story to make sure that I have included the most important points for the reader." Through modeling, the teacher demonstrates the value of reflection. Soon, children begin to internalize the teacher's language and use the same prompts to guide their own work.

Finally, teachers can promote reflective activity by introducing writing checklists. During assisted writing activities, the teacher and children co-construct a checklist of relevant areas for monitoring the children's independent work. (Some examples of these charts are provided in Chapter 5.) Remember, this checklist is a temporary nonverbal scaffold that helps promote reflection. Like all scaffolds, it is eliminated when it has outlived its usefulness.

Closing Thoughts

In this chapter, we have emphasized the importance of language interactions for shaping children's minds. Language helps students take advantage of what they already know to construct new knowledge. During literacy events, teachers design instructional interactions that engage children's minds in using language as a tool for learning. Here are some key concepts to keep in mind.

- Language interactions are the raw materials of learning. Language is the tool for causing structural changes in the brain. Language strengthens the brain's executive control functions for planning, remembering, working out steps, and organizing thought.
- Language helps children develop categories for problem solving, reasoning, analyzing, and reflecting.
- Higher-level development occurs as a result of the problem-solving attempts. Neural growth happens because of the process, not the solution.

chapter three

A BALANCED LITERACY CURRICULUM

Learning to read is a cognitive and social process that is shaped through interactions with more knowledgeable others. An enriched environment provides children with many opportunities to learn about literacy. A balanced literacy curriculum consists of five interrelated components: (1) reading books to children, (2) independent reading, (3) shared reading, (4) writing about reading, and (5) guided reading. In this chapter, we discuss the first four components; guided reading has its own chapter. Both chapters focus on how the teacher creates instructional opportunities in three areas:

- activating background knowledge
- integrating four cueing systems
- applying problem-solving strategies

Activating Background Knowledge

First, background knowledge is grounded in our concrete (sensory) experiences, which form the foundation for new learning. Our brain is biologically structured to learn from the environment, but the learning can be accelerated through meaningful and intentional teaching. Simply put, the goal of teaching is to help children pick up cues (sensory information) from the environment, integrate these sources with existing information, and construct new knowledge. This process is facilitated through the use of problem-solving strategies for initiating plans, making predictions, searching for additional information, and self-correcting when meaning breaks down (see Dorn and Soffos 2005). Further, this cognitive activity is orchestrated by motor functions (speaking and writing) that make thinking more visible and open for reflection.

The learning is facilitated by a responsive teacher who creates opportunities that build on children's background knowledge while simultaneously engaging their minds in problem-solving strategies that lead to the construction of new knowledge.

Here is a simple explanation of a complex process: *background knowledge plus strategic knowledge leads to the creation of new knowledge*. Teaching requires careful observations of what the learner knows so that learning can occur. The ultimate goal of teaching is to put the learner in charge of the thinking. Mediated learning describes how the teacher arranges the environment and facilitates the conditions that lead the student to make new discoveries. To accomplish this, the teacher must understand what the student already knows and provide scaffolds to help the student learn something new. During literacy events, the teacher and students share mutual responsibility for the construction of new knowledge (see Figure 3.1).

Teacher's Role	Student's Role
Select meaningful materials and arrange environment to arouse student's attention.	Access relevant and meaningful cues from the environment.
Activate background knowledge to understand new information.	Link background knowledge to new information.
Prompt for the integration of old and new information.	Integrate cues and use strategies to problem-solve with new information.
Use motor activities (speaking and writing) to promote thinking.	Apply motor function (speaking and writing) to express thinking.

Figure 3.1 The Construction Zone

If children are struggling in reading, many assessments focus on identifying their weaknesses and then designing instruction to remedy those areas. This theory of learning is in direct opposition to what research tells us about how the brain acquires information and then organizes related information into larger networks. Cognitive apprenticeship emphasizes the importance of using known information as a bridge to acquire new knowledge (Rogoff 1990). From this point of view, the old knowledge has the potential to activate new connections and to stimulate higher-level processes in the brain.

Let's apply this theory to our own learning experiences. Think of a topic you feel uncomfortable with (i.e., you don't have the background experiences for making sense of it) and imagine yourself in a class where you are expected to learn new information that relates directly to it. You might compensate for your inadequate background by recording and memorizing the basic information and thus be able to satisfy the teacher's requirements. But memorizing information that the brain does not understand forces you to use lower-level systems (Luria 1982; Healy 1990). In Chapter 1, we discussed the importance of building self-regulatory systems that enable young learners to use their current skills and strategies to initiate new learning. We can assume that a solid foundation based on conceptual understanding is the tool for promoting higher-level processing in the brain. In contrast, instruction that is based on inadequate background is grounded in a deficit model, which may force young learners to rely on low-level processes.

An important assumption underlying this theory is that teachers must identify the strengths of young children and use this information as the basis for designing rich learning experiences that emphasize problem solving. Clay (1991) describes how all teachers have a general theory about reading that guides their instructional interactions with their children. She explains that if a teacher's theory is in conflict with her observations of children, the teacher should be prepared to change the theory.

Children need us to be knowledgeable about the reading process. The teacher's role focuses on helping children become self-regulated readers with a repertoire of strategies for independent reading. Instructional interactions are based on the theory that children become proficient readers as they engage in strategic activity that integrates four sources of information—semantic, syntactic, graphophonetic, and pragmatic—in text. Together these four systems make communication possible, and children use all four systems simultaneously as they read. The teacher's ability to observe the children's processing behavior and to respond accordingly is a critical factor in developing strategic readers.

Integrating Four Cueing Systems

A reader who is reading independently is attending to many sources of information—or cues—in the text:

- Meaning, or semantic, cues. These derive from the reader's background knowledge and understanding of particular concepts as they relate to the author's purpose and intended message. Reading should always be message driven. An underlying question will be, Does my reading make sense in accordance with what the author is trying to tell me?
- Structural, or syntactical, system. These derive from the reader's control of oral language and exposure to book language. Grammatical substitutions are the most common cue used by young readers. This is not surprising when we remember the ease with which young children manipulate the structures of oral language when learning to talk. While reading, the reader applies structural cues to the text by asking, "Does it sound right if I say it this way?"
- Graphophonetic cues. These derive from the letters and their corresponding sounds. If the reader's response shows evidence of attention to visual cues, then we can assume that the reader has accessed some level of the visual information present in the text. Attention to visual cues may be triggered by a leading question: What have I noticed about this word?
- Pragmatic cues. These derive from the social and cultural aspects of language use.

When children who speak nonstandard English encounter texts written in standard English, they will often translate what they read into their dialect.

For example, a sentence written, "They are going to school" might be read aloud as "They be goin' to school." As children acquire more experiences with book language, they monitor their speech by asking, "Is this the way it would sound in a book?"

A successful reader integrates all four cues as he reads fluently and expressively with a focus on comprehension. The struggling reader has not learned how to integrate multiple sources of information. Instead, he views reading as an isolated process whereby he overly relies on one source of information at the expense of others and is deprived of important feedback from these other sources. The struggling reader must therefore build networks of information and learn how to use these mental storehouses for checking and confirming his responses to the text.

Applying Problem-Solving Strategies

Reading is a process of constructing meaning for the text based on the reader's background knowledge, purpose, available strategies, and understanding of the task and purpose. Strategies are enabling processes that promote effective reading because they are mental resources for students to use. We cannot observe strategies (i.e., in-the-head processes), but we can collect evidence of reading behavior that indicates that a child is engaging in mental problem-solving activity. Children who are employing strategies as they read are engaged in what Clay (2001) refers to as "reading work." Effective readers apply a repertoire of strategies to comprehend the author's message, including these:

- Use background knowledge to predict information.
- Monitor by rereading.
- Cross-check one source of information with another.
- Search for additional information.
- Self-correct when cues do not match.
- Read fluently and with expression.
- Reflect to comprehend at deeper levels.
- Regulate reading behavior (slow down or speed up) to meet reading goals.

All of these processes are brought into play efficiently and automatically by the strategic reader. However, the low-progress reader has developed a

processing system that is either ineffective or inefficient. In planning the child's literacy program, it is critical that the teacher observe and take notice of which strategic operations the child is initiating and which ones she or he is neglecting.

To examine strategic use, the teacher will analyze the running record and look closely at cues that the reader used or ignored (see Clay 2000 for how to use running records as well as Johnston 1992). The teacher must determine whether the child used a strategy to help herself make predictions and confirm or reject the predictions based on other information. To that end the teacher examines the running record for evidence of what the child did at the point of difficulty:

- Did the child stop at an unknown word and make no attempt?
- Did the child appeal for help?
- Did the child reread to gather more information?
- Did the child articulate the first letter of the problem word?
- Was the child using meaning cues (semantics), structural cues (syntax), visual cues (graphophonics), or some combination of these?

What Strategic Reading Looks Like

Each of the following examples of reading behavior demonstrates that the child is well on her way to becoming a proficient reader. In each case, the child is actively involved in the process of constructing meaning based on her own prior knowledge and personal language structures. To move the child to a higher level of processing, the teacher uses language to promote cue integration and reading strategies. Reading for meaning is the ultimate goal.

√ √ √ <u>big</u>   √   √   √   <u>right</u> √ √
I saw a —— brown horse looking ——at me.

Here the child is using his language structures to make sense of the text. He is aware that reading must make sense. However, the teacher knows that the child must gain control of one-to-one matching, so the teacher prompts the child to "read it with your finger and make the words match." If the child experiences difficulty, the teacher assists with the matching process.

√   √   √   <u>a</u>   √
The lion and the giraffe

√   <u>a</u>   √   √   √   √
and the elephant wanted the radio.

Here the student introduces a substitution that makes sense with the text. Because the miscue is insignificant, the teacher chooses to ignore it.

√   √   √   √   √
And the pumpkin seed grew

√   √   <u>sprig</u>
a pumpkin sprout.

Here the reader substitutes a word that is meaningful and structurally appropriate and also contains some visual similarities. Based on previous observations, the teacher realizes that the child possesses visual knowledge for investigating the word *sprout* further. Therefore she uses the miscue as an opportunity to direct the child's attention to searching behavior, prompting, "Try this again." The accuracy of the word is not the issue; rather, it is the opportunity the word offers the beginning reader to apply problem-solving strategies.

√   √   √   √   √   √   √   √
"I've made some cookies for tea," said Ma.
√   √   √   √   √
"Good," said Victoria and Sam.

√   <u>hungry/starting/SC/R</u>
"We're starving."

In this final example, the reader uses a range of problem-solving strategies as she works diligently to create a match between meaning, structural, and visual cues. First, she makes a prediction that is based on meaning and language structures but quickly rejects this information because of the inappropriate visual match. Next, the reader taps into her visual storehouse (her knowledge of *st* and *ing* patterns) and uses this knowledge to initiate a new response to the text. When the reader realizes this second attempt does not make sense in the story, she searches further for a new word that will satisfy her expectations for meaning and visual matches. This process results in the self-correcting (SC) activity. In a final transaction with the

text, the reader repeats the pattern "We're starving" with an emphasis that indicates a full understanding of the author's intended message. During this short process, we see the reader engaged in self-monitoring, searching, and self-correcting behavior that is driven by the desire to create a meaningful story.

These readers all made miscues, but the errors in each sample preserved the meaning of the text. Each reader used a strategic process to anticipate what the text would say, but each one was at a different level in his or her control of the reading process. In order to move the child to a higher level of reading development (a) the teacher must be a good observer of the child's processing behavior and (b) the teacher must have a good understanding of the reading process.

Accuracy Versus Problem Solving

The language a teacher uses when responding to a child's miscues should help beginning readers build effective processing systems for learning how to read. When teachers pose questions to young readers, they should consider the value of today's prompts for tomorrow's problem-solving actions: How can I prompt the child in such a way that he can use this information as a tool to help himself later when he encounters an unknown word?

The type of prompts a teacher uses can be a determining factor in how a child perceives the reading process. The reading behavior in the previous examples is evidence that these children view reading as a process of gaining meaning from the text. In contrast, the following example emphasizes "word level" response at the expense of constructing meaning.

A child is reading a predictable story with a cumulative pattern that builds on the actions of several animals that swim to a rock to take a nap. The story ends when the crocodile swims to the rock and eats the animals for lunch. As the child reads the text, he comes to the unknown word *lunch* and hesitates. The teacher prompts the child with an off-task question that focuses on getting the word correct: "What are we getting ready to eat?"

The child exclaims, "Lunch!"

The teacher praises the child's response: "Yes! Lunch! Good job."

The trouble with this interaction is that the child has missed an opportunity to predict a meaningful event based on logical expectations for how this story might end. At the same time, ineffective behavior has been reinforced so that the child develops an inappropriate definition of reading that will influence his reading behavior tomorrow. In this example, the child did not apply any textual information to help solve the unknown word. The prompt "What are we getting ready to eat?" has absolutely nothing to do with the story and has no value for decoding the visual information.

How can we prompt beginning readers to use visual information in a productive process that leads to new learning? We know that reading is a process of integrating multiple cues from text in order to construct meaning for the author's message. We also know that we must pay attention to visual information, for the printed symbols on the page are graphic signals whereby the message is communicated. Without the visual information, reading cannot occur. Teachers must therefore help young readers learn how to use visual information in fluent and flexible ways.

Using Known Parts to Solve Unknown Words

The children in Cathy's guided reading group have just finished reading a story about a baby bird. Cathy observes that several children are having difficulty with the word *something*. She decides this word is a good example for helping children use known parts to solve an unknown word.

In preparation, Cathy passes out small dry erase boards for each child in the reading group. Then she records a sentence from the story—"I must get something for my baby bird to eat"—on a large dry erase board at the front of the reading table. As she points to the word *something,* she remarks, "I noticed that several of you were having a little trouble with this word when you were reading." As she runs her finger under the word, she adds, "Let's take a good look at some things you already know that will help you solve this tricky word."

Cathy then guides the children so that they will learn how to access known information and use it to help them decipher unknown words. First she instructs the children to write the word *come* (a known word) on their individual boards. Then she asks them to erase the *c* from *come* and put an *s* in front of it. Simultaneously, Cathy performs this simple analogy at the large board so the children can confirm their attempts with her work. "What new word did you make?" she asks.

"*Some!*" the group responds.

Then Cathy says, "Jeremy, frame the word *some* in the sentence at the board." Next she models for the children how to learn a new word (*thing*) by manipulating two known parts (*th* and *ing*) from two other known words (*the* and *going*). She uses precise language and clear demonstrations to make the process of learning new words through analysis and integration explicit. After the demonstration, Cathy tells the children, "Now read the sentence and see if the word makes sense and looks right to you."

Learning About Multisyllabic Words

The children in Beth's transitional guided reading group already know a lot about word patterns. They understand how to use word chunks to solve unknown words. Today, Beth presents a word study lesson for multisyllabic words that builds on the student's knowledge of spelling patterns.

In preparation, Beth writes the five-syllable word *indescribable* on the board. She models how to use known parts to decipher each syllable break. She explains her thinking as she draws a line between each known part. "In the first part, I see the chunk *in*, like in the word *into;* I can use the word *decode* to help me with the next part, *de;* the third part, *scr,* begins like in the word *scream;* and the last two parts, *a-ble,* have the same ending as the word *fable.*" Last, she guides the children to say the new word together as they blend the five parts into a meaningful word. "The word *indescribable* is based on the word *describe,* which means to explain something. So, what do you think the word *indescribable* would mean?"

The children respond, "Hard to describe!"

"Yes," Beth acknowledges. "So now you know what the word means, and you also know how to use parts to read it. Let's try this strategy with a new word."

Beth understands that learning depends on the children's ability to generalize a strategy to use it for a different task, and that the new word should provide an opportunity for practicing the strategy. She has chosen the word *mathematical* because it contains five known parts and the math concept is meaningful. She says, "This is a new word, but you should recognize the parts within the word. And you already know the first part." The children quickly recognize the base word *math*. "Where do you think the word would be divided?" Beth asks. "Draw a line between each part, and see if you can figure out the whole word." As the children solve the word, Beth provides scaffolding to support their learning. At the end of the session, she guides the children to blend the parts together, say the whole word, and describe the strategy used.

A Balanced Reading Program

A balanced reading program includes a range of literacy activities, carefully selected materials for each activity, and a responsive teacher who knows how to structure literacy interactions that move children to higher levels of understanding. In an apprenticeship approach, the teacher asks the following questions:

- What can the children do alone? What can the children do with my help?
- What types of materials will support the children in applying their current knowledge, strategies, and skills?
- How does each type of literacy activity support the children in building effective reading systems?
- What sort of guidance do I provide the children in each activity?

The components of a balanced reading program would include many opportunities for children to learn about the reading process through the following:

- *Reading Aloud.* This allows children to interact with more complex language patterns, vocabulary, literary features, and world concepts. The teacher engages the children in an interactive experience that builds on their background knowledge while exposing them to new learning in a supportive context.
- *Independent Reading.* This allows children to practice cue integration, fluency, and strategy application on materials within their reading control. When children select interesting texts with familiar concepts and vocabulary, their background knowledge provides a scaffold for them,

thus motivating them to practice effective strategies while reading for meaning.

- *Shared Reading.* This allows children to learn about conventions of print, text features, and literary structures within a group-assisted activity. As the teacher shares an enlarged text with a group of children, she creates instructional conversations that engage children in talking about the text while prompting them to apply specific strategies for understanding written language.
- *Writing About Reading.* This allows children to record their ideas in print. Writing slows down the reading process and promotes reflective analysis. After a reading event, the teacher prompts the children to respond to the text by writing in their reading logs. Writing about the text increases reading comprehension; it also provides opportunities for children to practice spelling strategies in context.
- *Guided Reading.* This allows children to practice effective reading strategies on texts at their instructional level with the guidance of their teacher. As the children read supportive texts with a minimum of new challenges, the teacher observes their processing behavior and adjusts her degree of support to accommodate their problem-solving actions.

The overlapping and reciprocal benefits of the five types of reading events are illustrated in Figure 3.2. The rest of this chapter and Chapter 4 examine the teacher's role in each of these components.

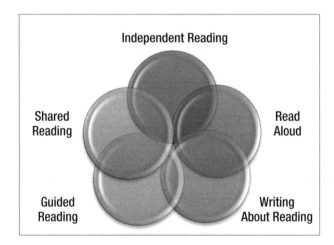

Figure 3.2 The five types of reading experiences work together to promote reading proficiency. Each reading event provides a different level of reading control.

Reading Stories to Children

A well-balanced literacy program includes opportunities for children to hear texts that they are unable to read for themselves. Reading aloud to children appears to be the single most important factor for building critical concepts about reading (Anderson et al. 1985). We know that young children who are exposed to book experiences in interactive literacy settings develop a complex range of attitudes, concepts, and skills that form the foundation of school-based literacy (Teale 2003).

Reading to children introduces them to the language of books, which is different from the language of speech and conversation. As children hear texts read to them, they acquire knowledge about book concepts, text structures, literary language, and vocabulary, and begin to anticipate that particular structures will occur within written language. They discover recurring relationships between various texts and language patterns. This knowledge gives children a personal foundation for making meaningful predictions as they read stories on their own.

During read-aloud experiences, children's brains are actively engaged in learning. The very act of listening to a book and talking about it with others (1) engages their attention and increases their concentration span, (2) stimulates their ability to visualize images, (3) develops their spatial and sequential memory functions, and (4) enhances their capacity to solve problems. Furthermore, the experience increases children's receptive (listening) and expressive (speaking) comprehension, which provides a critical language foundation for reading and writing success.

Teale (2003) describes reading books aloud as one type of social interaction from which the child can internalize features necessary for reading and writing. Listening to stories provides the child with important tools for building bridges to new learning. The purposes of reading aloud to children are to

- provide a good model of fluent and expressive reading;
- expose children to a wide variety of story structures, genres, characters, and writing styles;
- provide opportunities for writing;
- provide opportunities for discussion;
- increase children's concept and vocabulary knowledge; and
- promote an enjoyable experience with books.

Read-aloud should include a balance of literary and informational texts. Informational texts help children build the background knowledge they will need to experience success with future reading materials. Children are naturally curious, and informational texts can stimulate their minds to ask questions and seek answers to interesting things.

During read-aloud, the teacher encourages the children to use their background knowledge to develop understanding of the text. At appropriate points, she invites the children to discuss particular parts of the text and ask questions. The read-aloud experience can be integrated throughout the curriculum and extended to research projects, book discussions, and writing activities (see Wadsworth and Laminack 2006).

Independent Reading of Familiar Texts

As young children read books within their control, they learn how to become successful readers. For beginning readers, reading familiar texts can play a supportive role in promoting early reading behavior. Familiar texts give them opportunities to integrate cues and apply strategies in a known context. With each rereading, the child is able to anticipate the textual response more quickly, simultaneously freeing the brain to focus attention on constructing higher-level understanding about the story.

The familiarity of an easy book allows the child to practice fluent processing behavior. Clay (1991, 184) describes it this way:

> When readers are allowed to reread familiar material, they are being allowed to learn to be readers, to read in ways which draw on all their language resources and knowledge of the world, to put this very complex recall and sequencing behavior into a fluent rendering of the text. The orchestration of these complex behaviors cannot be achieved on a hard book.

The teacher can use the context of a familiar book to teach the child how to search for graphophonetic information. For example, the teacher can direct an emergent reader's attention to frequently encountered words with prompts such as, "Can you find the word *the* on this page?" and "Can you find the word *The* with a capital letter?" To help children connect reading and writing, the teacher can prompt the child to notice links: "Can you find a word on this page that you know how to write in your stories?" After the child has written the word, the teacher might ask the child to compare the two words: "Take a good look at the word in your story and look at the word you just wrote. Do they look the same?" In this way, the teacher enables the child to develop a more conscious awareness of the reciprocal relationship between reading and writing.

In summary, the reading of familiar materials enables the child to

- make meaningful predictions that can be checked against visual information,
- practice effective strategies on easy material,
- read with fluency and expression,
- experience the pleasure of revisiting favorite stories,
- become more knowledgeable about story structure and vocabulary, and
- problem-solve independently.

The teacher's role in organizing familiar reading is crucial. Books should be selected based on observations of the children's processing behavior across time, not left to chance or based entirely on the children's preferences. Children must have appropriate materials that build on their current knowledge and promote successful reading strategies, so the teacher prepares baskets of familiar books that include specially selected texts that the children can read with at least 95 percent accuracy. The children then select their familiar reading books from this collection of texts. As the children read, the teacher circulates and observes.

Some examples of familiar reading material are chart stories, alphabet books, poems, Big Books, and reproductions of shared stories that may be hanging around the room. The only selection criteria are that the children be familiar with the texts and that they enjoy reading them.

Independent Reading of Easy Texts

Beginning readers should have many opportunities to read books at their independent level. Volume reading of a wide variety of texts builds children's background knowledge, increases their vocabulary, and allows them to practice strategies on texts within their con-

trol. Based on a child's running records, the teacher might select three or four easy books from fiction and nonfiction categories, plus one familiar book for fluency practice, and assign these texts for independent reading. Additionally, the teacher should place tubs of interesting, easy-to-read texts in the classroom library where children can self-select books.

Shared Reading

Shared reading is an apprenticeship approach where the teacher uses an enlarged text to model, coach, and scaffold the children's learning about written language. Shared reading can occur in whole-group or small-group settings. During this event, the teacher reads with the children, and they actively contribute to the reading with the teacher's guidance. As the children become more familiar with the story, the teacher's support fluctuates in response to her observations of the children's developing control. She uses the familiar context of the shared book as a tool for directing the children's attention to new problem-solving activity.

Children enjoy shared reading because it enables them to begin reading successfully from their first day of school. It is an important experience for less able readers who enter school with limited exposures to books and print. Shared reading is a nonthreatening and enjoyable way to strengthen the language skills of struggling readers. When children read supportive texts over and over, they build literacy skills without boring, repetitive worksheet drills.

Choosing Texts

Choosing the right text is important: it needs to provide a supportive context that helps young children learn about the reading process. Many teachers use a variety of materials for shared reading:

- Big Books
- poems on charts
- enlarged texts
- nursery-rhyme charts
- raps
- favorite songs
- finger plays
- wall stories written during interactive or writing-aloud activities

Choosing a text that both the teacher and children will enjoy should be the first consideration. Books that have predictable story lines, make use of repeated phrases, include rhythm or rhyme, and incorporate natural spoken language are the ones children will want to read again and again. Overall, teachers need to create a relaxing, supportive reading experience for young readers.

Another crucial consideration when choosing texts is the size of the print. Ideally, children should gather closely around the teacher in an effort to simulate the intimacy of parents reading to their children. However, the text must be enlarged so that each child will be able to follow the print. Too often, teachers gather their entire class around a commercial Big Book that has tiny print rather than oversize print, too many lines of text per page, or unusual placement of text on the page. This hinders the children's ability to build their knowledge of print conventions. It is important that teachers keep in mind the needs of the children and the purpose of reading as they select texts.

Shared reading should be a daily component of a balanced literacy program. However, the amount of time the teacher devotes will vary from day to day, depending on the text and the depth of the strategy instruction. Most shared-reading blocks range from twenty to twenty-five minutes. This important block of the day provides the opportunity for the teacher to involve students in the text and focus on a variety of aspects, both visual and cognitive. Both the teacher and the students have important roles. As a result of shared reading, students will improve their abilities to choose appropriate, interesting texts for independent reading, and develop literacy skills in the essential areas of phonological awareness, phonics, vocabulary, comprehension, and fluency.

We recognize that each student develops on an individual time line. When well planned and executed, shared reading is a developmentally appropriate way to differentiate instruction in a whole-group setting. As teachers gradually release responsibility, the students begin to see themselves as readers. Drawn in by the text's content, they take on more and more active roles in the reading process.

Conducting a Shared Reading

In this section, we look at the four components of shared reading: (1) introducing the story, (2) reading the story, (3) discussing the story, and (4) subsequent readings. Then we share specific examples from various classrooms.

Introducing the Story

During the first reading, the teacher introduces the story to the students. This is where she "sells" the story so the children will want to read it again and again. The teacher engages the students in a conversation about the title, the cover illustration, the title page, and the children's own experience. She guides the children to form expectations about the story and its characters, which will be confirmed or disconfirmed when they acquire more details from the actual reading. Open-ended questions, such as the following, promote the prediction process:

- What do you think the story is about?
- What is on the book's cover?
- How would you feel if you were the character?
- What do you think will happen next?
- What else do you see in the picture?

Reading the Story

When reading the story for the first time, the teacher reads the entire text, pausing only to engage the students in constructing meaning. For example, the teacher might invite the students to predict a word or phrase, or to explain what might happen next in the story. Remember, the goal of the first reading is to understand the author's message and to enjoy the story; later this framework will provide a scaffold for problem solving on words and print concepts within a meaningful text.

Discussing the Story

After the reading, the teacher engages the students in a thoughtful discussion of the text. Talking about the text not only stimulates deeper comprehension, but also builds communication skills.

Subsequent Readings

Subsequent readings involve the students more and more. Because the texts are usually repetitive, students can join in on a repeated phrase. Repeated readings also provide teaching opportunities for students to learn about letters, words, punctuation, vocabulary, and print conventions.

A Specific Example of Shared Reading

This example involves a small group of six children in a first-grade class. As the teacher works with the group, the remaining children in the class pursue a range of independent activities: familiar or easy reading, illustrating the text of a class-written book, writing stories on the computer, and listening to books on tape.

The teacher has carefully selected *Goodnight, Goodnight* (Parkes 1989) and examined the book for supportive and challenging features in relation to the children's strengths and needs. (The amount of teacher support required during a first reading varies, depending on the number of experiences that the children have had with books, the type of text, and the particular concepts about print on which the teacher intends to focus.)

The teacher introduces the children to the book by setting the scene. First, she reads the title and asks the children to look at the picture on the cover. "What will happen in this story?" she wonders.

Several children respond, "The little girl is going to bed." The teacher validates this response and encourages the children to make further predictions as they look at the pictures and discuss the story's development:

Teacher: She's going to bed, isn't she? Because she has her nightgown on and she's in the bedroom. Do you see anything else in the picture?

James: She has her teddy bear in bed.

Kelly: She's reading a book to her animals.

Teacher: In this story, the little girl is reading some bedtime stories, and she has a dream about some of her nursery-rhyme friends who come out to play with her. Let's look at the first two pages and see who might come out of the storybook.

Thomas: There's a lady in her room!

Teacher: Yes, there is a lady. Where do you think she might be looking?

Kelly: In that door.

Tanisha: That's a closet!

Thomas: She's looking on the floor in the closet!

Teacher: Those are all good predictions from looking at the pictures. Let's read and see if we can find more clues about who this lady is and what she is doing in the story.

The teacher reads several pages with expression and without interruption. As she reads, she points to each word, thus modeling the relationship of spoken to written language. After hearing the repetitive pattern only two or three times, the children are able to initiate some of the reading on subsequent pages. The teacher helps this along by pausing at predictable points in the story, inviting the children to take over. She continues to direct their attention to the pictures and the rhyming patterns of the language as ways they can predict and confirm their responses:

Teacher: *(Reading story)*
"I love to read in bed at night.
Then Teddy and I turn out the light.
And as we dream the night away,
our storybook friends come out to play.
Who's that looking in my cupboard?
It's my friend Old . . ."

Tanisha: Mother Hubbard!

Teacher: What makes you think it might be Old Mother Hubbard?

Tanisha: Because it said *cupboard*. That's like *Hubbard*.

Teacher: Let's try it together.

All: "Who's that looking in my cupboard?
It's my friend Old Mother Hubbard!"

Teacher: Were you right?

Children: Yes!

The next page gives the children another opportunity to predict a word that sounds the same:

Teacher: "Jump on the bed and join the fun.
There's lots of room for . . ."

All: Everyone!

Teacher: That's good listening. You thought of a word that makes sense and rhymes with *fun*! *Everyone.* Let's read it together.

Similar interactions occur throughout the reading of the text. The children's repeated exposure to the structure of the story enables them to make predictions more quickly. They are learning how to apply two important strategies to their reading: (1) predicting from picture cues and language structures and (2) listening to the rhyming patterns of words. The teacher guides the reading so that the children can practice fluent and expressive phrasing of language, thus serving as a personal model for how reading should sound.

Teaching Opportunities

The teacher uses the supportive context of shared reading to
- model and teach early concepts about print, such as directionality and one-to-one matching;
- find some known words and letters;
- predict some letter/sound correspondence;
- teach reading strategies such as rereading to monitor, predicting and confirming responses, cross-checking one cue against another, and searching for additional information to resolve conflict;
- teach book conventions such as title, table of contents, author, and illustrator.

In addition to multiple readings, the teacher uses quick, focused activities to direct the children's attention to specific features of the text and to show them how to apply problem-solving strategies. The following tools are helpful here:
- a pointer
- framing cards
- masking questions
- cloze procedures
- sentence strips
- word cards

These activities should be done sparingly and quickly; the teacher will choose only two or three teaching points for each shared reading.

Framing Cards and Masking Questions

Framing cards and masking questions help children notice specific concepts about print. Masking questions

are prompts the teacher uses to direct the children's attention to a particular aspect of the text, which they then isolate with a framing card (a card with a "window" in the middle of it). The windows in framing cards are of different sizes in order to isolate different visual aspects of the text (one letter, a two-letter word, a four-letter word, a phrase, and so on). In the excerpt below, the teacher uses this technique to help the children apply their knowledge of beginning sounds (onset) and ending patterns (rime) to find a new word in the text. (See Chapter 7 for explanations of *onset* and *rime*.)

Teacher: Who can find a word that starts like *house* and rhymes with *dad*? *(Andrew raises his hand.)* Okay, Andrew. Use the framing card to tell us the answer.

Andrew: *(Framing* had*)* *Had*.

Teacher: Great job! *Had* starts like *house* and rhymes with *dad*. Now let's read it in the story.

Frames can be used to find
- known words,
- rhyming words,
- specific letters,
- frequently encountered words,
- punctuation, and
- word endings.

Cloze Procedure

Sometimes teachers use a cloze procedure to help children predict a word based on meaning or to apply cross-checking strategies. A simple way to do this is by placing a sticky note on top of words at various points in the text. The teacher reads the story up to that point and asks the children to make a prediction that makes sense. Then she asks the children to predict the letter they would expect to see at the beginning of their word. The teacher writes all the letter predictions on the board. Next she uncovers the first letter of the word, and the children confirm or reject their prediction based on this additional information. Then the teacher articulates the word slowly and encourages the children to make further predictions based on the sounds within the word. Throughout this process, the teacher guides the children to apply predicting, confirming, cross-checking, and searching strategies.

Here's a specific example using a poem:

Teacher and Children: (*Reading together*)
"Rabbit
My rabbit has two big ears
And a funny little _____.
He likes to nibble c_____
And he hops wherever he goes."

Teacher: "My rabbit has two big ears and a funny little . . ." Who can think of a word that would make sense in this sentence?

Terry: Nose!

Justin: Tail!

Eli: Mouth!

Teacher: Those are good predictions because they all make sense.
"And a funny little nose."
"And a funny little tail."
"And a funny little mouth."

Notice how the teacher validates the children's responses in two ways: (1) she praises them for making good predictions and (2) she repeats each response so that the children can hear how they all make sense. As the dialogue continues, the teacher pushes the learning to a new level by prompting the children to use first-letter cues to confirm or reject their initial response:

Teacher: What letter would you expect to see at the beginning of the word *nose*?

All: *N.*

Teacher: What letter would you expect to see at the beginning of the word *tail*?

All: *T.*

Teacher: What letter would you expect to see at the beginning of the word *mouth*?

All: *M.*

Teacher: Well, you all made good predictions based on what would make sense in the poem. Now we need to check further by looking at the first letter in the word.

At this point, the teacher uncovers the first letter of the word and the children apply strategies for confirming or rejecting their initial responses.

James: Oh, mine's not right!

Eli: Neither is mine.

Teacher: How do you know?

Eli: Because it doesn't start with an *n.*

James: Because there's no *t* in it.

Teacher: Could this word be *nose*?

Terry: Yes!

After the children confirm the word based on first-letter cues, the teacher prompts them to check their choice with meaning cues. She asks, "Can anyone think of another word that starts with an *n* and would make sense in the sentence? 'My rabbit has two big ears and a funny little n- n- n- . . .'" When the children say *nose,* the teacher highlights the importance of using multiple sources of information during reading: "So the word *nose* makes sense in our story, and it starts with the right letter. You found two ways to check on the word."

The dialogue below focuses on helping the children listen to the sounds within the word and predict the letters associated with these sounds.

Teacher: Before I uncover the whole word, can you tell me any other letters that you might expect to see in the word *nose*?

Terry: *S.*

Eli: *O.*

Teacher: Let's look. (*Uncovering the word and reading*) "My rabbit has two big ears and a funny little nose." Were you right?

Figure 3.3 Using word cards to match the text of a familiar poem.

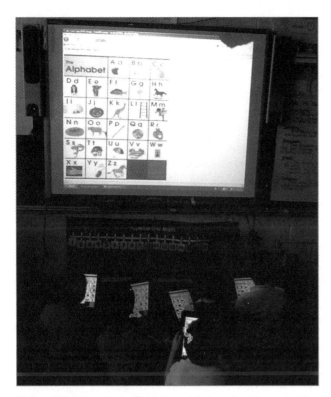

Figure 3.4 A shared reading of an alphabet chart from a whiteboard and individual iPads.

Figure 3.5 Learning how to build sentences and stories by assembling cut-up words from familiar texts.

All: Yes.

Reading an Alphabet Chart

A common activity in kindergarten or early in first grade is for the teacher and children to participate in a shared reading of an enlarged alphabet chart. The purpose is to help the children acquire letter-sound alphabet cues they can use when they are reading and writing. Each child has a reduced version of the chart, which they also use during independent writing.

The children and the teacher gather around the chart, and the teacher leads the children in saying the name of each upper- and lowercase letter and pointing to an adjacent drawing of something beginning with that letter (*A, a, apple, B, b, ball,* and so on). The letters are read fluently, and the teacher pauses occasionally to allow the children to say the letters or the name of the picture symbol. As the children become more competent, the teacher increases the difficulty of the task:

- "Read the tall letters only."
- "Read the lowercase letters only."
- "Read the picture cues only."
- "Read the rounded letters only."

Sentence Strips, Word Cards, and Pocket Charts

Teachers use sentence strips and word cards to extend the shared-reading experience. The text of a familiar story is gradually rebuilt as the teacher prompts the children to match the text fragments to the story by placing sentence strips into pockets on a chart. First the teacher passes out strips of paper containing individual sentences from the story. Then she asks, "Who has the first line of our story?" The child with this line of text goes to the chart and places her line in the first pocket. After each line is added, the teacher guides the children in rereading the sentence strips to see what should come next. Each child contributes his or her sentence until the story is completed. Finally, the teacher prompts the children to reread the story on the chart and check it against the published version.

The same activity can be adapted for word cards. First, the teacher and children read a sentence from the shared book; then, the teacher passes out cards containing individual words from the sentence. The children rebuild the words into the sentence. Each time a word is added, it is important that the teacher and children reread the sentence to predict which word is needed next. Below, we share some ways that teachers can use pocket charts and word charts to promote children's literacy skills.

Activities for Emergent Readers
- Match text on top of text.
- Match text underneath.

- Match text to illustrations.
- Match illustrations to text.
- Match high-frequency words on top of words in text.
- Use cut-up sentence strips or word cards to fill in missing word from text.
- Act out the word or phrase—copy phrases or words from text and have students rebuild the text.
- Write or highlight a word from the text—invite students to generate other words that begin the same, rhyme, or end the same; write words on cards and have students sort words in pocket chart.

Activities for Early and Transitional Readers

- Reread text on sentence strips for enjoyment.
- Use cut-up sentence strips or word cards to fill in missing word from text.
- Match photographs to captions.
- Match heading to text.
- Act out the text—copy text (sentences, phrases, or individual words) and have students rebuild the text.
- Write a word from the text and invite students to generate other words that begin the same (blends, consonant clusters, diagraphs, prefixes); rhyme; or end the same (diagraphs, suffixes, rime pattern).
- Write generated words on cards and have students sort words in pocket chart (visual, sound, meaning).
- Highlight charts, maps, sidebars, headings, labels, and/or captions to written text on sentence strip.
- Use highlighter tape or colored transparency to highlight special nonfiction features (for example, bold words, italicized words).
- Highlight words from text that indicate text structures (such as cause/effect, problem/solution).
- Locate a word and generate synonyms, antonyms, or homophones.

Cut-Up Poems

Poems are frequently used for shared reading. Once children have heard a poem many times, the teacher can photocopy the poem and cut it into meaningful chunks that can be "rebuilt." Children reassemble the poem by using the familiar language structure to pre-

dict and confirm the visual features of print. The jigsaw format is self-correcting. (The cut-up poems can be stored in zippered plastic bags and placed in poetry centers where children can work independently.)

More on Shared Reading with Poetry

Poetry provides young children with rich opportunities to hear the rhythm of language and to develop phonological awareness of sound patterns. Oral language is a natural foundation for learning how to read. When children expect particular language patterns to occur in text, they have a reliable means of relating the structure of language to its visual features. The teacher guides the process by using prompts that direct the children's attention to cue integration. In Figure 3.6, we share a few examples of activities that teachers can use to promote children's phonological awareness through the shared reading of poetry.

Word Awareness—Ask children to listen to one line in the poem. Prompt them by asking, "How many words do you hear in this sentence?"

Word Rhyming—Name one word in the poem, and ask children to provide a word that rhymes with it.

Sound Matching—Pronounce two words from the poem and ask children if they begin with the same sound. Or ask children to name two words in the poem that begin the same.

Sound Isolation—Using selected words from the poem, ask children to name the first sound of the word.

Phoneme Blending—Slowly articulate a word from the poem. Ask children to blend the word together.

Sound Addition or Substitution—Choose a word from the poem to show that a new word can be created by the addition or substitution of a letter. Ask children to add the new sound to make a new word.

Sound Segmentation—Choose selected words from the poem. Ask children to tell you what sounds they hear in each word.

Phoneme Manipulation—Ask children to manipulate phonemes from selected words in the poem. For example, "Take away the first sound in *me* and add the /h/ sound. What's the new word?" (*he*)

Figure 3.6 Developing phonological awareness with shared reading of poetry.

In elementary classrooms, shared reading of poetry is a daily activity (see Figure 3.7). During poetry reading, the teacher reads the poem once without stopping so students can hear the pacing, cadence, and meaning of the language. On the second reading, the teacher invites the students to read along, using this whole-group experience to direct children's attention to concepts of print. When she thinks the students have learned the poem, the teacher gives them a copy to read in pairs or in small groups, or to engage in poetry performance. We encourage teachers to expose young children to hundreds of poems, thus building a rich storehouse of language patterns for supporting reading development.

Figure 3.7 An interactive whiteboard is a great way to display poems and engage children in shared reading. Teachers can also upload the poems to children's iPads for independent reading practice.

Shared Reading of a Nursery-Rhyme Big Book

Angela, a first-grade teacher, gathers the children around her to introduce them to a new book. The *Great Enormous Watermelon* (Parkes 2009) recounts the antics of nursery-rhyme characters who work together trying to pull an enormous watermelon out of the ground. Angela begins by talking about nursery rhymes.

Angela: What do we know about nursery rhymes?
Suzy: They always rhyme.
Angela: That's right. What is an example of a nursery rhyme? Who knows?
George: "Jack jumped over the candlestick."
Angela: (*Validating George's knowledge and prompting him to remember the language pattern*) "Jack be nimble . . ."
George: (*Chanting in rhythm*) "Jack be nimble. Jack be quick. Jack jumped over the candlestick."

Angela and George share the experience of reciting the poem. Angela's supportive language helps maintain the integrity of the rhythm and rhyme associated with poetry.

Angela: "Jack jumped high . . ."
George: "And Jack jumped low.
Jack jumped over and bumped his toe."

Angela next invites other children to share favorite nursery rhymes. She modulates her voice and pauses at appropriate points so that the children can predict upcoming language patterns.

Angela: Do you have a favorite nursery rhyme, Dexter?
Dexter: "Hey, Diddle Diddle."
Angela: "Hey, Diddle Diddle, the cat and the . . ." (*Pausing with a slight rise in her voice to stimulate the next response*)
Dexter: " . . . fiddle!"
Angela: "The cow jumped over the moon."
All: "The little dog laughed to see such a sight. And the dish ran away with the spoon."

During the lesson, Angela pulls out familiar poems that have been written on large colorful posters and leads the children in fluent rereadings. The children are exposed to poetry's specialized vocabulary and literary patterns. For example, when the children read the line "rapping at the windows," Suzy asks, "What does *rapping* mean?"

Dexter responds, "It's just another word for knocking."

"Old Mother Hubbard" provides another opportunity for vocabulary development. When the word *bare* is read in text, the children develop a new understanding of its significance in regard to the fate of the characters:

CC: What does *bare* mean?
Dexter: It means empty.
Angela: Yes, the cupboard was empty. There was nothing in it.
Suzy: What did she eat?
Angela: I guess nothing. The cupboard was bare, so she didn't have anything to eat, and neither did the dog.
George: They're probably starving.

Remembering these familiar nursery-rhyme characters has set the stage for the shared reading of the new book. Angela now holds up the book; the cover has a picture of an old woman pulling a large watermelon out of the ground.

Angela: Let me show you what today's book is going to be about. It's called *The Great Enormous Watermelon.* We've been talking about nursery rhymes, so what do you think this book is going to be about?
Suzy: A watermelon.
Angela: (*Confirming Suzy's prediction while encouraging more ideas*) Well, it has a watermelon on the cover. What else do you think this book is going to be about?
Dexter: I think they are going to try to get it out.
Angela: Who?
CC: Some people.
Angela: (*Continuing to prompt for more information*) Do you have any idea who the people might be?
George: Some nursery-rhyme people!
Suzy: (*Leaning forward and pointing to the old woman on the cover*) She's going to pull it out.
Angela: (*Prompting Suzy to justify her prediction*) How can you tell?
Suzy: Because she's got some water there on her face.
Angela: Because she's sweating? Is she pulling so hard that she's sweating?
Several children in unison: Yeah!

The dialogue above is characteristic of an apprenticeship approach to literacy. Angela prompts the children to use clues from the cover and from their background experiences to establish a predictable framework for the story.

Angela: This story is called *The Great Enormous Watermelon.* What does *enormous* mean?
CC: It means bad.
George: No. It means really, really big.
Angela: (*Prompting the children to explain their predictions*) Well, how do you know what the word means?
Suzy: (*Pointing to the large watermelon on the cover of the book*) Because it's really big. Because *big* means big!
Angela: Yes. That is a really big watermelon! So, we can call it an enormous watermelon.

Next Angela introduces the concept of "retelling."

Angela: This story is retold by Brenda Parkes.
Brandon: Retold? What's *retold*?
Angela: *Retold* means that someone else wrote it a long time ago, and Brenda Parkes decided to redo it herself. So she retold the story in her own words.
CC: She just put in some words? And put some things in it?
Angela: Well, maybe she just changed the story a little bit, retold it in her own words. Like if you wanted to tell the story to a friend or write about it in your journal, you might use your own words to tell about it. (*Prompting the children to listen carefully to her next question, which focuses on the main character*) Now here's a really important question. (*Points to the old woman on the cover*) Who do think this old woman is? Who have we been talking about today that this might be?
Brandon: Old Mother Hubbard!
Angela: Do you think this could be Old Mother Hubbard planting a watermelon seed?
Suzy: (*Aware that an author may pull from different sources when retelling a story*) She probably got that out of a nursery rhyme.
George: Or Old Mother Goose.

As the shared reading continues, the children focus on creative ways for helping Old Mother Hubbard pull the enormous watermelon out of the ground.

They express excitement as familiar characters from nursery rhymes appear in the pages of the story. Brandon comments that Humpty Dumpty looks different in this book. Angela explains, "That's not the important thing in the story. Every illustrator draws their pictures a little different."

When a pail of water appears in one corner of the page, Suzy points to the bucket and comments, "That's Jack. That gives us a clue."

Angela reinforces this behavior, saying, "Yes, that does give us a clue, doesn't it. On every page, we have a pattern of clues. Let's look for more clues as we turn the pages."

As the story ends and the enormous watermelon remains in the ground, the children offer advice. Suzy indicates her impatience with the characters' efforts to continue with a plan that seems to be getting them nowhere. In a slightly irritated voice, she exclaims, "They need to try something a little bit better than that!"

About that time the watermelon comes out of the ground, and all the children seem relieved. As the characters return to the house with the watermelon, Angela asks, "What do you think they are going to do when they get inside?"

Several children respond, "Try to eat it," but Brandon remarks, "Get a drink of water."

This response is a logical prediction because the characters have worked so hard to get the watermelon out of the ground; a drink of water might be the first thing on their minds! However, as the last page of the story is turned, the children confirm their predictions and the group exclaims in unison, "They ate it!"

Brandon says, "I would eat it, too!"

The Importance of Informational Texts

Nonfiction Big Books should be included in the shared-reading framework. Informational topics make up a large majority of what we read about every day. The topics of nonfiction are varied with vivid photographs. Children are drawn to real-world knowledge. These books also allow children to draw on their personal experiences to activate prior knowledge, to build vocabulary, and to expand their knowledge of the world. For some it also gives motivation and interest to read. When we include nonfiction in shared reading we are building academic literacy.

According to Short and FitzSimmons (2007, 2), academic literacy

- includes reading, writing, and oral discourse for school;
- varies from subject to subject;
- requires knowledge of multiple genres of text, purposes for text use, and text media;
- is influenced by students' literacies in contexts outside of school;
- is influenced by students' personal, social, and cultural experiences.

Shared reading is an ideal place to teach young children how to navigate nonfiction text and how to learn about new topics. To be efficient readers, students need to understand how expository texts work. They need to learn the organizational structures and signal words used to convey meaning. Shared reading offers explicit opportunities to teach children about the specific features associated with nonfiction texts.

Effective readers of nonfiction texts need to understand (1) how visual literacy combines with the written text to convey specific information, (2) how information in captions and labels combines with the text to communicate specific knowledge, and (3) how strategies are used to activate prior knowledge and facilitate interaction with the text.

Highlighting Text Features

During the past three days, Vicki and her first-grade students have been reading *The Life Cycle of a Butterfly* (2009) by Margaret McNamara, a nonfiction text with a variety of text features that illustrate the butterfly's life cycle. She wants her students to realize that meaning is embedded in these visual aids and that they must understand these features in order to comprehend the content. As the children encounter a new feature within the shared reading, Vicki guides them in adding the term and the definition to a large chart titled "Text Features." After the shared reading, she instructs the students to visit the classroom library, search through nonfiction texts for examples of text features, and record these examples in their reader response log. In Figure 3.8, we share examples of text features, organizational structures, and language cues that are associated with nonfiction texts.

Fonts and Special Effects
- titles, headings, subheadings
- boldface and color print
- italicized words
- bullets
- captions
- labels

Text Organizers
- index
- preface
- table of contents
- glossary
- appendix

Graphics
- diagrams
- cutaways
- cross sections
- overlays
- distribution maps
- word bubbles
- charts, tables, graphs
- framed text
- illustrations and photographs

Text Structures
Cause and Effect, and Problem and Solution
- because
- since
- therefore
- consequently, after
- when
- then
- finally
- as a result
- if, then

Sequence
- on (date)
- not long after
- now
- as
- before
- while

Description
- to begin with
- most important
- also
- in fact
- for instance
- for example

Comparison and Contrast
- however
- but
- on the other hand
- instead
- either, or
- although

Figure 3.8 Examples of text features, organizational structures, and language cues associated with nonfiction texts.

An Example of Shared Reading of Nonfiction Text

In this final example, Hannah, a second-grade teacher, has selected the book *Habitats Around the World* (Castor 2009) as today's nonfiction shared reading. She displays the cover of the book, reads the title and the author's name, and invites the children to predict what they think the book will be about. The photographs provide clear evidence of animal homes, and Hannah builds on the children's responses by saying, "This book is about animal habitats—places where animals live."

Teacher: Do you think this book is fiction or nonfiction?

Lauren: Nonfiction, because it has photographs of real things.

Teacher: Yes, nonfiction books provide information. As you read a nonfiction text, you need to make sure you understand the information. Ask yourself, what are the most important ideas that the author wants me to understand? This is sometimes called a main idea.

Then Hannah turns to the table of contents and prompts the students to look at the first chapter. She asks, "What do you think the first chapter is about?" When Megan responds correctly, Hannah probes further. "What page will we begin reading?" Then she encourages predictions: "What kind of animal might live in this habitat?" Hannah accepts all responses with her remark, "Let's read to find out."

After the first reading, Hannah prompts, "What did we learn about a savanna? Turn to your partner and share at least two details." The teacher allows the students time to discuss their knowledge with a peer; then she brings them together to share their ideas with the whole group. As the children share their information, Hannah records the main idea and details on a graphic organizer. The next day, the class will read Chapter 2, and the teacher will scaffold the students to articulate the main idea and find the details for animals that live in this habitat.

Closing Thoughts

A balanced literacy program provides an integrated context for promoting children's literacy development. An essential goal of self-regulation is for children to be able to transfer their knowledge, skills, and strategies across multiple contexts for different purposes. When this occurs, old knowledge is transformed into new knowledge, and the children's understanding of a literacy concept moves to a conceptual level.

chapter four

GUIDED READING

A balanced literacy program includes opportunities for students to receive whole-group, small-group, and one-on-one instruction. During small groups, the teacher creates a learning context that is based on children's instructional needs. It is important to remember that individual children within the group will progress at different rates; thus teachers need to group (and regroup) based on careful observations of how children are applying their skills, knowledge, and strategies while they are reading and writing.

In guided reading, the teacher works with a small group of children with similar instructional needs. The teacher's role is to predict the type and amount of support the group needs to be able to read and understand the book or story. She prompts them to apply reading strategies, regulating her assistance according to the developing control of the individual children in the group. She intervenes only when a student is unlikely to problem-solve independently, is frustrated, or is in jeopardy of losing meaning and does so by asking questions that relate to the reading process. She also provides specific feedback that praises an appropriate processing behavior: for example, "That helped you to return to the beginning of the sentence and reread that tricky part."

Guided reading helps children develop an appreciation and understanding of the story and at the same time stimulates problem-solving conversations about how to apply reading strategies in context. Competence as well as independence is encouraged as the teacher models ways of responding when one encounters difficulty in text. The goal is to provide students with a toolbox of resources they can use to read a wide range of text with full comprehension.

When Do I Begin Guided Reading in My Classroom?

Although there isn't a pat answer to this question, there are observable characteristics that indicate that children are ready to participate in these more formal groupings:

- Do they have many of the early concepts of print almost under control (i.e., can they distinguish between text and illustration)?
- Do they have some understanding of directionality?
- Do they have some knowledge of one-to-one matching?
- Do they know the difference between letters and words?
- Do they know most of the letters of the alphabet and a few frequently encountered words (such as *I, the, a*)?
- Do they actively participate in shared reading by predicting events and language structures that show an awareness of comprehension, rhythm, and rhyme?
- Do they spend time reading and noticing a few details of print?
- Do they explore the print on the classroom walls?
- Do they notice that the same words appear in many different contexts?
- Do they link sounds with symbols when they write?
- Do they articulate words slowly as they write?

If the answer to some of these questions is yes, chances are that children are ready to learn more about how printed language works. Some children are ready to begin guided reading in kindergarten, whereas others need more opportunities and experiences with print before reading a book in a small group.

Planning for Guided Reading Lesson

The student's success during guided reading is dependent on the teacher's ability to plan and execute a lesson that is based on three theories:

1. **Theory of the Task:** What are the specific components of a guided reading lesson? What are the procedures for each lesson component? How are these procedures implemented? What is the rationale behind each procedure? How will these routines (procedures) provide a predictable structure for promoting the students' independence?

2. **Theory of the Prompts:** What are some language prompts that I can use to activate the students' successful problem solving? Are my prompts clear and goal oriented? Are they focused on strategies or items? When should I use these prompts? What is the least amount of support I can provide? Am I prompting for independence and transfer? How can I use nonverbal prompts to scaffold the learner?

3. **Theory of the Learner:** What does the child already know that he or she can bring to the problem-solving task? Where will I need to fill in the gaps through the book orientation and my levels of prompting? How can the learner's background be helpful? How might it hinder? How will I use my theory of the child to ensure a successful reading experience?

The teacher's theory of instruction will influence how she organizes her teaching. A well-designed lesson planner (see Appendix C-2) can provide a scaffold for planning instruction that incorporates the three theories described above. As the students read independently, the teacher writes observations of their problem-solving behaviors. Some teachers like to use the back side of the planner for recording the reading behaviors of the group. Other teachers prefer to write their observations on a sticky label and then file this evidence in an assessment section for each child.

Regardless of the method, it is important for teachers to study how their guided reading instruction is influencing their students' learning.

Elements of a Guided Reading Lesson

Guided reading follows a predictable structure with built-in scaffolds for supporting student needs. In this section, we share examples of guided reading lessons with emergent to fluent readers.

Book Selection

Book selection is critical. Books need to be chosen based on children's interests, prior knowledge, and competency. When selecting books for young readers, teachers should consider important factors such as text layout, specialized vocabulary or concepts, the child's oral language facility, and his potential to apply problem-solving strategies to figure out the words he is unlikely to know. A carefully selected book enables a child to learn more about reading each time he reads.

The teacher should select a book that the child can read at 90 percent accuracy or better. Analyzing running records of previously read texts (see Clay 2000; Johnston 1992) helps teachers make good decisions about a student's reading ability. When reading accuracy falls below 90 percent, the child may be unable to retain the meaning of the story.

Many books that might be considered easy for some children can be too difficult for others. Reading is a problem-solving process by which the reader creates meaning through interacting with the text. Meaning is created as the reader brings prior knowledge and personal experience to the page. The physical design of books and the way their stories are constructed are critical elements in the process. Children begin school with varied literacy backgrounds—some have so little experience that they may not understand that the print conveys the message. Limited experiences in a child's environment may hinder his or her understanding of the content. (For example, if a child has never been to a zoo, he may be unfamiliar with some of the animals in a zoo book.) Therefore, teachers must be very careful to select books for beginning readers that not only meet the goal of instruction but also support the children's level of knowledge and experience. For example, are the picture cues clear? Is the type large enough? Is the layout of the text easy to follow? Does it require knowing about certain concepts?

For a child to be able to read a book effectively, the book needs to contain more supportive features than challenging ones. Answering the following questions should help you select an appropriate book for guided reading:

1. Does the book allow the child to construct meaning?
2. Does the book contain structural patterns that are within the child's language control?
3. Does the book include letters and some words that the child can use to monitor his or her reading?
4. Does the book allow the child to use his or her current strategies and skills to problem-solve?
5. Does the book promote fluency?
6. What are the supportive features of the book?
7. What are the challenging features of the book?

As teachers select guided reading texts, they should be reminded that levels are fallible. Teachers should consider the children's prior knowledge about the topic as an important factor in text selection. If prior knowledge is limited, the teacher will need to select another book or provide a higher degree of scaffolding through the book introduction.

Focus of Lesson

In literacy apprenticeship, the teacher is the more capable person. Through sensitive observation, she is always aware of the cutting edge of her children's development. The focus of a guided reading lesson is determined by the strengths and needs of the children in the group. The teacher can use the following questions (Clay 1991; Fountas and Pinnell 1996) to help her set the proper focus for instruction:

1. Does the child attend to print (for example, use one-to-one matching, notice known letters or words within text, apply directional movement on two or more lines of print, and so on)?
2. What strategies does the child use (for example, rereading, searching pictures, using first-letter cues, noticing chunks in words)?

3. What strategies does the child neglect?
4. What does the child do at point of difficulty (for example, appeal to the teacher, sound out the word, reread, correct himself)?
5. What sources of information (meaning, structure, visual) does the child rely on?

As children become competent readers, the focus of instruction may shift to deepening their understanding of the text. For example, the teacher may ask questions about specific content, the author's writing style, characteristics of the genre, text features, or literary devices the author uses to express meaning.

Book Orientation

Before a group reads a new book, the teacher provides an orientation to the text. The orientation prepares children to read the text by creating a supportive context for building meaning. The teacher activates the children's background knowledge, invites them to make predictions about the book, and identifies the title, author, and illustrator. In her orientation, the teacher prompts the children to integrate meaning, structure, and visual cues. She helps the children build meaning by giving a brief overview of the message and prompts them to discuss the pictures. She exposes them to structure by identifying recurring language phrases and patterns, being careful to use the precise vocabulary of the text as she and the children talk about it. She introduces the children to visual cues by having them find a frequently encountered word they know or predict a letter at the beginning of an unknown word. As the children gain more control, she might ask them to predict letters in ending and medial positions as well, and she provides more opportunities to think about the message at higher levels of comprehension.

The book orientation provides a framework for children to use as they explore the written message. The teacher sets the purpose for reading and quickly discusses with the group how to overcome possible challenges within the text. This reminder encourages the children to consider alternatives and to make informed decisions in order to gain meaning. Their attention is freed so they can concentrate more closely on the visual details of words when they need to.

The level of support in the introduction diminishes as the children move toward self-regulated reading. During the emergent reading stage, the teacher provides a rich introduction with active discussions around the pictures, the sentence patterns, and the text sequence. As the children move into the early stages, the introduction may be reduced to a summary statement, a few selective questions, and a purpose for reading. By the transitional and fluent levels, the children have acquired strategies for orienting themselves to the text, and they apply previewing techniques for surveying the text and constructing meaning. Figure 4.1 illustrates how the teacher adjusts her degree of support as children develop greater control over the reading process.

Oral Reading and Teacher Conference

In the elementary grades, oral reading is an essential component of the guided reading lesson. The first reading is an opportunity for children to apply their skills and strategies with the assistance of a support-ive and responsive teacher. Each child reads aloud at his or her own pace, and the teacher provides tailored support based on the strengths and needs of the individual. Many times the teacher helps the children apply problem-solving strategies to visual information in context, such as letters, chunks, rhyming patterns, whole words, affixes, roots, or sound sequences. The goal is for the reader to integrate multiple sources of text information and to apply flexible strategies for comprehending the author's message.

Guided Discussion After First Reading

After everyone has read the book, the teacher convenes the group for an interactive book discussion. She guides the group to discuss the meaning of the text, while keeping the focus on the purpose for reading. Then, she selects one or two important teaching points that will boost the children's learning to a higher level. These points are based on careful observation of the children's processing behaviors during the first reading.

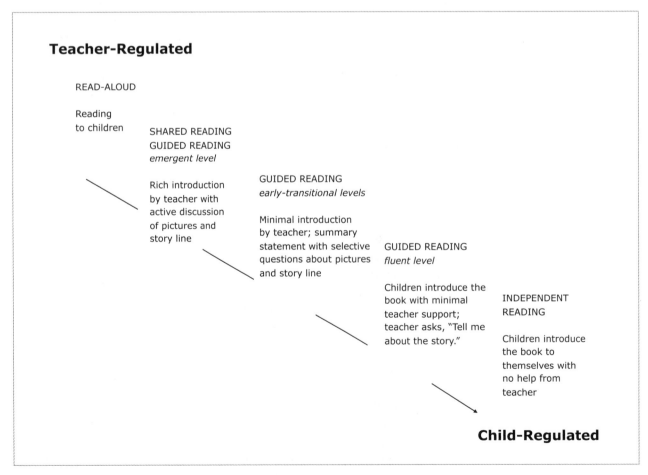

Figure 4.1 Degrees of support in the reading process.

Guided Silent Reading and Teacher Conference

As children become more competent readers, the teacher provides opportunities for them to incorporate more silent reading into the guided reading experience. Generally, this transition occurs in second grade: the lesson includes a balance of oral and silent reading with sensitive scaffolding from the teacher. A simple scaffold might look like this: (1) the teacher sets a purpose for reading a particular passage, (2) she tells the children to follow along silently as she reads aloud, (3) she engages the children in a conversation about the message, and (4) she guides them to locate and read orally those specific sections that support the message. As the children gain more experience with silent reading, the teacher prompts them to read silently for a specific purpose. For example, "Read to find how Tina felt when the storm hit the island." If the children are reading an informational text, she might prompt them to locate specific information; for instance, "Read to locate three important facts about Earth." After the book orientation, the teacher conducts one-on-one reading conferences with each student, during which she interacts with them about the meaning of the text and encourages them to read aloud particular passages to check on their reading fluency and problem-solving strategies.

Guided Discussion After First Reading

The silent reading activity is followed by an interactive discussion about the message, as well as selective oral reading of specific passages to support the meaning-making process. As children move into the intermediate grades, they are expected to engage in sustained silent reading; therefore, it is important for elementary teachers to scaffold this process through guided reading experiences.

Subsequent Reading Activities

At the emergent and early levels, the teacher provides opportunities for the children to reread the text independently. This experience promotes reading fluency, allows children to practice reading strategies comfortably, and frees their attention to notice new information. For beginning readers, rereading familiar texts plays a critical role in learning about written language.

By the transitional and fluent levels, the children have acquired a repertoire of strategies and word knowledge and need opportunities to apply this information to new texts within their control. Volume reading is directly related to reading success; therefore, children need to increase their reading power by reading many different books independently. Reading a new book (in contrast to a familiar book) enables the competent reader to apply flexible strategies in novel contexts, as well as to expand vocabulary and background knowledge through new text experiences. In all cases, the teaching goal is to find books that children can read without teacher assistance, so that they can practice effective reading strategies on materials within their control.

Regardless of the guided reading level, writing about the text provides a powerful opportunity to increase the children's reading comprehension. After the guided reading discussion, the teacher provides the children with a comprehension prompt that extends the discussion to deeper thinking. For instance, in Figure 4.2, a child at the early reading level writes about *Tabby in the Tree* (Randell 1996b), a story about a cat named Tabby who is stuck in a tree. The teacher prompts the children to "think of a way that Kate Green [the cat's owner] could get Tabby down from the tree if she had no fish." The child's written response indicates her ability to generalize beyond the text. In Figure 4.3, a child at the transitional reading level writes about an expository text by using bullets to list important facts about ants.

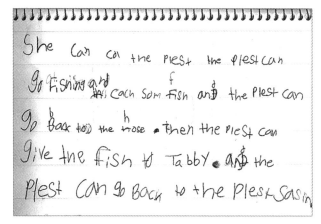

Figure 4.2 An early reader writes a personal response to a fiction text. ("She can call the police. The police can go fishing and catch some fish and the police can go back to the house. Then the police can give the fish to Tabby and the police can go back to the police station.")

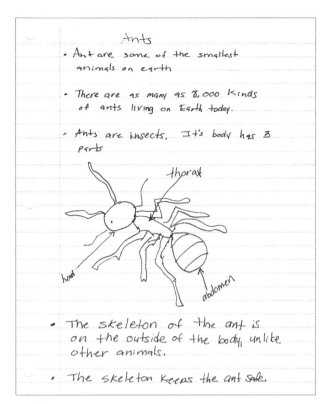

Figure 4.3 A transitional reader writes an expository text by using bullets to list important facts about ants.

Levels of Guided Reading

Next we provide examples of guided reading interactions at the emergent, early, transitional, and fluent levels. Successful guided reading interactions depend on the teacher's ability to (a) observe the children's processing behaviors and respond accordingly, (b) use language prompts that focus on cue integration and effective processing strategies, and (c) select appropriate materials that support reading development.

Emergent Guided Reading

Children in kindergarten and the beginning of first grade are typically emergent readers. They are used to "making sense." Their oral language provides additional cues, as well as the things they remember about the story to guide their interactions with the text. The observant teacher uses information from the Observation Survey (Clay 2006) and ongoing documentation of children's processing behavior (as recorded during shared reading, interactive writing,

and independent writing and on running records) to determine the aspects of print to which children are attending and thus come up with an appropriate focus for small-group instruction. Although at this level the pictures provide major cues to reading books, the teacher wants the children to realize that the story resides in the text. She directs their attention to the print by asking them to point to the words, locate known words, and search for unknown words based on their knowledge of a beginning-letter/sound relationship. The children's behavior is observable evidence that they are learning about the processes of reading: they send signals that they are aware something is wrong and they begin to search for alternatives to resolve the problem. The sensitive teacher is alert to these signals and responds accordingly. Emergent readers are learning to attend to print and may exhibit the following reading behaviors:

- self-monitor or check on reading, using known letters or high-frequency words
- point to words with one-to-one matching on one and two lines of text
- use directional movement with return sweep on two or more lines of text
- read some high-frequency words fluently
- articulate first letter in unknown words
- notice unknown words and search for cues in pictures and print
* reread to cross-check first letter with meaning and structure cues
- segment sounds in one-syllable sequence (consonant-vowel-consonant pattern)
- discuss the story with the teacher; ask questions about information and events in a text; describe the connection between two events or ideas in a text

Book Selection

For a guided reading group at the emergent level, the teacher uses ongoing assessments such as running records and samples of children's writing to help her select a new book that is within the children's zone of proximal development. As the teacher analyzes the children's processing behaviors in both reading and writing, she is collecting data that will drive her instructional focus during guided reading, assisted writing, and word-building activities. Figure 4.4 describes some typical reading and writing behaviors of emergent learners (adapted from Dorn and Soffos 2001a, 2001b).

Emergent Readers . . .	Emergent Writers . . .
use background knowledge and oral language structures to predict the author's message.	use background knowledge and oral language structures to compose the written message.
retell familiar stories; identify characters, settings, and key elements in a story.	incorporate language from texts into written compositions.
respond to reading through guided discussions, storytelling, and dramatizations.	use a combination of drawing, dictating, and writing to respond to reading.
hold predictable patterns in memory while attending to print; reread to restore meaning.	hold simple sentences in memory while transcribing the message; reread to restore meaning.
attend to print using some known letters; use known letters and words to monitor reading.	notice when known letters or words are written incorrectly; monitor by crossing out incorrect form and attempting to self-correct.
point to words in a one-to-one match throughout one to three lines of patterned text.	use spaces between words with greater accuracy.
recognize the link between known letters and sounds; articulate sound for first letter in an unknown word.	recognize the link between known sounds and letters; say the word slowly to identify sound-to-letter match.
fluently read some high-frequency words in easy texts; begin to acquire a reading vocabulary of about twenty frequently encountered words.	write a few high-frequency words with accuracy; begin to acquire a writing vocabulary that reflects attention to print during reading.
notice unknown words and predict the meaning from pictures or how words are used in text.	include new words from reading in writing of text.

Figure 4.4 Typical reading and writing behaviors of emergent learners.

Let's look at a typical emergent guided reading group. Kimberli, the kindergarten teacher, realizes the importance of selecting books that will help the children build a reading foundation (see Appendix D-7). She is aware that the children are still relying primarily on the pictures. Looking through the books that have been identified as being at the emergent level,

Kimberli notices that most texts have only one sentence or line per page. The sentence usually matches what is seen in the picture. She also observes that most have a picture on both the left-hand and right-hand pages, with a single line of print positioned at the bottom of the page. Kimberli knows that the position of the text is critical for emergent readers: when they open a book, the first thing they should notice is the print on the left-hand page. Therefore, she searches through the books for ones with the print on the left-hand page and the picture on the right-hand page. She wants the children to discover that the message is in the print, not the picture.

Continuing to analyze the books, Kimberli looks for those in which the spacing of the letters and words on the page will give the children room to move their finger from word to word as they read. In some emergent-level books the spacing between words is so small that the children cannot practice the speech-to-print match successfully. Kimberli believes this supportive feature will serve as a conceptual model the children can apply to other reading and writing contexts.

Narrowing her choice still further, she looks carefully at specific words and letters. She has observed that the children are becoming more aware of particular letter formations as they write and read daily. She wants to select a text that will give them the opportunity to use their limited knowledge of print to check on their own reading. Finally, Kimberli selects a book that contains the following features:

- Print begins in the upper-left corner. This directs children's attention to an appropriate starting point.
- Each line of text begins with a high-frequency word.
- Pictures are placed on the right-hand pages. Children will look at the print first, then at the picture.
- Print is large and spaces are bold. The children will be able to pay attention to one-to-one matching.
- Simple, repetitive language pattern occurs on each page, with only one word changing each time. The one-word change is supported by the picture.
- One or two frequently encountered words are repeated throughout the text.
- Several known letters are used in the context of the repetitive pattern.
- The concepts are familiar.
- There are some familiar high-frequency words.
- There are one or two new high-frequency words.

Setting the Purpose

After carefully analyzing the children's reading and writing behavior, Kimberli sets an overall purpose for the group that will take them to a higher level of cognitive development. She knows that the children must learn how to use what they know to check on their own reading progress. She realizes they are inconsistent with their one-to-one matching. For instance, instead of using known words in texts to monitor their responses, the children rely on their oral language and their memory. Kimberli wants the children to use their finger to guide their speech-to-print matches. With these goals in mind, she is ready to introduce the new book to the emergent reading group.

Book Orientation: *Balloon Ride*

During the book orientation, Kimberli introduces the children to specific concepts they will encounter in the story. Her aim is to create anticipation and to construct a meaningful framework for the story. First, she shares the cover of the book, *Balloon Ride* (Bryson 2010) and gives a brief summary of the story: "Today we are going to read a story called *Balloon Ride*. Rabbit goes up in a hot air balloon. Rabbit tells us about the things that he can see." Next, Kimberli asks the children to close their eyes and visualize the kinds of things Rabbit might see as he is up in the air. By encouraging the children to close their eyes and visualize, Kimberli activates strategies of visualization and prediction. Next, she gets them to discuss the pictures on each page in the book, simultaneously planting the language of the text in their minds: "Let's look at the pictures and see what Rabbit can see."

Several children exclaim, "He can see a house!"

Kimberli validates these responses and at the same time adjusts the language to accommodate the words in the text. "Yes," she comments, pointing to the words as she says them, "I see the house."

Finally, Kimberli passes out individual copies of the book to the children and prompts them to apply phonological skills for predicting a first-letter cue in an unknown word:

Kimberli: (*Stressing the initial sound of the word* band *during pronunciation*) Who can tell me what letter *band* begins with?

Children: *B*!

Kimberli: Yes. Can you find the word *band* in your book on page ten?

As the children locate the word and frame it with their fingers, Kimberli observes to see whether they are successful. When Sarah experiences difficulty, Kimberli increases her level of support: "Find the word that starts with a *b*." She is prepared to pull out a magnetic letter if Sarah needs additional support. After all the children have located the word, Kimberli prompts them to confirm their response: "Check it with your finger to be sure it is the word *band*." Confirmation is a critical part of the reading process.

To promote further attention to visual information, Kimberli puts magnetic letters on a large magnetic board and shows the children the word *see*. Then she instructs them to locate the word *see* in the story. She selects *see*, a partially known word, for two important reasons. First, the word is encountered frequently and she wants the children to notice it. Second, she believes the structural position of the word (it falls in the middle of the repeated pattern) will give the children a strong anchor for one-to-one matching. The children already have control of the word *I*, which is the first word on each page of the story, and they can use a strong picture cue to get the last word of the repeated pattern. After the children locate the word *see*, Kimberli says, "This is an important word in your story. I want you to use it to help yourself when you are reading." With this prompt, Kimberli is sending a critical message: the children must use known words as anchors in the text to monitor and guide their reading.

First Reading

Before asking the children to read the text, Kimberli tells them, "Use your pointing finger to help you as you read." Then she circulates among them while they read. She observes their behavior and prompts them toward constructive activity: "What is happening in the picture?" "Can you find a word that you know?" When the reading is completed, Kimberli uses her observations of the children's reading behavior to emphasize three carefully selected teaching points:

- Teaching Point 1 (validating a previously learned response): "That's good that you used your finger to point to the words while you were reading. That helped you to match your words, didn't it?" Here Kimberli acknowledges the children's attempts at one-to-one matching.

- Teaching Point 2 (activating a new response): "Also, I noticed that when several of you came to the word *lake* on page fourteen, you started to say *ocean*. How did you know the word was not *ocean*?" Here and in the next teaching point, Kimberli illustrates the importance of using first-letter cues to monitor one's reading.

- Teaching Point 3 (activating a new response): "You all know that the word *lake* starts with an *l*, don't you? Let's take a look at some other words that start with *l*."

Subsequent Readings

The books are now placed in the children's familiar reading baskets, and over the next few days they are encouraged to reread the story several times. The children who read independently during the first reading are ready to share their book with a partner or to read it by themselves.

Early Guided Reading

As children develop and refine their reading skills, they integrate cues and apply flexible strategies for solving new words. They exhibit behavior that indicates they are using visual information to check on the printed message (for example, they rely less on the pictures). They are less dependent on their finger for matching speech to print, and the teacher encourages this greater control, prompting them to "read it with your eyes." Precise and deliberate matching is replaced by more fluent reading. The breaks between the words disappear, and the children read groups of words with correct phrasing and intonation. The stories are read more naturally and sound more like the language that children use every day. By the end of the early level, competent readers would exhibit the following behaviors:

- Read for meaning and return to reread when meaning breaks down; integrate meaning, structure, and visual cues.

- Use pictures, illustrations, and details to describe characters, events, or setting; distinguish between information provided by pictures or illustrations and information provided by the words in a text; identify the main topic, main ideas, and key details of a text.

- Self-monitor reading with greater ease: use known words and patterns to check on reading.

- Search through words in a left-to-right sequence; blend letters into sounds; repeat as if to confirm; take words apart at the larger unit of analysis.

- Read high-frequency words quickly, fluently, and automatically.

- Become faster at noticing errors and initiate multiple attempts to self-correct.

Book Selection

Janice, a first-grade teacher, selects a nonfiction text called *Families* (Burton, French, and Jones 2010) as an appropriate text for a guided reading group at the early level. Her choice is based on a careful analysis of the children's processing behavior as documented on previous running records, her observations of their reading strategies during independent and guided reading, and her observations of their problem-solving strategies during assisted and independent writing. (See Figure 4.5, Dorn and Soffos 2001a, 2001b.) Janice knows that texts of the right difficulty help move children to the next level of reading development. Some characteristics of an early text level are as follows:

- Familiar concepts are made accessible through introduction.
- Text layout supports fluency and phrasing.
- Illustrations and photographs support content.
- High-frequency words build and extend vocabulary.
- Children are allowed to use their current strategies and competencies to problem-solve unknown words.
- There are more supportive features than challenging features.
- Varied language patterns are based on oral language and meaning.

Early Readers . . .	Early Writers . . .
integrate knowledge sources to interpret the author's message.	use background knowledge to construct written messages.
hold more information in memory when solving problems at points of difficulty; return when meaning breaks down; hold longer sequences of meaning in memory when reading.	hold more information in memory when transcribing the message; return to reread when meaning breaks down; develop and maintain a sequence of ideas when transcribing a meaningful message.
respond to texts through oral retellings and guided discussions.	respond to reading through writing about the text; keep a reader response log.
ask and answer questions about key details and events in a text; describe characters, settings, and significant events in a story; compare and contrast two or more versions of the same text.	include more details in writing; use graphic organizers to plan and develop writing; use illustrations and text aids to support the message.
use known words and patterns to monitor reading; acquire a reading vocabulary of 150 words from easy and familiar texts.	begin to notice common misspellings in writing; acquire a writing vocabulary that reflects reading experiences.
search through words in a left-to-right sequence; blend letters into sounds; repeat word to identity.	say words slowly to analyze sequence of sounds and to record corresponding letters; segment and blend sounds in words.
take words apart at the larger unit of analysis (consonant digraphs, onset and rime, blends, inflectional endings).	construct words using larger units of sound-to-letter patterns.
read high-frequency words quickly and fluently.	spell high-frequency words correctly.

Figure 4.5 Typical reading and writing behaviors of early learners.

Setting the Purpose

The teacher always has two purposes for reading. The most important purpose is to understand the message and enjoy the reading. A second purpose is to apply useful strategies for solving words as they read for meaning. Based on her analysis of the children's reading and writing behaviors, Janice concludes that they need more opportunities to apply problem-solving strategies when examining words during reading. She knows that it is critical for the children to have flexible ways to analyze unknown words at points of difficulty.

Book Orientation: *Families*

Janice introduces the title and directs the children to the photograph on the cover by saying, "We can see from the photograph on the cover that the little boy has a small family." She engages the children in a short discussion about the people in their own families. Then she provides a clear summary of the book. "This book tells about many kinds of families. It also tells us how important families are and how they help us." This brief introduction about families sets the stage for reading the book.

Next, Janice and the children have a short conversation about the text while making predictions based on the photographs and concepts in the text. When Dillon predicts the word *large* for *big*, Janice accepts his response because it will give the children an opportunity to problem-solve and initiate cross-checking behavior when they read the text.

To incorporate structure, Janice has anticipated that the children might have difficulty with some of the language or specialized vocabulary of the text; thus she uses these words in her orientation to the text. For example, as she points to the photograph on page 7, she explains, "Look at this building. It is an apartment building. Some families live in an apartment." Finally, Janice directs the children's attention to the visual information in the text and demonstrates how to use a known chunk to get to an unknown word.

Janice: If you were going to read the word *small,* what chunk would you expect to see at the end of the word?

Children: *All.*

Janice: (*Makes the word* all *with letter cards, then puts the chunk card* sm *in front of it*) That's right. If I put the *sm* in front of *all,* what new word did I make?

Children: *Small.*

Janice: Can you think of other words that begin like the word *small*?

Children: *Smoke, smell.*

Janice: That's right. When we get to a word that we do not know, we can look for a part that can help us, just like the chunk *all* in *small.* Now look on page two and let's read the whole sentence.

First Reading

As the children read the story independently, Janice moves among them and listens. She keeps interruption of the reading to a minimum. Janice intervenes only when a child appears to be in jeopardy of losing the meaning of the text. She then uses language prompts, according to each child's need, to help children apply problem-solving strategies at points of difficulty. She varies her instructional interactions with the children and uses the strengths and needs of the individuals to determine the nature of those interactions.

After the children finish reading the story, Janice praises them for using specific strategies. She leads them in a quick review of things to do to help themselves when they are reading.

Janice: What are some things that you can do when you get stuck on a word?

Child: Go back and reread.

Another child: Think about the story and look all the way through the word.

Another child: See if there is a part of the word you know.

Janice: Yes, it helps you to do those things as you read. Now, I want you to take your book and read the text with a partner. When you have both read the book, please put it in your familiar-reading basket.

Subsequent Readings

During subsequent readings, the children might re-read the book with a partner or read it alone. The important thing is that they be given the opportunity to practice fluent rereading behavior.

A Few Words About Text Supports

In designing a supportive book introduction, the teacher must consider the influence of the text on the student's reading success. If a text is not supportive of the reader, the teacher will need to fill in the gaps by providing more scaffolding. However, with a more supportive text, the child can assume more responsibility for regulating his performance during reading.

In Figure 4.6, we share some guidelines for teachers to consider as they select appropriate texts for emergent and early readers. The characteristics of text supports for late early readers involve greater complexity as they move closer to the transitional reading level.

Text Supports for Emergent Readers (A–B/C)	Text Supports for Early Readers (C–F)	Text Supports for Late Early Readers (G–J/K)
• Consistent placement of text with supportive layout. • Placement of high-frequency words within repeated sentence patterns to promote attention to print. • Large print with ample spacing to support one-to-one matching. • Naturally occurring language structures that support or duplicate oral language and promote meaningful predictions. • Simple story line that focuses on a single idea; many topics relate to personal experience. • Use of simple punctuation (period, question mark, exclamation point). • Direct correspondence between text and pictures. • One–three lines of text.	• Clear print with obvious spacing. • Repetitive use of high-frequency words to promote automaticity. • Words with blends, diagraphs, inflectional endings, and so on provide more opportunities to apply visual searching strategies. • Concepts are within student's background experiences. • Illustrations are supportive (more attention to print is required). • Sentences are longer with more complex language structures. • More varied use of simple punctuation (period, quotation marks, commas, question marks, and exclamation point). • Simple dialogue. • Three–six lines of print.	• Greater number of episodes or events. • Expanded vocabulary. • Punctuation supports phrasing. • Character development. • More opportunities for problem solving on multisyllabic words. • Complex sentence structures. • Dialogue is presented in a variety of ways. • Literacy language is mixed with typical oral language structures. • Generally three–eight lines of print per page.

Figure 4.6 Text supports for emergent and early readers.

Transitional Reading Level

By the transitional reading level, children have participated with their teacher in many book introductions. In the process, they have been apprenticed in how to introduce books to themselves. Now they know how to make predictions based on the title, author, and genre; they make meaning as they look through the pages, ask questions of the author, and make connections to other texts as well as to their personal lives. Further, transitional readers have acquired more flexible strategies for solving problems within texts, their vocabulary has increased, their word knowledge is more automatic, and they exhibit greater independence during the reading act. They read longer texts with greater accuracy and fluency, they apply higher-level comprehension strategies, and they are more metacognitive of the reading and writing relationship (Figure 4.7).

At the transitional level, the teacher provides more opportunities for children to practice silent reading as a component of their guided reading group. Silent reading enables children to increase reading speed and comprehend at deeper levels. Let's look at two examples of transitional readers who are developing their silent reading skills during guided reading lessons.

Book Selection

Christie, a second-grade teacher, selects a beginning chapter book, *Frog and Toad Are Friends* (Lobel 1970), for her transitional reading group. The children have read several books in the Nate the Great series written by Marjorie Weinman Sharmat, and they understand the layout of transitional chapter books. The Frog and Toad series consists of the following characteristics (Dorn and Soffos 2001b):

- small-book format divided into sections that resemble chapters
- simple illustrations to break up the text and promote comprehension
- simple plot with one main event and one or two main characters
- lots of dialogue to move the plot along

Book Orientation: *Frog and Toad Are Friends*

Christie introduces the book *Frog and Toad Are Friends* to her transitional reading group. Together, they read the title and the name of the author and illustrator on the cover. Christie explains that the book is an anthology of adventures about two very good friends named Frog and Toad. She turns to the table of contents and briefly notes the different stories in

Transitional Readers . . .	Transitional Writers . . .
use knowledge of text and genre structures to predict, monitor, and self-correct reading; read diverse texts (such as beginning chapter books, fairy tales, and information) and engage in book discussions.	use knowledge of text and genre structures to plan and organize writing; write for different purposes and for diverse audiences.
ask and answer questions such as who, what, where, when, why, and how to demonstrate understanding of key details and events in a text.	include important details in logical sequence to communicate a comprehensible message for the reader.
develop an awareness of how to read silently; use oral and silent reading strategies to promote comprehension.	find that writing strategies are becoming more silent; understand how to shift from silent processing to oral reading when writing for the reader.
expand reading vocabulary; show interest in unfamiliar words.	expand writing vocabulary; include new and unusual words.
solve multisyllabic words by noticing larger parts within the words.	attend to syllables when writing unknown spellings.
read longer texts with great accuracy and fluency.	write increasingly longer texts with greater accuracy and speed.
use words' meanings (e.g., suffixes, roots, compound parts) to solve unknown words.	show flexibility with words (prefixes, choice; try out different ways of saying a message with the same meaning; revise word choices in writing).

Figure 4.7 Typical reading and writing behaviors of transitional learners.

the book. Then she informs the children that today they will be reading the first story, "Spring."

Next Christie taps into the children's background knowledge by initiating a discussion about hibernation. The children talk about animals that sleep during the winter months and awaken in the springtime from their long winter naps. This provides a supportive framework within which to introduce the story. Christie says, "In today's story, Frog tricks Toad into waking up too soon from his long winter nap." Then she coaches the children to think of ways Frog might trick Toad into doing this. Christie records the children's predictions on a chart and comments, "After you read the story, we will check to see if you were right."

Next Christie sets a purpose for reading the story: "I want you to read the story silently and find out how Frog convinces Toad to believe it is about half past May and time to get up." She is careful to plant the language chunk "half past May" in the introduction, so that the children can hear this unfamiliar phrase. "What do you think is so important about 'half past May'?"

One child responds, "That's when it's time for Toad to get up from hibernation." Several children express their agreement.

Before the children begin reading, Christie also initiates a brief conversation about ways the children can problem-solve independently: "When you come to a difficult word, what are some things you can do to help yourself?"

The children's responses indicate their understanding of problem-solving strategies: "Search for chunks in words." "Notice how the word starts, and check to see if the word makes sense and looks right."

Christie reminds the children to try various ways to solve the problem but tells them that if their attempts are unsuccessful, they can mark the word with a sticky note: "We will help you figure the word out after you finish reading the story."

First Reading

The transition from oral to silent reading is a new behavior, and the children will need a high degree of scaffolding. Christie explains, "Sometimes we read out loud, and other times we read silently. As we read longer books, it will be important for us to use silent reading strategies." Then she invites the children to think of times during the school day when they are required

to read silently. This brief interaction sets the purpose for the silent reading experience. Christie says, "I'll read the first two pages aloud, and you read silently with me." After the reading, she engages the children in a meaningful discussion and sets the purpose for the next episode of silent reading. "Now you will read the next six pages in your head. As you read, think about how Frog felt when Toad would not get out of bed." As the children read silently, she observes their behavior and conducts brief conferences to check on their comprehension. After the children have completed the six pages, Christie engages the group in a discussion around the feelings of both Frog and Toad. She accepts all responses while prompting the children to read orally those specific passages that provide evidence of their thinking. When she is sure the children understand the message, she says, "Now, finish reading the story silently to find out how Frog finally got Toad out of bed." As the children read, she meets with individual children to check on their comprehension and to prompt for word solving if they need it.

Subsequent Reading Activities

Once they have finished the story, Christie directs the children back to their original predictions from the chart. They confirm or discount their initial predictions with supportive passages from the text. Next, she asks them to locate any word that they had difficulty with during the first reading. She selects one or two words for group problem solving. Christie coaches the children to apply strategies for solving the problem. Afterward, she encourages them to return to the text and read the problematic part within the context of the story. Then, taking the textual experience to a new level, Christie asks the children to discuss whether they feel the trick was fair and to predict what they think will happen if Toad ever finds out it really is not "half past May." These lively discussions lead to writing connections that allow the children to explore feelings and story elements.

Book Orientation:
The Tale of Peter Rabbit

Judy, the second-grade teacher, introduces a picture book, *The Tale of Peter Rabbit* (Potter 2002), by building on background experience: "Have any of you ever done something your mother or father told you not to do?" Several children relate their personal experiences. Next, Judy presents a brief overview of what the story is about: "Well, in this story, Mother Rabbit warns Flopsy, Mopsy, Cotton-tail, and Peter not to go into Mr. McGregor's garden, or something terrible might happen to them, like it did to their father." Then she encourages the children to make predictions:

Judy: What do you think might happen if the rabbits go into the garden?

Ryan: The scarecrow might scare them.

Lisa: They might get poisoned from bug spray or fertilizer.

Jarred: No! I think another animal will eat them, like a dog or a cat.

Judy: (*Praising the children's predictions*) Those are all terrible things that might happen to the little rabbits if they don't mind their mother.

Next Judy provides the children with enough detail to stimulate their interest and leave them wondering what will happen to the rabbit: "Well, unfortunately, one of the rabbits disobeyed Mother Rabbit and went into Mr. McGregor's garden anyway. Needless to say, he ran into a lot of trouble. Several things happened to him that really frightened him and made him wish he had listened to his mother."

First Reading

Now that the children are familiar with the overall theme of the story, they are eager to begin, and Judy prepares them for a silent reading. First, she sets a purpose for reading: "I want you to read pages two and three in your head and find out why Mother Rabbit didn't want the young rabbits to go into Mr. McGregor's garden." After the children silently read the pages, Judy asks, "Who can find the part that tells why Mother Rabbit didn't want her bunnies to go into Mr. McGregor's garden?"

Lisa reads, "Your father had an accident there; he was put in a pie by Mrs. McGregor."

Judy responds, "Well, no wonder Mother Rabbit didn't want her babies to go in there."

Next Judy prompts the children to read pages 4 through 7 to find out what happened to one of the rabbits as he squeezed under the gate of Mr. McGregor's

garden. After they've read these pages silently, Judy starts a discussion:

Judy: On page four, what did Peter do when he entered the garden?

Lisa: He ate the vegetables in the garden.

Judy: (*Prompting the children to provide evidence from the text*) Read the part that describes what happened to Peter in the garden.

Ryan: "First he ate some lettuces and some French beans; and then he ate some radishes. And then, feeling rather sick, he went to look for some parsley."

Judy: (*Coaching the children to think beyond the text*) Why do you think Peter went to look for some parsley?

Lisa: He ate so much that he got a tummy ache.

Nicholas: Yeah, and the parsley will make him feel better.

The children continue to predict their way through the text and use rereading to confirm or discount their predictions. At appropriate places, Judy guides the children to make further inferences: for example, "How do you think Peter felt when he had to face his mother?" She prompts them to relate these textual events to their own lives: "Have you ever disobeyed like Peter and had to face your actions? What happened to you? How did you feel? What lesson did you learn?" These questions are thoughtful and are naturally interspersed with extended stretches of reading.

The discussion during the first reading does not deter the children from comprehension or the sheer enjoyment of reading. It simply engages them in the reading process as they learn to read for the author's intended meaning. As children gain experience and expertise in silent reading, they are encouraged to read increasingly longer passages at one time, until they can manage a whole book.

Fluent Reading Level

As children progress through the transitional level, they are on their way to becoming fluent readers. Generally, the fluent period begins around third grade and develops in sophistication and complexity as children progress through the grades. At the end of third grade, the competent reader has an extensive reading vocabulary, reads longer texts with specialized content and unusual words, and learns new words daily. She applies knowledge about word meaning across different texts, distinguishes literal from figurative language, and refines word knowledge as she responds to reading numerous texts. The fluent reader is self-regulated, with the capacity and motivation to read independently for sustained periods of time. As a result, the fluent reader has developed a self-extending system that empowers her to improve with each reading experience.

Selecting Books

Selecting books for the fluent reader is based on a much wider range of criteria, such as interest, content, thematic units, and genre. At this level, readers must be able to deal with diverse materials that include various text structures, figurative language, academic vocabulary, writing styles, and longer texts with fewer pictures. Books might be clustered under units of study, such as text types (for example, literacy, expository, argumentative), genre (for example, myths, fairy tales, mysteries, biographies), author studies (for example, Eve Bunting, Patricia Polacco, Chris Van Allsburg), chapter books (for example, Cam Jansen, Junie B. Jones, Bailey School Kids), content areas (for example, solar system, life cycles, human body), or themes

(for example, African-American history, sports, natural disasters). Fluent readers have accumulated a set of literary knowledge that can be generalized across reading and writing, have developed longer attention spans, and are more intentional in how they plan and organize their learning (see Figure 4.8).

Setting the Purpose

The fluent reader is a self-regulated reader who applies flexible reading strategies to fulfill a range of purposes. Therefore, the focus of instruction varies according to the topic or subject matter. The focus may include (but is not limited to) learning how information is presented in a variety of ways (maps, drawings, charts, tables of contents, indexes, glossaries, headings, subtopics, diagrams, and labels); making comparisons and contrasting information between texts; exploring the author's craft and structure; increasing mastery of story elements (setting, main characters, plot, problem, resolution); and applying higher-level comprehension strategies (synthesizing, critiquing, and evaluating). The range of possibilities in setting a focus for a fluent guided reading group is immense, as are the opportunities for moving children to a higher level of competency. Let's look at an example of a fluent guided reading group for a unit of study on the Cam Jansen mystery series.

Fluent Readers . . .	Fluent Writers . . .
use knowledge of text and genre structures to comprehend texts; understand common features of literary texts (such as legends, myths, fairy tales) when speaking about classic stories from around the world.	use graphic organizers (such as writing guides) for planning and writing literary pieces based on text readings.
describe the main characters in a story (for example, motivations, feelings, traits) and explain how they contribute to the sequence of events; compare and contrast the plots, settings, and themes of stories written by the same author about characters in a collection (such as Junie B. Jones).	keep a reader response log and write thoughtful responses to the text (for example, analyze the character, identify the theme, compare and contrast different books within a series, summarize key points, make predictions).
ask and answer questions to demonstrate understanding of a text, providing evidence from the text as the basis for the answers.	demonstrate knowledge that authors write for readers and that writing should be logical and coherent.
apply self-reflective strategies during reading (such as questioning the author, generalizing, critiquing, evaluating).	use self-reflective rubrics to assess the quality of writing according to proficiency indicators.
adjust their reading rate according to purpose, apply silent reading strategies for deeper comprehension.	adjust their writing purposes, work on multiple pieces of writing at the same time.

Figure 4.8 Typical reading and writing behaviors of fluent learners.

Introduction to the Series

Renee, a third-grade teacher, understands that the children are familiar with the mystery genre and invites them to share what they already know about mysteries. As they contribute, Renee records these characteristics on an anchor chart titled "Mystery Genre." She holds up one book in the Cam Jansen series and tells the children they will engage in a mystery unit of study over the next three weeks. She introduces Cam, the main character, who has a photographic memory; Eric Shelton, Cam's best friend, who works with her to solve mysteries; and David Adler, the author, who has based Cam's character on an elementary classmate who was thought to have a photographic memory. Last, she holds up five books in the Cam Jansen series, provides a brief summary of each one, and asks the children to select the three they would most like to use for the mystery unit of study. The children select *The Mystery of the Stolen Diamonds* (2009) as the first choice in the mystery unit. The remaining two books are placed in the classroom library for independent reading.

Book Orientation: *The Mystery of the Stolen Diamonds*

Renee passes out a copy of *The Mystery of the Stolen Diamonds* and prompts the children to look at the introduction on the back cover. She says, "I'll read the introduction aloud and you read it silently." As she reads, she models her questioning process: "Cam sees the thief, but the police arrest the wrong person. I wonder how Cam will catch the real thief. Will her photographic memory help her?" Then she directs the children to the inside blurb and instructs them to silently read the short excerpt from one of the chapters.

After the reading, Renee guides the children to ask questions based on key statements in the passage. The children ask, "Do you think he is an innocent man? If so, why would he be running away from them? What happens if he sees them? Will the police rescue them? How will they catch him?"

Renee records the questions on a chart tablet and explains, "It is important to ask yourself questions before and during your reading. Keep these questions in mind as you try to solve the mystery."

First Reading

The first reading is a balance of silent reading, oral reading, guided discussion, and charting ideas. The teacher informs the children that they will read and discuss the first two chapters of the mystery. She explains, "The story has a lot of dialogue that keeps the action moving. In the first chapter, we are introduced to the main characters, Cam and Eric, and we learn about Cam's photographic memory. At the end of the chapter, Parker's Jewelry Store is robbed, and Cam and Eric witness a man running from the store." Then she sets a purpose for the first reading: "Read to learn more about the traits of Cam and Eric." The children read silently, and the teacher observes their reading behaviors. Do they seem engaged? Are some children reading more slowly? Do they subvocalize as they read? If a child appears to struggle, Renee confers with the child, prompting him to tell about the story. After the first reading, she prompts the children, "What did you learn about Cam? About Eric?" As the children identify character traits, Renee asks them to read orally the passage in the book that supports their statement. When she is confident that the children understand the purpose of reading, she tells them to read the next chapter silently. She reminds them to ask new questions about the story, and to look for clues that might help them solve the mystery. As the children read, she conducts one-on-one conferences to listen to each child's oral reading and to check on comprehension. At the end of the chapter, she convenes the group for a guided discussion. Finally, she sets the purpose for the independent reading of the next two chapters.

Subsequent Reading Activities

The children read the assigned chapters independently and record their thinking in their reader response logs. After the children have read all three books in the mystery unit, they may select other Cam Jansen books from the classroom library.

A Few Words About Text Supports

Earlier, we discussed the infallibility of leveled texts. This is even more evident with books at the transitional and fluent levels. However, teachers should consider how particular text features are related to text complexity. Here are a few typical characteristics of texts at these upper levels:

- blurbs for previewing the text
- book and chapter leads
- continuation of chapters or stand-alone chapters
- tables of contents and titles
- multiple settings and characters
- genre structures
- changes in time
- point of view
- mood or tone
- descriptive and figurative language
- complexity of story elements

Closing Thoughts

In this chapter, we have shared how guided reading moves along a continuum of emergent to fluent reading levels. In an apprenticeship-type context, the teacher creates opportunities for children to engage in meaningful and strategic learning experiences with her guidance. As children become more competent readers, the teacher adjusts her levels of scaffolding to match their strengths and needs. The goal of guided reading is to ensure that all children are successful readers, an approach that requires a sensitive and observant teacher who understands how children learn.

chapter five

ASSISTED WRITING

An apprenticeship approach to literacy requires us to spend time observing changes that indicate that children are moving in appropriate directions. These are the data we need so that we can make informed decisions about what types of assisted writing activities will promote advanced learning.

As teachers of young writers, we recognize the vast range of experience and ability that children bring to the task of writing. In apprenticeship settings, teachers provide children with guided opportunities to learn how to use things they know (skills, strategies, facts) to initiate problem solving in different situations. During assisted activities, the teacher uses language prompts and adjustable levels of support to enable children to accomplish writing tasks they would be unable to accomplish alone. During follow-up writing activities, children are given important opportunities to apply their personal knowledge to independent work. As a child's understanding of the writing process increases, responsibility is transferred from the teacher to the child. Simultaneously, the child moves to a higher level of intellectual development. Clear demonstrations and guided practice are the basis of apprenticeship learning.

Teachers must therefore keep ongoing documentation of what children know and can do. With this information they can validate children's knowledge and activate the problem-solving processes we want them to access each time they pick up a pen. This process of validation and activation is an important concept in helping children acquire higher-level understanding about the writing process.

The following writing conference illustrates the complementary relationship between validating and activating knowledge. Harriet (the teacher) and LaShala are talking about LaShala's story (see Figure 5.1).

Figure 5.1 LaShala's story. ("He couldn't get burned.")

Harriet observes that LaShala is able to write the words *He* and *burned* independently. She also notes that LaShala is hearing consonant sounds (*c, n* in *couldn't; g, t* in *get*). She thinks LaShala should be able to hear the *t* in *couldn't*. She thinks that perhaps the middle symbol in *get* may be an attempt to self-correct the *t* to *e*. Harriet's teaching conference focuses on praising (validating) and initiating (activating) LaShala's knowledge about writing. Harriet validates LaShala's knowledge by pointing out the words and letters that LaShala wrote independently. Then she activates LaShala's problem-solving ability by asking her to listen to the ending of *couldn't* and practice writing the word *get*. LaShala is able to accomplish both activities successfully. However, if LaShala had experienced any difficulty, Harriet was prepared to increase the level of support to ensure that she was successful.

Harriet's first activating prompt (AP): Say the word *couldn't* slowly. What can you hear at the end of the word?

LaShala: *T.*

Harriet's second AP: Yes, say *couldn't* and *get (stresses the t sound).* How do they sound alike?

LaShala: They both end with *t.*

Harriet's third AP: Now, take a good look at the word *get.* You heard the *g* and you heard the *t,* but there's something about it that doesn't look quite right. Can you find it?

LaShala: That needs to be an *e.*

Harriet's fourth AP: Write it on your board and see if you can make it look right.

LaShala writes the word *get* correctly on her dry erase board.

Children's writing development is shaped by experiencing different types of writing activities in assisted situations, which are then followed by independent practice. Using an apprenticeship approach, the teacher designs instructional interactions that evolve around children's current knowledge, skills, and strategies. The goal of assisted instruction is achieved when the children apply this knowledge to guide and regulate their independent writing.

This is accomplished by instructing children in numerous writing activities aimed at their zone of proximal development. The teacher provides the children with opportunities to practice things they know (at their independent level), while simultaneously supporting them as she guides them down new learning paths (in their zone of proximal development).

An early-literacy writing program should incorporate a range of assisted activities, each one designed to help young children reach higher levels of understanding about the writing process. During assisted writing activities, children are mentored into how to use language and resources to support their writing development, including how to draft, revise, and edit their pieces. An observant teacher documents children's progress and plans transitional moves that reflect the children's increasing control. Assisted writing activities occur in two settings: (1) interactive writing and (2) writing aloud. Independent writing and writing conferences during these assisted experiences are discussed in Chapter 6.

Teacher support and explicit instruction are essential elements woven throughout all levels and types. However, the teacher glides in and out, depending on how much the children can contribute or attain with their current abilities and what new learning must be introduced to activate their processing abilities.

What Is Interactive Writing?

A common characteristic of struggling writers is their reluctance to take risks with their writing. Their stories are often controlled by the words and letters they know, rather than the message they want to share. This overdependency on a limited number of words and letters does not give children enough opportunity to try out new learning and confirm or reject their responses based on old knowledge. John Dewey (1935, 62) reminds us, "The old and the new have forever to be integrated with each other so that the values of the old experiences may become the servants and instruments of new desires and aims." This is a lesson that struggling writers have not yet learned. These children need us, as their teachers, to help them acquire problem-solving strategies that they can use to advance their own learning to higher levels.

The goal of writing is to communicate a message, and writing consists of putting conventional marks on paper to express this message. During instructional interactions with a more knowledgeable person, children acquire important learning that they can use to communicate their thoughts in a readable way. The purposes of early writing activities are

- to create a situation that promotes risk taking,
- to demonstrate effective writing strategies, and
- to help children learn how to apply their existing knowledge to problem-solve in different places and with new information.

One form of assisted writing is a collaborative-writing technique known as interactive writing (Dorn and Soffos 2011; Pinnell and McCarrier 1994; Fountas and Pinnell 1996). Interactive writing helps beginning writers develop early reading and writing strategies. It is a shared experience between the teacher and children who collaboratively write a text. The teacher transcribes the text on a group chart and invites individual children to record a few known words on the chart as well. As the teacher records the message, she models how to problem-solve using early reading and writing strategies, and she prompts the children to write known letters and/or words from the text on their individual dry erase boards.

For interactive writing to be productive, the teacher must know the children's strengths and give them opportunities to use this knowledge in the writing process. In this way the teacher is able to validate the children's current understanding and provide specific and explicit feedback to further that understanding. The teacher's interactions with the children focus on developing early reading and writing behaviors:

- directional movement and one-to-one matching
- concepts of letter, word, and punctuation
- sounds in words
- letter knowledge
- familiarity with some frequently encountered words
- rereading and predicting strategies

The teacher's conversation throughout these interactions moves children forward. The teacher is continually using the children's strengths, never doing anything for them that they can do alone. Furthermore, the teacher demonstrates and models powerful strategies that will carry over into children's individual writing.

Organizing for Interactive Writing

Interactive writing can be implemented with the whole class or with a small group of children who need more tailored support (see Chapter 8 for sample schedules). Whole-class instruction is a natural component of a reading and writing workshop—an opportunity for all students to learn about grade-level concepts. For whole-class interactive writing, the teacher models critical literacy behaviors and engages all children through techniques such as writing words on individual dry erase boards and talking to a partner about literacy concepts. For children who need more tailored scaffolding, the classroom teacher provides an interactive writing lesson for three to six children for approximately twenty minutes—the same amount of time that is allotted to the guided reading groups.

For struggling learners, the school's reading specialist or special education teacher can provide interactive writing as a supplemental small-group intervention (see Chapter 10; also Dorn and Soffos 2011a, 2011b).

Typically, the teacher's materials for interactive writing include books or poems for read-aloud, a large chart tablet, a black marker and eraser, a large alphabet chart, a large writing checklist, and a pointer. The children's materials include a reduced copy of the alphabet chart, magnetic letters, a small bowl to hold letters, a personal word dictionary, a small dry erase board and marker, and an unlined writing journal with a practice page at the top (see Figure 5.2). Examples of interactive writing formats include a short story (a few sentences), a dialogue bubble, a menu, a recipe, a list, a literary response, a short retelling, a nonfiction text, and a brief description of a meaningful event.

Figure 5.2 The teacher has created a well-organized space for an interactive writing lesson.

Risk taking is a prerequisite of learning. Many teachers place a dry erase board next to the interactive writing chart; children can practice something on the board before writing it in the group story. In addition, we encourage teachers to give each child a dry erase lapboard, dry erase marker, and magnetic letters for individual problem solving. This is important for two reasons: (1) the teacher has an opportunity to see how different children are processing print, and (2) the teacher is able to guide an individual child toward an appropriate response before a wrong letter or word is written in the group story. Children's approximations are praised. However, because the stories will be reread, it is important that the words be spelled conventionally. Therefore, correction tape is occasionally used to mask any preconventional attempts.

All assisted writing lessons include an independent-writing component. In Chapter 6, we share more details about independent writing and teacher conferences.

Interactive Writing with Emergent Writers

Interactive writing uses a predictable framework for scaffolding young writers. In this section, we apply this framework to lessons with emergent and early writers.

Generating the Message

After reading the predictable text *I Like . . .* (Cutting 1988), Harriet, the teacher, guides a small group of kindergarten children in constructing a simple story. (In emergent writing, a story may consist of a single sentence.) Harriet uses each child's personal knowledge and oral language background, as well as the language of the book, to jointly construct a story based on things they like to eat.

Harriet: What are some of the foods you like to eat?
Paul: Pizza!
Damion: Candy!
Melissa: Ice cream!
Julie: Hot dogs!
Larry: French fries!
Harriet: Yum! Those all taste good. Which one do you like best?
All: Pizza!
Harriet: Me too! So, in our story, we can write, "I like . . ."
All: "Pizza!"

Next Harriet gives the children an opportunity to hear and rehearse the language of the story, thus supporting the students' memory of the language pattern for future predictions. This remembered message is critical, because the children will use it to self-monitor their writing.

Harriet: "I like pizza." Let's all say the story together.
All: "I like pizza."

Writing the Story

Harriet repeats the language pattern fluently; then she prompts the children to attend to the concepts "first" and "word":

Harriet: "I like pizza." What is the first word in our story?
All: *I.*

Next Harriet focuses the children's attention on where to begin writing and the left-to-right directional movement across print:

Harriet: Where do I start to write the word *I*?
Damion: Right there *(pointing to the left side).*
Harriet: I want everyone to point on your own board where to write the word *I*. *(The children point to the appropriate starting points on their dry erase lapboards.)* Which way do I go now? Show me on your board. *(The children demonstrate left-to-right movement on their lapboards.)*

Harriet repeats the language pattern and gives the children an opportunity to write a known word:

Harriet: "I like pizza." You all know how to write the word *I*. Damion, come up and write *I* in our story. Everyone else can practice writing the word *I* on their board.

Harriet goes on to prompt the children to recall the story, confirm their knowledge, and demonstrate the process of slow articulation of sounds within a word:

Harriet: What does our story say?
All: "I like pizza."
Harriet: Yes, "I like pizza." L—i—ke. Now, everyone say the word with me very slowly, and let's listen to the sounds we can hear in the word.
All: L—i—ke.

Harriet prompts the children to monitor their writing by rereading to recall their story (a message level) and then asks them to think about the next word (a word level) in the story. She again demonstrates the process of slowly articulating the sounds within a word (emphasizing but not segmenting the sounds). The children must now predict the letter for the sound they hear (a graphophonemic level). She also helps the children attend to important conventions of print: word, space, letter formation, first, next.

Harriet: After writing the word, we have to go back and reread our story and think about what we want our story to say.

All: "I like pizza."

Harriet: What word are we writing next? "I . . . (*She pauses to invite the correct response.*)

All: *Like*!

Harriet: Yes. The next word in our story is *like*. Where do I need to write the word *like*? Julie, can you come up and show us? (*Julie comes up to the chart and points to the space beside the word* I.) Good for you! Before we write the next word, we need to leave a space like it looks in books. That makes it easier for us to read. Julie, can you make us a good space with your finger?

Next Harriet concentrates on hearing and recording sounds in words. She validates the children's contribution of the ending sound of *k* while simultaneously directing their attention to the importance of listening to the sounds in sequence. She emphasizes the beginning sound, that of the letter *l*, in three ways: (1) she stresses the first letter, (2) she compares it to the beginning letter in Larry's name, and (3) she links it to the appropriate letter on the alphabet chart.

Harriet: Say the word *like* very slowly. Let's stretch the sounds.

All: L—i—ke.

Harriet: What can you hear in *like*? Write the sounds you hear on your lapboard. Paul, come up and tell me what you can hear.

Paul: *K.*

Harriet: Good listening! There is a *k*. You hear it at the end. Now, everyone say the word *like* and listen to what you hear at the beginning. L-l-l-l-ike.

Larry: *L*! Like my name!

Harriet: Yes, it starts like *Larry*! Can everyone hear it? Can you feel it in your mouth? L-l-l-ike. L-L-Larry. (*Harriet and the children say the two words together.*) Now who can find a picture on our ABC chart that starts like *Larry* and *like*?

Damion: Ladder!

Harriet: That's right. *Larry, like,* and *ladder* all start with *l*. Damion, will you come to the chart and point to the *l* so everyone can see how it looks? (*Damion finds the* l *for* ladder *and chants the letter and picture cue.*) Now Larry can write the *l* in our story. The rest of you can write it on your lapboard. (*She quickly adds the letter* i *in the word, and then calls Paul up to the chart to add the* k.) Paul, you heard the *k* at the end of *like*, so come up and write it in our story.

Analyzing new words by saying them slowly and predicting the sequence of sounds is a productive activity for helping children learn how to create links between sounds, letters, and words. In this lesson, Harriet makes it easy for the children to hear known sounds within the articulation of a new word. In other lessons, she will look for opportunities to help the children generalize their knowledge about sounds to beginning, middle, and ending positions within a variety of words. In the current lesson, Harriet held the children accountable only for things they already knew—she incidentally supplied the *i* in *like* because it was an unknown item, and she added the ending of the word. However, as she contributed the unknown ending, she used language that channeled the children's attention toward noticing a new feature about print: "Now, I'll write the *e* on the end of the word *like*. We don't hear that sound, but we need it to make the word look right."

Expanding the Text

During the writing of this simple message, the children are practicing directionality, one-to-one matching, and return sweep on a single line of text. The next step in the lesson is to expand the text based on the repetitive pattern, which will provide the children with an opportunity to practice return sweep and to develop fluency with two high-frequency words, *I* and *like*.

Harriet: Now let's add two new foods to your story. What foods would you like to add?

After some teacher negotiation, the children agree that ice cream and hot dogs are their favorite foods, in that order.

As the message is being rehearsed, Harriet quickly considers (1) which letters and sounds within words are good exemplars for demonstrating slow articulation and letter/sound match, (2) which letters she will contribute without explicitly teaching them, and (3) which letters and words provide opportunities for modeling how to use resources. She uses explicit language and accompanying actions to highlight critical concepts of print.

Harriet: Let's return to the beginning of our sentence and get our mouths ready to say the next word. (*As she rereads, she articulates the beginning sound for the letter* h *in* hot.)What do you hear at the beginning of the word *hot*?

As several children make the sound for the letter *h,* Harriet directs their attention to the large alphabet chart. "Yes," she affirms, "you are making the *h* sound, just like the word *horse* on your alphabet chart." She quickly records the two letters *h* and *o* in the word, then prompts, "Now let's say the word *hot* slowly. I believe you can hear the last sound in the word."

The children respond with confidence and enthusiasm, "It's a *t!*"

As the lesson comes to closure, Harriet wants the children to record the words *like* (a known word) and *hot* (a partially known word) in their word dictionaries. First, she directs their attention to the large alphabet chart: "What is your picture cue for *L*?"

Without hesitation, the children respond, "Ladder!"

Then she prompts, "Get out your word dictionary and turn to the *L* page."

Harriet wants the children to be able to locate letters in their dictionary without turning individual pages. However, she knows this is new learning for the children and that they will need a high degree of scaffolding to acquire this skill. She asks, "Where is the *L*? Is it at the beginning (*pointing to the upper section of the chart),* the middle (*pointing to the middle section),* or near the end of the alphabet (*pointing to the last few lines of the chart)*?" She wants them to notice that the *L* is near the middle of the alphabet, but the children's uncertainty is evident as they yell out different responses. She increases the scaffolding, modeling once again the sections of the alphabet and lingering on the *L* section. "Is the *L* in the middle of the alphabet?" she asks.

"Yes," the children respond.

Harriet: Now that you know where to locate the *L* in the alphabet, let's see how quickly you can find the *L* page in your word dictionary. Don't turn the pages one by one. I'll help you if you need me.

The children require varying degrees of scaffolding, but in the process, they are learning an important lesson about efficiency, which will have implications for reading fluency. As they locate the *L* page, Harriet prompts them to write the word *like* on the page; then she applies the same procedures to adding the word *hot* to the dictionary. As the children carry out the task, Harriet adjusts her scaffolding to ensure that each child is successful. During subsequent lessons, the children will add other high-frequency words to the appropriate pages.

Over the next few lessons, the teacher and children will create an ending to the story—one that will break from the pattern (for example, "I will eat them all"), and also present new opportunities for the children to learn. The interaction between teacher and children is similar to a dance, where the teacher orchestrates the movements according to what the children know and what the teacher needs to contribute. Within this apprenticeship context, the children display confidence and excitement as success is guaranteed.

Through repeated readings of this simple text, the children are exposed to the visual features of the word *like.* Their ability to analyze the beginning and ending consonants form a framework for learning the visual features (the *i* and *e*) that are needed to make the word look right.

Because Harriet realizes the children need to become familiar with some frequently encountered words, she extends this knowledge to their guided reading lesson. First, she prompts them to locate the word *like* in their book. Next, she encourages them to take a good look at the word and then shut their eyes and look at the word in their head. When Melissa enthusiastically exclaims, "I see the *l*," Harriet prompts her to locate its position point within the word: "Where do you see it?"

Julie says, "I see the *l* at the beginning and the *k* at the end."

Finally, Harriet says, "Now open your eyes and check to be sure that your word *like* looks the same as the word *like* in your story." After the children confirm their response, Harriet passes out the appropriate magnetic letters for constructing the word *like* on their individual dry erase boards.

Harriet: Make the word *like* with your magnetic letters. After you have made the word, what do you need to do?

Daniel: Check it with your finger. And say it.

Harriet: That's right. Check it with your finger and say the word as you check it. That will help you remember the word.

In the apprenticeship approach, it is critical that all children be actively involved in the literacy event. When an individual child contributes a letter or word to the group story, the teacher simultaneously engages the other children with appropriate prompts: (a) "Say the word slowly." (b) "Locate the letter on your alphabet chart." (c) "Write the letter on your lapboard." (d) "Trace the letter with your finger on the carpet." Throughout the lesson, Harriet guides the children to participate actively in the learning experience. Her flexible prompts are based on her understanding of how the brain organizes information and provides feedback by which children can confirm their response (see Chapter 1). In the previous example, the children were not only learning a frequently encountered word (*like*), but were also acquiring an effective strategy for learning new words.

We use interactive writing for a special purpose: to support the development of early reading and writing behavior. The literacy demonstrations are very clear and focused in order not to overwhelm the children with new learning. As soon as the children demonstrate that they can use the behavior in their independent reading and writing, the assisted writing lessons are adjusted to reflect this increasing control.

Interactive writing gives children opportunities to practice critical aspects of print under the guidance of an observant and responsive teacher. They work within their zone of proximal development—that is, they are able to apply knowledge and strategies with the help of the teacher that they would be unable to accomplish alone. Children develop higher-level understanding as they become more aware of the power of their own knowledge in solving new problems. The teacher must therefore know how to adjust her assisted activities to accommodate the child's understanding of the literacy process. In the next section, the teacher "ups the ante" in interactive writing to reflect the children's new understanding about written language.

Interactive Writing with Beginning Early Writers

Having learned how to brainstorm ideas and generate simple messages gives children a very supportive framework for acquiring critical concepts about written language. An important shift occurs at this point: children become more conscious of their own mental processes and begin to use early checking strategies to guide and confirm their initial response to print. To keep children working at the simple sentence level would inhibit opportunities to learn more about the writing process. Children now need experiences in creating longer pieces of writing similar to that used in texts.

In the following example, Judy is working with a small group of first graders. Her observations of the children's independent reading and writing behaviors indicate that they are ready to begin constructing longer texts. On this particular day, the children are very excited because they have just finished cooking a large pot of chili for a class project. This is a perfect context for learning how to add details to a story while simultaneously practicing problem-solving strategies.

Judy initiates the conversation. "I could smell your chili cooking this morning. Tell me how you made it." Several voices join together as the children describe the ingredients. As the children talk, Judy records key ingredients on a chart: tomatoes, hamburger meat, beans, V-8 juice. This list will become a resource when the story is written.

Now Judy guides the children to begin composing the message: "How do we need to start our story? What is the most important thing about the story?"

Again, a chorus of voices says, "We made chili."

Judy confirms this while encouraging the children to expand on their simple statement: "That's right. But tell me more. When did you make the chili? Where did you make the chili?" As the children elaborate, Judy listens and encourages them to expand even further. "Why did you make the chili? How did you make the chili?" Through guided participation, the teacher and children are finally ready to compose the complete message. Judy starts the composition process while seeking approval from the children.

Judy: Okay, let me see if I have your story right. Today at school we made chili for a class project. We put in tomatoes, beans, hamburger meat, and V-8 juice. It was so good! Yum, yum!"

Several children: Yes. Let's write it now!

With this activity, Judy elevates the assisted writing to a new level by introducing the children to five key words—*what, when, where, why,* and *how*—that provide a scaffold for adding details to a simple message. At this level, the teacher provides a high degree of scaffolding by clearly modeling the process and using the key words to engage the children in talking about the details in their story.

Judy: These five key words can make your story more interesting for your reader. Let's go back to your story and think about how you answered these questions for your reader.

As she writes the word *what* on the anchor chart, she asks, "Now what did you do?"

The children respond, "We made chili." She records this statement next to the key word and continues to probe further until all key words and corresponding statements are recorded on the anchor chart. This simple exercise provides an early foundation for adding details to writing. An additional benefit is that children are being exposed to important high-frequency words—those *w* words that can be so confusing for many beginning readers.

On another day, Judy revisits the interactive writing text and uses it to demonstrate simple analogies.

First she asks the children to locate and frame (with a framing card) the word *we* in the story. When Darin notices that there are two *we*'s in the story, Judy confirms this fact and makes certain everyone is looking at the same word: "Yes, there are two *we*'s—one with a capital letter and one with a lowercase letter. Who can find the word *we* with a lowercase letter?" Next Judy distributes the appropriate magnetic letters and asks the children to change the first letter of this known word to make a new word:

Judy: Make the word *we* with your letters. Now I want you to take away the first letter from *we*. What letter are you going to take away?
All: *W.*
Judy: Yes, put an *h* in front of the *e*. You have just made a new word. Who can tell us what this word is?
Several children: *He*!
Judy: What would I do if I wanted to make the word *we*?
Several children: Take away the *h* and put back the *w*.
Judy: Let's try that and check it to see if it works.

Now Judy prompts the children to make another word: "Now make a word that starts like *mouse* and ends like *he*." Because Judy knows that the word *mouse* is a familiar cue—it is on the ABC shared reading chart—she believes the children will have no trouble making this new word. Although the prompt represents higher-level processing, Judy provides the children with strong external support—the appropriate magnetic letters and the letter/picture cue for *m*. The goal of the activity is to ensure a meaningful and successful performance.

After numerous experiences with interactive writing, children should demonstrate control of early concepts about print: starting position, spacing, letters, and so forth. In addition, they should know how to analyze and record sounds within words. They should be able to write several important frequently encountered words and apply simple analogies for using what they know about a known word to write an unknown word. Finally, children should be writing two- and three-sentence messages that demonstrate their ability to use punctuation to support meaning. Their writing should reflect their early understanding about how print works.

Some Comments About Resources (Tools)

An important goal of interactive writing is the use of anchor charts, checklists, and rubrics. At the emergent and early levels, these tools are used during shared reading experiences. The teacher creates the tools and models their benefits as a writing resource while immersing the children in the experience. It is important that the language on the tool match the language used during the interactive writing experience. Here is an example of a shared reading checklist that aligns with the assisted writing experience (see Dorn and Soffos 2011b):

1. Did I start in the right place?
2. Did I leave good spaces between words?
3. Did I say the words slowly?
4. Did I reread to help me with the next word?
5. Did I use my practice page to help me with tricky words?

When the children have internalized the language from the checklist, they are given a personal copy to use during their independent-writing time. At the early and above levels, children are introduced to anchor charts, editing and revising checklists, and matching rubrics. These nonverbal resources are used to assist children's planning, monitoring, and reflecting behaviors in writing.

Making the Transition to Writing Aloud

At this point the teacher introduces the "writing-aloud" concept. In this type of assisted writing, the teacher vocalizes her thoughts as she composes text, inviting the children to contribute at selected points. Her invitations are grounded in her knowledge of children's processing behavior, and her focus is on promoting effective problem-solving strategies that will carry over to new situations. While writing aloud, the teacher's primary goal is to demonstrate the importance of composing a meaningful, coherent message for a particular audience and a specific purpose. Taking an apprenticeship approach, the teacher gives the children clear demonstrations and good models that they can use as standards when they direct their

own writing activities. Through guided participation in these assisted demonstrations, the children acquire important tools for learning how to write more sophisticated and conventional messages.

Organizing for Writing Aloud

As with interactive writing, the writing-aloud lesson can occur in a whole-group or small-group setting. The workshop framework (see Chapter 8; also see Dorn and Soffos 2005) provides an authentic context for delivering the writing-aloud lesson to the entire class. In this case, the teacher selects a universal topic that would appeal to the class and guides them through the process of drafting, revising, crafting, and editing the group composition. The writing piece is developed over a period of several days as the teacher models the writing continuum and the children apply the knowledge, skills, and strategies to their independent writing.

For children who need additional assistance in writing, the teacher provides the writing-aloud lesson in a small group. The small-group lesson is approximately twenty minutes, spanning several days in order to carry a writing piece through the writing continuum. For the children who are struggling the most in literacy, the reading specialist or special education teacher can provide writing aloud as a supplemental small-group intervention (see Chapter 10; also see Dorn and Soffos 2011a, 2011b).

The teacher gathers the following materials for the writing-aloud lesson: a large chart tablet for group composition, large laminated writing guides and checklists, a dry erase board and marker, and a dictionary. Some teachers compose the message on an interactive whiteboard. Most of the children's materials are smaller versions of the teacher's materials.

In the writing-aloud activity, the teacher is the scribe. She also leads the discussion. She deliberately encourages children to contribute, expand, and sequence their ideas logically, because her goal is to help them develop an understanding of the writing process. Writing aloud also gives children opportunities to learn effective strategies for solving unfamiliar words.

To begin, the teacher takes a moment to describe the purpose of the activity and the teacher-student roles:

- She emphasizes that her main reason for writing is to create a story that others will enjoy. She tells the children they will help her compose her story and add details. As she writes, she asks clarifying and extending questions that focus on building meaning.

- She tells the children that her first copy is her draft, that her main concern is the quality of her message, and that when the story is completed, she will reread it to ensure that she has communicated her message in an effective and descriptive way. She informs the children that they will help her with this process.

- She tells the children that she will show them some important ways to solve particular words as she writes the story: she will use her practice board to work on a few selected words, and they will help her.

- She instructs the children to listen to how she applies a wide range of problem-solving strategies and resources as she composes her message.

- She emphasizes that the main purpose of writing is to construct a meaningful (and interesting) message, so she will reread her story after she has worked on a new word or added a new detail to keep her mind on the composing process.

- She tells the children they will help with this rereading and make predictions about logical events that could occur next in her story.

Writing aloud provides children with shared opportunities to learn how to construct and organize ideas for particular purposes and how to solve words on the spot. It can emerge from read-alouds, storytelling, hands-on experiences, shared readings, and content-related topics. The extensiveness of the prewriting discussions will depend on the type of writing. A writing-aloud activity, such as the example below, can span several days.

Writing-Aloud Lesson with a Small Group of Early Writers

Writing aloud follows a predictable structure for engaging students in the writing process. In this section, we share examples of writing-aloud lessons with early to fluent writers.

Prewriting Discussion

Carla has chosen an enjoyable topic that will maintain the children's attention. Using the book *The Very Quiet Cricket* (Carle 1990), her own personal experience, and the children's background knowledge about fishing and crickets, Carla tells her students a story about the night she searched for crickets and invites them to help her compose the message.

Composing and Writing the Story

Carla: I want you to help me write my story. When do you think I went out to look for crickets?

DeMario: One night.

Russell: One dark night!

Carla: (*Writing*) "One dark night . . ." What did I do?

Kevin: Went walking.

Carla: (*Rereading*) "One dark night (*writing new text*) I went walking . . ."

Because Carla's emphasis is on the message, she is able to write the story fluently. There is active discussion throughout, and the children contribute; however, Carla is the primary scribe. She focuses on composing and also on thinking aloud as she models conventions of writing and strategies for solving new words. Her demonstrations foster writing proficiency. They are brief, on the spot, and purposeful attempts to call attention to a particular source of knowledge the children possess and can use to solve new problems. Early in the lesson Carla reminds the children of a word they have recorded in their word dictionary.

Carla: Yesterday we put the word *light* in our dictionary. Do you remember the chunk that was at the end of *light*? It can help us with this word *night.*

Tania: I.

Carla: I what?

All: G—h—t.

Carla: I-g—h—t. (*Writing* light *on the practice board next to the story*) Now if I erase the *l*, what do I need to make the word *night*?

All: N.

Carla: (*Writing* night) So if I know *light*, that can help me to write *night*.

Carla now directs the children to reread and predict what could happen next in the story. She encourages them to expand the story and uses revising techniques to illustrate the process. She directs the children's attention to the importance of using things they know from one situation to help them in a new situation.

Carla: Help me read what we have written so far.

All: "One dark night I went walking."

Carla: Where?

DeMario: By a pond.

Carla: "By a pond." (*Writing this quickly*) Now, let's read it again.

All: "One dark night I went walking by a pond."

Carla: What did I have with me when I was walking by the pond?

All: A flashlight!

Carla: Do I need to add that in there? Would that make my story better?

Kevin: Yes, because it was dark and we need to know you had a flashlight.

Carla: Okay, what do I need to cross out to add that?

All: The period.

Carla: The period, because I'm not finished. (*Rereading*) "One dark night I went walking by a pond with . . ." Adrianna, you can help me with that word *with*. You made that earlier with the magnetic letters. (*As Adrianna spells the word, Carla writes it in the story.*)

Negotiating the Text

Carla has the students monitor the message by rereading the text after each new addition. She encourages story expansion with questions that provide a scaffold from which the children can develop a well-organized story. In the next negotiation, Carla leads the children to incorporate book language into the story. She asks, "What kind of noises did I hear?" When the children respond "Cheeps" and "Chirps," Carla fluently writes, "I heard chirping noises" into the text.

Carla also looks for productive opportunities to direct the children's attention to strategies for analyzing words, always keeping her primary focus on the fluent construction of a meaningful story.

Carla: (*Prompting*) What did I do then?

Kevin: "I flashed my . . ."

Carla: (*Writing* I flash) What do I put on the end of *flash* to get *flashed*?

All: *E-d.*

Carla: (*Adding* ed *and rereading*) "I flashed my" (*writing* light) toward the what?

Andy: Problem.

Carla: (*Writing* problem; *writing a new sentence*) "I saw some crickets." (*Prompting*) What did I say I was going to do the next time?

Tania: Get a jar.

Carla: (*Writing* The next time I go walking, I need to take a j—) *Jar* is like another word that I know. *Jar* is like the word . . .

All: *Car*!

Carla: (*Writing* car) So if I know *car*, I can change the *c* to a what?

All: *J.* Jar!

Carla: (*Rereading*) "I need to take a (*writing*) jar so I can . . ."

All: "Go."

Carla: (*Prompting*) "So I can . . ." What am I going to do with that jar?

DeMario: Catch some crickets.

Carla: (*Rereading and writing*) "So I can catch some crickets." (*She slowly says the word, emphasizing the* ck *chunk, and then writing the word* crickets.) Then what will I do?

Kevin: Go fishing.

Carla: (*Rereading and writing*) "Then I can go f . . ." Help me with *fishing.*

All: *I-s-h.*

Carla: (*Writing* fish) What's on the end of *fish* to make *fishing*?

All: *I-n-g.*

Carla: (*Writing* ing *and rereading*) "Then I can go fishing (*writing*) and catch a . . ."

All: "Big fish!"

Notice how Carla engages the children in a collaborative dialogue during which they jointly use problem-solving strategies at both the message and the word level. At the message level, she asks leading questions (when? what? where? why? prompts) that keep the composing process in motion. She balances this by fluently recording particular patches of language and asking questions that prompt the children to use their own knowledge of analogies and spelling patterns to solve specific words. This is social dialogue, in which Carla prompts the children to assume responsibility for whatever aspects of the writing process they are able to control. It is through these interactions that the children will gain strategies for their independent writing.

As today's story comes to an end, Carla returns to the goal of writing, which is to create a meaningful message for the reader. She directs the children's attention to the writing chart as a resource for their individual work.

Carla: Now before I do anything else, what do I need to do with my story?

Andy: Go back over it.

DeMario: Read it again.

Carla: I want to read my story and make sure it makes sense (*pointing to the first step on the writing chart*) and that somebody who reads my story will understand it. So, let's read my story to see if it makes sense.

The teacher and children reread the story in unison and agree that it makes sense. However, in her final comments, Carla emphasizes that a story can be added to even after we think it is finished: "Tomorrow we can put this on the interactive whiteboard and add to it to make it even more interesting." She writes the word *draft* on her story and says, "My draft just needs to make sense so that when I read it to somebody, they will understand it."

Revising and Editing

Revisions are perhaps the toughest activities to do with children who are programmed to make perfect attempts. We believe children should be taught how to solve words so that they will take risks in writing interesting and longer texts. One way to accomplish this is through teacher demonstrations of problem-solving strategies. Explicit talk and action give children a good model for solving words while keeping the focus on composing meaningful text. The emphasis should not be on an individual word itself; rather, the word is the means by which to demonstrate important strategies the child can apply to new situations when writing independently. The child thus moves from the interpsychological plane (group problem solving) to the intrapsychological plane (individual problem solving) as he internalizes effective processes for moving his development forward.

The first step in revision is to examine the message for meaning: the teacher and children reread the text to see whether the story makes sense. The teacher instructs the children to listen for transitional words that move the story forward.

Carla: How many transitional words did you hear?

Kevin: There are three. *Next, so, then.*

Carla: Everybody read it together, and Kevin can circle them.

As revision continues, the teacher and children cross out or change words and insert new words or phrases. Carla channels the children's attention toward the relationship between an appropriate title and the text:

Carla: What do I need to put at the top?

DeMario: "Night Crickets."

Carla: Is that what you think would be a good title? Yes, it is. (*Writing the title*) That is a very good title. It tells me exactly what is going to be in the story. I know that when I read "Night Crickets," somebody is going to be out at night, and what are they going to see?

All: Crickets!

At the end of the session, Carla tells the children she will make a copy of the story for future revision. Her explicit demonstrations of writing behaviors and her gentle scaffolding at the children's level of understanding have helped them learn how to revise their work. She has not followed a script. Instead, she has made a number of flexible decisions based on her observations of and interactions with the children. Her teaching priorities will promote gradual shifts in the children's writing behaviors over time. Through critical teaching decisions such as these, the children gain control of and take more responsibility for their own writing. The goal of assisted writing is achieved when the children begin to use the skills and strategies they have encountered in group demonstrations to monitor and regulate their own thinking processes when writing independently.

Children need frequent opportunities early on to revise and edit their work. Crossing out words when they have changed their minds and using carets to insert missing words and phrases are just some of the revision techniques children need to acquire. They also need to learn how to edit their writing for grammar and spelling. This crucial behavior is taught during instructional interactions with an observant and responsive teacher. With more experience, early writers become fluent writers willing to work on an evolving piece of writing.

When children revise a piece of their own writing, they focus on communicating the message to their reader in the clearest way possible. They may do any of the following:

- add meaningful information to clarify content
- add missing words to make the sentence sound right
- add details to expand and enhance the message
- cross out unnecessary words and phrases
- use good word choices, including concrete nouns and strong verbs
- vary sentence lengths to create fluency rhythms
- use figurative language to create images

When children edit a piece of their writing, they focus on spelling, punctuation, and grammar functions. For instance, they

- capitalize the first letter of every sentence,
- correct misspelled words, and
- use appropriate punctuation.

Through clear demonstrations and small-group or one-on-one conferences, the children learn that writing is not something that is done at only one time or in only one place. Their confidence and writing ability increases as the result of specific feedback. The successful teacher

- stimulates additional content ideas,
- prompts for clarity and meaning,
- elicits details and colorful words to make the story more interesting,
- models questions writers need to ask themselves when writing, and
- demonstrates proofreading and self-correcting skills.

Revision with a Group of Early Writers

During early revision sessions, we suggest displaying a child's text on an interactive whiteboard and modeling how to reread it with the intention of clarifying it. Listening to a rereading gives the writer personal feedback for monitoring meaning: the author will often hear a gap in her story that she did not notice while she was writing it.

Carla's opening remarks establish the importance of creating a meaningful text:

Carla: Today we are going to use Andy's story on the whiteboard. We all know that writers miss things when they read their own work and that they need listeners to help them. When we look at Andy's story, we are going to think about whether it makes sense and whether Andy has made clear what he wants to share with us. Andy, read your story to us.

Andy: (*Reading*) "Last night I went outside and I saw some frogs and I picked them up and I put them in a box."

Carla: Does Andy's story make sense?

Children: Yes.

Carla: Is there anything about Andy's story that you want to know more about?

James: Where did you find the frogs?

Andy: At the pond.

Carla: Andy, where would you add this in your story?

Andy: (*Rereading and adding new information*) "Last night I went outside and I saw some frogs by the pond." (*Carla adds a caret to the text and inserts the phrase* by the pond *into Andy's story.*)

Carla: Is there anything else you would like to know about Andy's story?

DeMario: Andy, are you going to let them go so that they can go back home?

Carla: Andy, would you like to tell us about that in your story?

Andy: Yes, I could say that at the end. (*Rereading and adding new information*) "Last night I went outside and I saw some frogs by the pond. I picked them up and put them in a box. Then I let them go."

Carla: (*Asking for confirmation before making any additions on the board*) Is that where you want to put it? (*Then, prompting for further expansion and clarification*) Is there anything else you want to ask Andy about his story?

Tania: I have a *when* question. Hey, Andy, when did you catch the frogs?

Andy: It was nighttime.

Carla: (*Probing further*) What was it like outside?
Andy: Dark.
Carla: Where are we talking about "outside"? Where could we add the new information, Tania?
Tania: We could put it after "last night."
Carla: Would that be a good place, Andy?
Andy: It needs to go after the part "I went outside."
Carla: Okay, let me add it right here (*after* outside) and let's read and see if it makes sense there.

Later Carla prompts the children to think of an appropriate title for Andy's story. After several children suggest titles, she says Andy should decide:

Carla: Those are all really good suggestions, but since this is Andy's story, he should decide what his title should be.
Andy: "Night Frogs."
Carla: Does that title tell us about the story?

Later in the conversation, DeMario comments that this is Andy's draft copy.

Carla: Yes, this is his first draft. And what has Andy done to his first draft?
Tania: First, he read it to see if it made sense.
Carla: Yes, Andy wants his readers to feel like they are right there with him at the pond. How does his story make you feel?
James: I could see it in my imagination.
Carla: Yes, you were seeing his story in your head.

Finally, Carla invites the group to reread the story together and thanks Andy for sharing his story with his classmates. The support offered by the members of this writing group is obvious, for everyone has played a role in working on Andy's revisions. At the same time, the rules of ownership were honored: each new suggestion was presented to Andy for his approval. This collaborative approach to revision is used daily until Carla observes that children are using these techniques when writing independently. After that, she holds more individual conferences. However, flexibility is important; Carla convenes a group conference whenever a common difficulty arises.

Editing for Spelling with a Group of Early Writers

In this example, Esther uses the interactive whiteboard to display a copy of Shanika's writing for a group editing lesson:

Esther: Shanika has written a wonderful story that she would like to read to us, and she would like us to help her prepare her story for publication. What are some things we need to check for before we publish any of our work?
Mya: We need to be sure we have capital letters and the right punctuation.
Roshon: Be sure to check the spelling.

Esther agrees with these suggestions and asks Shanika which one she wants help with today.

Shanika: I need help with my spelling.
Esther: What can we do first?
Kevin: We need to search for misspelled words and circle them.
Esther: That's right. We have to find them first, don't we? Shanika, read the first sentence, and everyone else check with your eyes to see if the words look right.

The point of group editing is to help the children identify misspelled words and then apply some problem-solving techniques to selected words. This is more productive than correcting all the misspelled words at once. As Shanika reads her sentences, Esther circles the words the children identify as being misspelled. Then:

Esther: Let's look at the word *brothr*. You noticed something about it that is not exactly right. What did you notice?
James: There should be an *er* on the end.
Esther: Let's write it and see how it looks. (*Writing the word* brother) What do you think? Does it look right, Shanika?
Shanika: Yes.
Esther: Good. Let's think of other words that look like *brother* on the end.

The children generate a short list of similar words and Esther records them under *brother*. The goal is not achieved until the children apply their learning beyond correcting the initial word.

At the end of the session, Esther reminds the children of other places to go for help:

Esther: You still have some words circled that we didn't work on today. Let's look at these words and think about where Shanika can go for help.

James: The word *was* is in the class dictionary.

Tania: Say *went* slowly. There's a letter missing in the middle.

Kevin: She could check the word pattern charts for *er* spellings.

Esther: These are all very good things to do to help with spelling. Shanika, after you have worked on your spellings, then come see me and I will help you with the rest of the words.

A Few More Thoughts on Writing Checklists

An editing checklist is a useful tool for helping young writers learn how to evaluate their writing according to conventional standards. The editing checklist is introduced during assisted writing activities, and students use it during independent journal writing.

For the checklist to be effective, it should be based on a continuum of learning. As children develop control of particular behaviors, the editing checklist is revised to shift attention to a new area. For example, an early editing checklist may emphasize the following areas: (a) include your name; (b) put good spaces between words; (c) start each sentence with a capital letter. When children gain control of these early behaviors, the new editing checklist may focus on these behaviors: (a) check for misspelled words; (b) reread for punctuation; (c) cross out unnecessary words. The editing checklists change to reflect the children's increasing understanding of writing conventions. As children become more competent writers, they internalize these rules and become less dependent on a checklist to assess their work. The teacher looks for evidence that the children are making this shift to higher-level processing.

A writing checklist is another supportive tool for beginning writers. Like the editing checklist, it is first introduced during assisted writing and eliminated when it is no longer needed. Here's an example:

1. Write your story and make sure it makes sense.
2. Add to your story or cross out what you do not want.
3. Read your story to yourself or a friend.
4. Edit for misspelled words. Circle words that do not look right to you.
5. Look up words in your dictionary or try out spellings on your practice page.
6. Put in punctuation marks.
7. Write the final draft.

Writing Guides

Writing guides are graphic organizers for planning a piece of writing according to a particular text type or structure. The guides are introduced during writing-aloud lessons as the teacher models how to use the appropriate guide for planning and subsequently assessing her writing. The teacher uses an enlarged version for demonstration lessons, and the children use small versions during their independent writing. The teacher's version is laminated, which enables her to use it multiple times for demonstrating varied compositions.

Text-writing guides fall under three broad text types: literary, persuasive, and informational. These types include a variety of conventional structures, such as problem/solution, cause/effect, descriptive, and procedural. Additional guides help writers organize their writing for particular purposes, such as summaries, character analyses, reports, or presenting arguments. Writing guides are important scaffolds for apprenticing young writers into academic writing through the writing process. (See examples of writing guides in Dorn and Soffos 2011a, 2005, 2001.)

Closing Thoughts

Two important principles contribute to successful group revision conferences:

- Children must be comfortable having their work displayed for group revisions and editing.
- Teachers must ensure a supportive environment that focuses on collaboration and problem-solving opportunities.

Children's writing ability is directly influenced by three important factors:

- the appropriateness and the quality of the demonstrations provided by the teacher
- the types of opportunities they have to apply revising and editing techniques
- the teacher's feedback during group and individual conferences

The teacher, as the more knowledgeable person, keeps the children working at the cutting edge of their intellectual development. As the children demonstrate they are moving to a higher plane of learning, the teacher creates new assisted writing situations that validate the old knowledge and activate new learning. At the same time, the teacher provides independent writing opportunities that allow the children to practice the skills and strategies they are acquiring from the assisted activities. Throughout, the teacher collects data that she uses to inform her next instructional move.

The social context is very important in developing new understanding. A balanced literacy program provides children with many opportunities to apply and expand their learning. The following principles are important factors in helping children become successful learners:

- Children acquire important concepts about writing during social and collaborative dialogues with more knowledgeable people.
- Teachers use explicit language and action to model critical concepts about the writing process.
- Teachers hold children accountable for applying their existing knowledge in new problem-solving activities during assisted writing.
- Teachers constantly adjust their levels of support in accordance with their observations of children's developing control.
- Children's cognitive processes are validated and activated during meaningful collaborative writing.
- Literacy learning needs to take place in the children's zone of proximal development if they are to internalize, appropriate, and generalize these strategies.

chapter six

INDEPENDENT WRITING

An apprentice works alongside a more knowledge-able person who assists him to successfully carry out carefully structured tasks. Progress is determined according to two levels of performance: (1) what the apprentice is able to accomplish in the zone of proximal development with the assistance of the more knowledgeable person, and (2) what the apprentice is able to accomplish independently. Vygotsky (1978) would say that what the child is able to perform today with assistance he will be able to accomplish tomorrow on his own.

During assisted writing (see Chapter 5), teachers provide demonstrations, clear models, and guided practice, followed by opportunities for children to apply the learning independently. In an apprenticeship approach, the transfer of knowledge cannot be over-stated. Therefore, if the student experiences difficulty in transferring the knowledge to the independent situation, the teacher should reflect on the appropriateness of her instruction during the assisted activity. Here are a few questions to consider:

- Was the assisted activity too difficult? Did the children have the necessary background knowledge to make sense of the instruction? Did the children understand what they were expected to do?
- Were the demonstrations clear and memorable? Did the teacher provide adequate opportunities for the children to practice the learning with assistance before the independent writing?
- Were the language prompts appropriate for the children's needs? Did the instruction focus on scaffolding the children to apply their knowledge to the new task? Did the children make the connection between the prompt and the task to be accomplished?

- Were the students adequately engaged and challenged with authentic tasks that kept them motivated to work independently?

Apprenticeships in Writing

As children interact with their teacher during varied writing experiences, they are learning to become writers. These experiences include assisted writing in a group setting, independent writing, and writing conferences with the teacher. Teachers must recognize children's writing behaviors as evidence of how they are responding to their teaching.

In assisted writing activities, the teacher provides instruction aimed at children's potential to learn. Through guided participation, the teacher presents clear and memorable models that provide children with high-quality standards for writing. The goal of instruction has been achieved when the teacher observes that the children are indeed applying this knowledge when writing independently.

Independent writing gives children personal opportunities to apply recently demonstrated techniques and strategies. The teacher has a chance to observe how the children use their skills, strategies, and knowledge on their own. By comparing the writing samples of a child across time, the teacher sees just how a child is regulating his or her own writing development. To assess children's writing development, teachers can ask questions such as these (see Dorn and Soffos 2001a):

- Do they understand the writing process, including prewriting, first draft, revising editing, and final draft?

- Can they select their own topic? Do they focus on a topic, respond to feedback, and add details to strengthen their writing as needed?
- Do they know how to use revising and editing checklists and rubrics to assess their own writing?
- Do they use resources, such as dictionaries, word charts, and thesauruses, to check their spelling and vocabulary?
- Do they attend to the writing techniques and language used by their favorite authors?
- Do they write for different purposes? Do they understand how to organize their writing to accommodate a particular audience? Can they use their knowledge of text genre to plan their writing?
- Do they use spelling, punctuation, and grammar that is appropriate for their grade level?

As the children write, the teacher observes how they problem-solve and apply what they know about writing. If a child doesn't apply a strategy the teacher believes he is capable of using, the teacher might stop by and nudge him in a more productive direction. For example, if a child is experiencing difficulty with spelling, the teacher might prompt, "Say the word slowly as you write it" or "Write the word in parts." If the message of the child's writing is unclear, the teacher might prompt the child to "reread that section again to make sure it makes sense to the reader" or to "add some details to clarify the message." In all cases, the teacher is aware of what the child can do and how she can scaffold him in transferring his knowledge to a new situation.

Assessing Writing Development

In order to follow children's progress effectively and instruct them according to their needs, teachers must be able to analyze and interpret change over time in children's writing development. Children's writing samples provide evidence of how they are learning from instruction. If a child is not progressing at the expected rate, the teacher must be prepared to examine her teaching and adjust her instruction if needed. In the next section, we share three continuums that represent change over time in writing development.

Writing Stages

Research shows that children move along a continuum of development reflecting increased control of written language and more conventional writing behavior. Heenman (1985) identifies five developmental writing stages that young children go through when they write:

1. *Scribble stage.* The child uses lines or scribbles to convey meaning (see Figure 6.1).
2. *Isolated letter stage.* The child strings together symbols, numbers, and letter formations with little or no sound-symbol correspondence. Generally, there is no spacing between these forms. The child may be able to read the message, but only with the help of the picture (see Figure 6.2).
3. *Transitional stage.* The child uses some correctly spelled words, but continues to use isolated letters, symbols, and numerals to represent meaning (see Figure 6.3).
4. *Stylized sentence stage.* The child begins to use repetitive patterns organized around known words. The child leaves spaces between words and shows evidence of letter-sound knowledge. The child can read the message without picture support (see Figure 6.4).
5. *Writing stage.* The child composes messages independently for a variety of purposes. The ideas are organized logically and chronologically. Sentences are more complex, varied punctuation appears, approximated and conventional spellings are used, and the writer's voice emerges (see Figure 6.5).

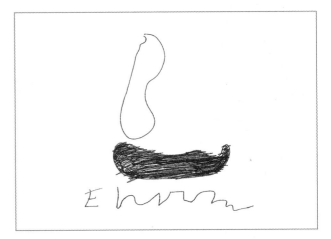

Figure 6.1 Scribble writing (telephone).

Figure 6.2 Isolated letters representing the names of family members.

Figure 6.3 Transitional writing. ("I live in a mobile home. I live in a brick house.")

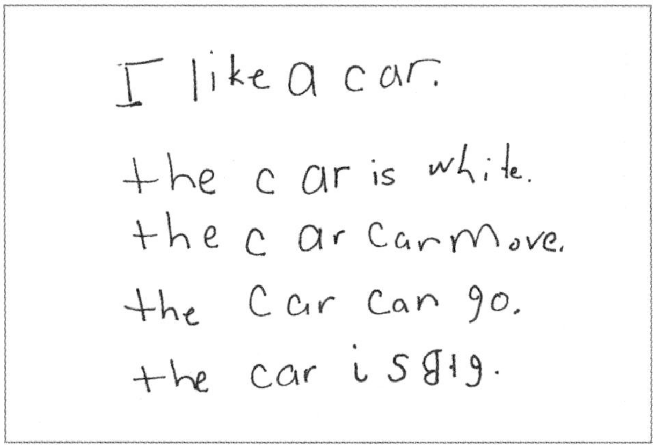

I like a car.
the car is white.
the car can move.
the car can go.
the car is big.

Figure 6.4 Stylized writing. ("I like a car. The car is white. The car can move. The car can go. The car is big.")

I woke up erly in the morning and got in black dress. We drove all the way to grandma Bettys house. Whene we got there we got rdy for granddadys funrle. I had gotten stiches I han been hurt and teased but this felt worst of all. I got in the Car we where redy to go we drove to the church as we drove I got a funny feeling inside of mo like I had smallowed a ice-cube Whene We got there I walked in and felt ows. is I where in a gost grave yard. I felt like crying but I felt so bad I cowlnot cry. Thene the prest started talking his words where slow and sorrowful. I couldnt stand it I was so sad I thaght to my self eWY did he have to smoke? Whene the funaral was over I spent hours just looking at his ashs. I know one thing and I will allways know it no one at all could ever replace him.

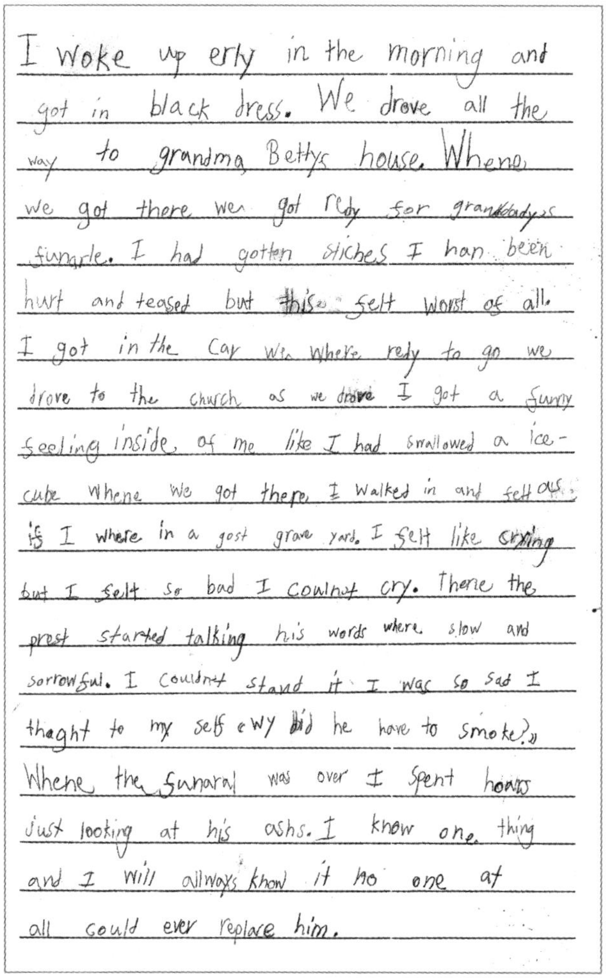

Figure 6.5 Writing stage.

Spelling Stages

Gentry and Gillet (1993) identify five stages of spelling development that are closely aligned with the stages of writing development.

1. *Precommunicative stage.* The child uses random and recurring letters with no letter-sound correspondence. The letters are strung together without spacing. Most letters are uppercase. The child may have an understanding of left-to-right directional movement in print (see Figure 6.6).

2. *Semiphonetic stage.* The child recognizes that letters have sounds, but may represent whole words with only one, two, or three letters. The writing shows a mixture of upper- and lowercase letters (with a preference for uppercase). Letter names are used to represent sounds or syllables (for example, *b* for *be*, *r* for *are*, *u* for *you*). The child begins to use spacing between words (see Figure 6.7).

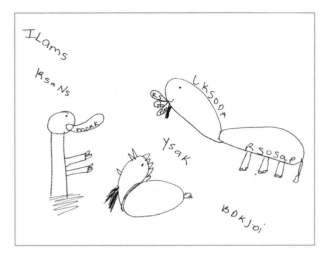

Figure 6.6 Precommunicative spelling.

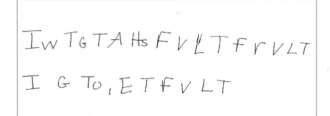

Figure 6.7 Semiphonetic spelling. ("I want to go to a house for Valentines. I go to eat for Valentines.")

3. *Phonetic stage.* The child records letters for every sound within the word. Spacing and left-to-right directional movement are generally under control. The writing at this time may contain a mixture of semiphonetically and phonetically spelled words, with some words spelled correctly (see Figure 6.8).

4. *Transitional stage.* The child begins to rely more on how words look visually rather than on how they sound. The writing at this time may include alternative spellings for the same sound, reversed order of visual patterns (for example, *ou* for *uo*), generous use of inflectional endings, vowels in every syllable, and flexible control of known words (see Figure 6.9).

5. *Correct stage.* The child's letter-sound knowledge is firmly established. The child uses a variety of word structures (prefixes, suffixes, compound words, and so on). The child is able to come up with alternative spellings when a word does not "look right" and is comfortable with using resources such as a dictionary and thesaurus for help. By now, the child has accumulated a large writing vocabulary (see Figure 6.10).

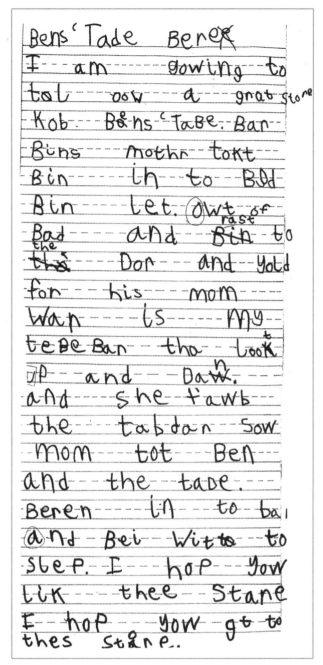

Figure 6.8 Translation:

Story Retelling for Ben's Teddy Bear (PM Reader)

"I am going to tell about a great story called Ben's Teddy Bear. Ben's mother tucked Ben into bed. Ben got out of bed and rushed to the door and yelled for his mom. 'Where is my teddy bear?' Then (she) looked up and down and she found the teddy bear so mom tucked Ben and the teddy bear into bed and Ben went to sleep. I hope you like the story. I hope you get to read this story."

Oun day (Wen) I was at my hous I saw a butfliy fliying thir the ayr I chrid to caych it but I (cued)

Figure 6.9 Transitional stage.

Writing Is a Generative and Recursive Process

It is important to remember that children's writing samples may indicate that several stages are occurring simultaneously. In Chapter 1, we discussed how children's progression through the zone of proximal development is characterized by both generative movements (where the child uses something known to learn something new) and recursive cycles (where the child temporarily ignores something known while problem solving). During the recursive cycle, the child may divert his attention from something he has used before and spend his time thinking about a new challenge. Although this may appear to be regression, it is actually progress. The teacher needs to direct the child toward internalizing the concept (such as the spelling pattern, the known word), so that the response occurs automatically, without conscious attention.

Alice Humphrey (1997, 74), a reading teacher working with first graders, found that her children did indeed go through generative-recursive cycles in acquiring word knowledge:

> Some [of Destini's] attempts captured clear evidence of the learning process. For example, Destini attempted the word *and* nine times. Her first attempt was correctly spelled. On the next attempt, she recorded only the last letter. Next, she recorded two ending letters in the proper sequence. Destini recorded the beginning and ending letters on her fourth attempt. On the next attempt, only the final letter was written. Destini did not write any letters on the sixth trial, but on the final three attempts, she consistently spelled the word correctly.

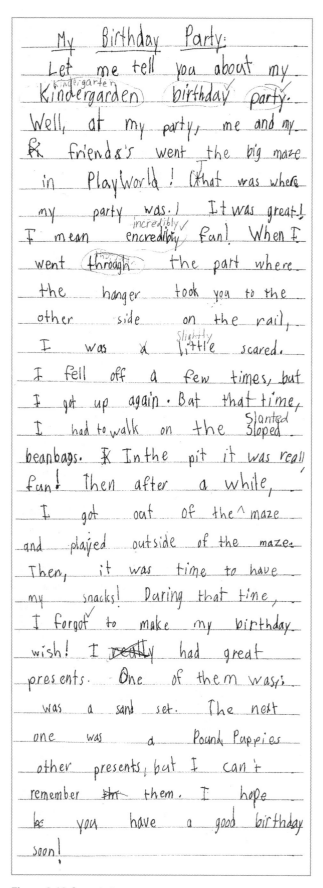

Figure 6.10 Correct stage.

To move children to higher levels of development, the teacher must understand the learning process. Teachers who work with struggling readers sometimes express concern because children know something one day but are unable to recognize the same information in a different situation or at another time. Too often, teachers view this behavior as a problem rather than as movement along a developmental continuum. The teacher's role is to observe where the child is in terms of graphophonemic awareness, spacing, directional movement, and letter formations, and to use this knowledge to lift the child to a higher level.

Writing Continuum

A writing continuum provides teachers with a practical and manageable tool for seeing the connection between standards, assessment, and instruction. The descriptors provide teachers, students, and parents with a common language for discussing students' progress in relation to learning expectations at benchmark periods. In Appendix D-10, the benchmark behaviors along the continuum increase in complexity as students acquire greater skills and knowledge about the writing process (Dorn and Soffos 2001a; 2011). Teachers observe the students' strengths and needs and provide scaffolds to stretch their learning to new levels. In Appendix D-10, the writing behaviors are a reflection of reading, indicating that students must have opportunities to read a variety of text types to be able to write in these modes (NGA/CCSSO 2010).

Teacher Assistance and Student Learning

The relationship between teacher assistance and student performance cannot be overstated. Surely, teaching is directly related to student learning. In other words, if a child is not responding adequately to instruction, then the teaching may be the problem. Furthermore, teachers must understand how to provide the right amount of guidance at the right time to ensure that the student is learning from the teaching opportunity.

To illustrate, let's look at one standard from the Common Core State Standards (NGA/CCSSO 2010) that addresses the role of teacher scaffolding in student learning. Notice how writing expectations increase in complexity as the student benefits from writing instruction across the grades.

- With guidance and support from adults, the kindergarten student will respond to questions and suggestions from peers and add details to strengthen writing as needed.
- With guidance and support from adults, the first-grade student will focus on a topic, respond to questions and suggestions from peers, and add details to strengthen writing as needed.
- With guidance and support from adults and peers, the second-grade student will focus on a topic and strengthen writing as needed by revising and editing.
- With guidance and support from peers and adults, the third-grade student will develop and strengthen writing as needed by planning, revising, and editing.

Independent Writing with Emergent Writers

After assisted writing, children are expected to write independently for fifteen to twenty minutes. As the children write, the teacher circulates among them and observes their performance. She focuses on the children's use of strategies that were emphasized during the assisted writing activities.

The following steps are used during independent writing:

- generating and rehearsing the story in the group
- writing the story independently with scaffolding from the teacher
- conducting an individual teacher-student conference after the story is complete

Emergent and early writers use an unlined book that is bound across the top. The children write their story on the bottom section and use the top section as a practice page for letter and word work. When children's writing becomes longer and more complex, their writing book is replaced with lined paper that is dated and filed in writing folders.

Before children begin independent writing, the teacher clearly models how to write in a journal. First she prepares a large chart divided into two sections. Then she asks a student to demonstrate on the chart where to write the story and where the practice page is. Thinking aloud, she talks about where to write her name and the date. She discusses important strategies, such as hesitating on the word *get* and saying, "I need to say that word slowly because that will help me hear the sounds." She uses language to illustrate how to space between words ("I'll put my finger between these words so I can leave a big space") and to model the importance of rereading to make predictions for the next word. She uses clear, repetitive language and explicit action to help children learn the process of writing in their own journals. After her demonstration, she asks the children, "Who can tell me some things I did to help myself when I was writing my story?" As the children respond, the teacher praises them and encourages them to use these types of strategies when they are writing in their own journals.

Once children have learned how to use their journals as repositories for productive writing, the teacher sets expectations for them based on her observations of the knowledge they demonstrate and the strategies they use during assisted writing. She uses this documentation in deciding when to shift the children to a higher level of assisted writing.

Generating and Rehearsing the Story

Children at the emergent level need to rehearse their story orally before writing it in order to have a language structure with which to monitor their work as they construct the story on paper independently. During the weeks before this interactive writing session, the teacher and children have read and discussed several books about being scared. The teacher now guides the children to generate and rehearse a short message:

Harriet: What are you scared of? Think a minute and then turn to your neighbor and tell him what you are scared of. (*The children turn and talk to each other.*) Who wants to be first to tell us what you are scared of?
Marlin: I am scared of a dinosaur.
Harriet: Me too! They are big and scary! Say it one more time, Marlin.

Marlin: I am scared of a dinosaur.
Harriet: Now, go get your journal and write your story.

Reading and writing are reciprocal processes. These simple and personal sentences introduce the children to important writing concepts that will simultaneously support their reading development. After the rehearsal, each child gets his or her basket of writing materials, which includes a journal, colored markers, an ABC chart, and a personal dictionary of known words. Working independently, each child helps herself or himself.

Writing the Story

Harriet circulates among the children and records their use of strategies as they write their stories. She realizes the fragility of early learning and is ready to support a struggling child with gentle reminders of effective strategies to use at points of difficulty. Noticing that Marlin has made no attempt to record any sounds for the word *scared* in his story, Harriet reminds him of a helpful strategy for analyzing sounds:

Harriet: Say the word *scared* slowly. What can you hear?
Marlin: Sssccared. I can hear an *s*.
Harriet: Where do you hear it?
Marlin: At the beginning.
Harriet: That's good listening. It helps you to say the word slowly. Say it again and write the sounds you can hear.

Participating in Writing Conference

Besides conducting these "drop-in" conferences with the children as they write, Harriet has follow-up conferences with different children each day. Children are always excited to have their work acknowledged in this way. These individual conferences allow the teacher to provide personal support for a child in a particular area. During early conferences, Harriet provides explicit praise by placing a light checkmark over the child's contributions.

Harriet: Read me your story.
Rashad: "It was a vampire."

Harriet: *(Responding to the message)* Oh, that's a scary story! You did some great work on helping yourself! Look at all you did. You wrote the word *it* all by yourself. *(She writes the word* it *and places a checkmark over Rashad's writing.)* And you heard the *w* in *was*. That's good listening. And you knew there was an *s* in *was*, didn't you? *(She writes the word* was *and places a light checkmark over the child's contributions.)*

Harriet builds on Rashad's partially correct attempt to write the word *was,* wondering whether it is based on a visual memory for how the word looks. She quickly makes the word with magnetic letters and says, "This is the word *was.* You wrote the *w* and the *s,* didn't you?" She then encourages Rashad to evaluate his own accomplishment: "Show me the letters you wrote by yourself." After this she asks Rashad to construct the word *was* two more times, carefully modeling how to check and confirm the word.

In this simple example, Harriet validates Rashad's contribution but also lifts him to a new level of visual attention. Her final teaching point is to instruct Rashad to point to the accurate version of the text and read the story with his finger, thus encouraging one-to-one matching on a familiar language pattern.

Rashad's independent work documents that he is able to hear and record consonant sounds in beginning (*w, v*), middle (*p*), and ending positions (*t, s, r*). His use of the chunk *ir* in the word *vampire* suggests he may be beginning to notice visual features within words. This will be an area where Harriet will need to collect further evidence. Rashad is also aware of two frequently encountered words (*it, was*) that he can add to his personal writing dictionary. Rashad's writing style is at the transitional stage: he is writing a simple sentence with isolated letters that represent letters and sounds. His spelling development is a mixture of semiphonetic and phonetic knowledge.

During tomorrow's interactive writing lesson, Harriet will need to focus Rashad's attention on spacing between words, a critical area for supporting his reading and writing progress. The explicit nature of interactive writing will continue to play a role in helping him gain greater control of early literacy behavior. Through guided participation, Rashad will have opportunities to refine his understanding of letter-sound knowledge and to acquire some new words. Rashad's independent writing indicates that he is ready to progress to writing longer stories (at least two or three sentences) during interactive writing.

Independent Writing with Emergent to Early Writers

To communicate a message, children must be taught some important strategies for helping themselves when they write. First, they must learn how to listen to the sounds within words and assign an appropriate letter for the sound they hear. They must also learn how to retrieve a message by rereading the text after they have stopped to solve a word. During interactive writing at the emergent level, the context of a simple sentence provides a natural backdrop for helping young writers acquire these strategies.

However, children must learn that writing consists of more than just one sentence, so the teacher models the process of writing texts with two or three sentences. The topics for assisted writing are deliberately varied; for example, they may be generated by a read-aloud, a personal experience, a retelling, a letter, a recipe, or a special event. Before asking students to write independently, the teacher invites them to share their message. This rehearsal serves two important purposes: (1) it places value on the child as having an important message to share with others, and (2) it enables the child to practice the story's meaning, which he can then use to monitor the written version.

In the following example, the children have been instructed to write about something exciting that has recently happened to them. Blake, who is in first grade and has been in an early literacy program for four weeks, writes the journal entry shown in Figure 6.11. It reflects his understanding that sentences must come together in a coherent and sequential pattern to communicate a message. This is a characteristic of Heenman's (1985) writing stage in the continuum of children's writing development. Blake's writing from previous lessons has given no evidence of stylized writing. Instead, Blake writes in single sentences for nearly four weeks before his writing changes to a three-sentence story. Angela, the teacher, notes that the change occurred two days after the assisted writing demonstrations on constructing longer texts.

Blake's spelling is generally at the phonetic level: he's able to hear and record the sounds of most of the consonants and able to spell several frequently encountered words correctly. He is also beginning to monitor his writing attempts (for example, *went, saw, animals, one*) by crossing out the incorrect response and trying the word again. In the first sentence, Blake writes the word *went* correctly. In the second sentence, he writes the word *went* for *we,* and then corrects his first attempt by crossing out the unnecessary letters (*nt*) to produce the accurate spelling of *we.*

Figure 6.11 Blake's independent writing sample. ("Me and my dad went to the zoo. We saw lots of animals. My favorite animal was the bear.")

Angela begins the follow-up conference by inviting Blake to read his story. Then she validates what he's written (the primary focus of the conference must be to respond to the child's message before attending to the words within the text): "I like bears too. I think they are such pretty animals."

Blake responds by expanding on his original message: "They are my favorite animal because they have fur on them and they look like a big teddy bear."

Angela says, "Well, tomorrow you might like to add that to your story."

Next Angela validates Blake's knowledge of words, praising him for the ones he is able to write correctly. Since she realizes Blake must be able to spell common words, she boosts his learning by using the words he already knows. First she says, "Find the word *the* in your story." Next she says, "Turn your paper over and write the word *the* quickly." Then she says, "If you know *the,* you can write the word *then.*" She shows Blake how the two words are the same except for the *n,* which Blake is able to hear. Then she asks Blake to put an *m* on the end of the word *the* and read the new word. Blake reads the word *them,* but adds a little stress on the final sound as though he is using the *m* to help himself with the

word. This teaching point shows Blake how to apply visual information from a known word (*the*) to auditory information from two known sounds (*n, m*) to create two new words (*then, them*). Blake is learning a strategy for working on new words during his writing. Before ending the conference, Angela makes a final comment about the story: "I hope you and your dad get to go back to the zoo again."

Independent Writing with Early Writers

The primary purpose for writing aloud in an assisted situation is to help young writers learn how to compose longer stretches of text for different purposes and audiences. A secondary purpose is to demonstrate some strategies for solving selected words within the text. As with any type of assisted writing, the teacher provides a follow-up opportunity to apply this learning in independent work.

After a writing-aloud lesson, the children's stories become longer and more elaborate. They may contain examples of literary phrases and specialized vocabulary from stories they've heard their teacher read aloud or those they've encountered in guided reading. Their writing is more organized and contains a logical pattern, including a beginning, middle, and ending. Their focus is still on meaning; however, visual patterns may be evident in their attempts to write particular words.

The children are encouraged to write about anything of interest to them. During earlier writing-aloud activities, the teacher and children have written about a favorite book, written a letter to a friend, and written about a personal experience. A specific time for story generation and rehearsal (as in interactive writing) is no longer needed.

Writing the Story

As the children write in their journals, their teacher, Carla, circulates among them and responds to their messages. She observes how the children are expanding their stories independently using composing strategies that have been demonstrated in assisted activities. She has noticed that Kelly's stories are always about books she has read, yet that morning Kelly told her a funny story about her baby sister. Carla drops in on Kelly and reminds her about this: "Kelly, you told me the funniest story this morning about your baby sister. Why don't you write about that today so everyone can read it? I know they will enjoy it." She and Kelly remember the story together, and Kelly then begins writing about her baby sister.

Nick is able to regulate his topics according to specific needs and interests. The examples in Figures 6.12 and 6.13 accommodate different messages for different purposes. However, in each case, Nick's writing shows that he understands story organization. In the example in Figure 6.12 Nick writes about losing his toy. His story follows a logical pattern that begins with one problem (the car won't start) and leads to another problem (he loses his toy). He includes details ("we went back to the car"), character dialogue ("'We will have to call dad so we can go home'"), language techniques for emphasis ("But no toy"), transitional words (but, when), and complex structural patterns. Nick's writing style can be classified at an early level of the writing stage (Heenman 1985).

Two weeks later, in the example in Figure 6.13, Nick uses the same language structure to retell a story from a guided reading lesson. In his version of Late for Soccer (Randell 1996a), Nick describes the setting, the time, the problem, and the solution. He effectively uses dialogue to support meaning and literary phrasing for emphasis ("They got to soccer on time thanks to Michael's dad and Tim's mom").

In both examples, Nick writes his stories fluently and independently. He revises his message on the spot using techniques such as crossing out words and inserting carets. He edits his spelling by circling words he is unsure of and using the dictionary to check and revise them. After Nick corrects the word, he places a checkmark over the spelling for confirmation. On Gentry's spelling scale, Nick's writing reflects a mixture of transitional and correct spelling.

Carla's follow-up conference for both writing sessions is similar. In each case, she praises Nick for his message and asks him a few clarifying questions. Then she focuses on helping Nick refine his editing and revising skills, particularly relative to punctuation. His stories include expressive language, but he does not use consistent and appropriate punctuation marks to support that language.

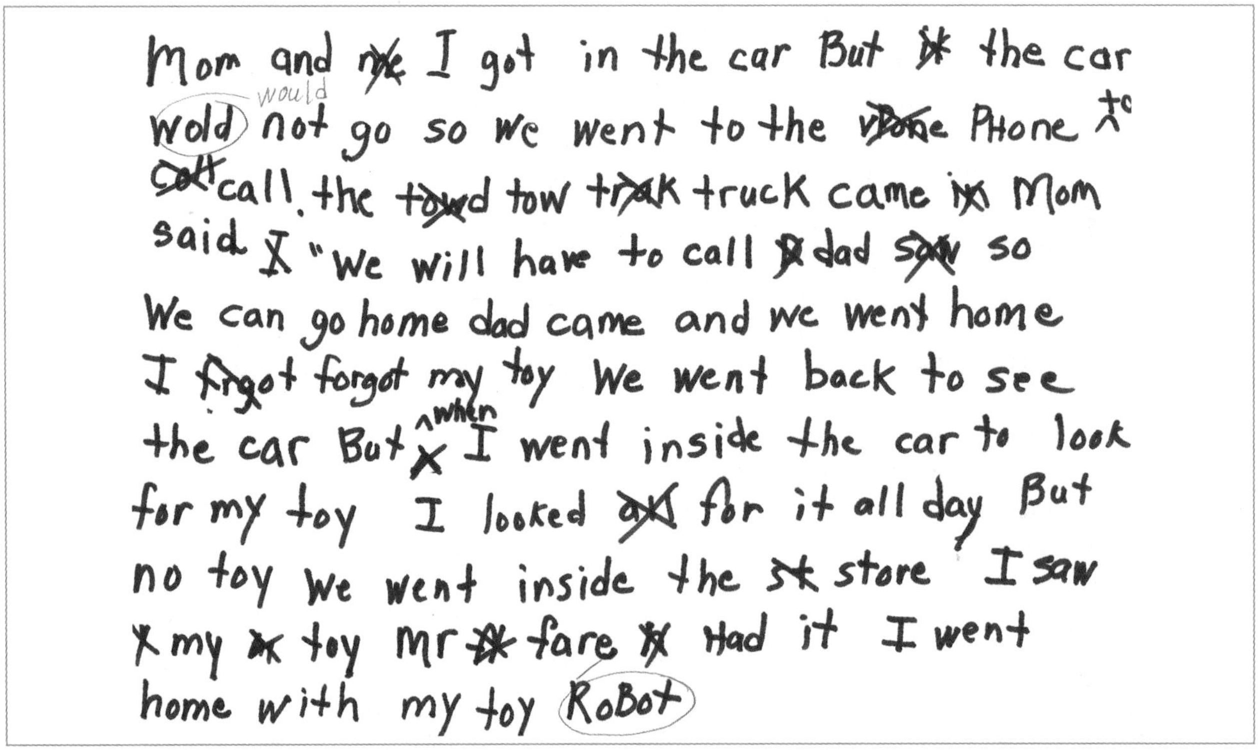

Figure 6.12 Nick's first-grade writing about a personal experience. ("Mom and I got in the car but the car would not go. So we went to the phone to call the tow truck. The tow truck came. Mom said, 'We will have to call Dad so we can go home.' Dad came and we went home. I forgot my toy. We went back to see the car but when I went inside the car to look for my toy, I looked for it all day but no toy. Mr. Fast had it. I went home with my toy robot.")

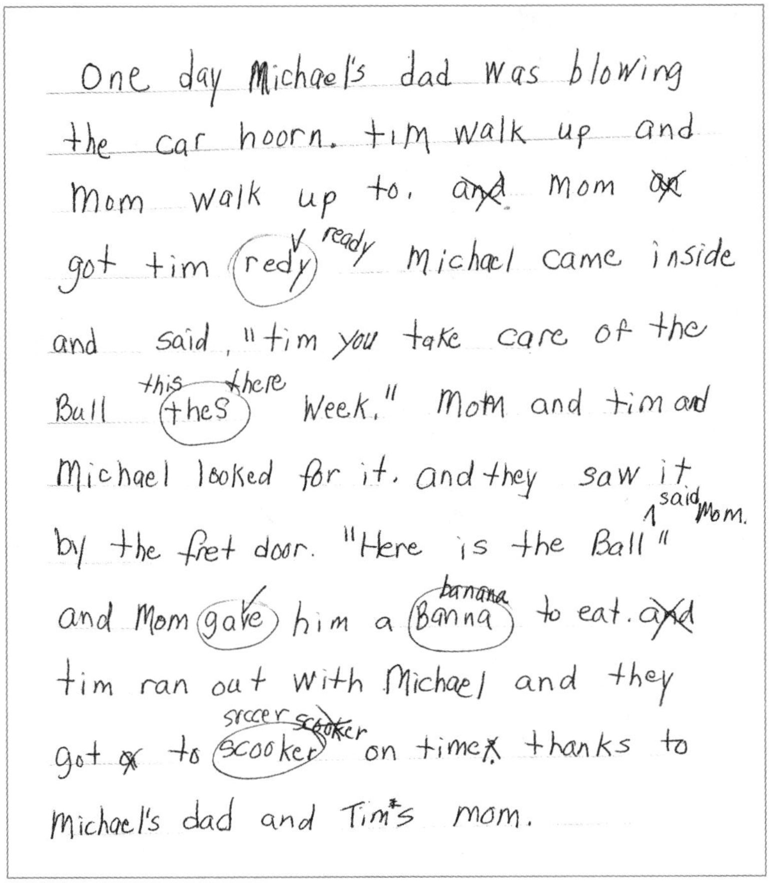

One day Michael's dad was blowing
the car hoorn. tim walk up and
Mom walk up to. ~~and~~ mom ~~ox~~
got tim (redy) ready Michael came inside
and said, "tim you take care of the
Ball (thes) this there week." Mom and tim and
Michael looked for it. and they saw it
by the fret door. "Here is the Ball" said Mom.
and Mom (gave) him a (Banna) banana to eat. ~~and~~
tim ran out with Michael and they
got ~~ox~~ to (scooker) soccer on time. thanks to
Michael's dad and Tim's mom.

Figure 6.13 Nick's first-grade writing of a story retelling. ("One day Michael's dad was blowing the car horn. Tim woke up and Mom woke up too. Mom got Tim ready. Michael's dad came inside and said, 'Tim you took care of the ball this week.' Mom and Tim and Michael looked for it. They saw it by the door. 'Here is the ball,' said Mom, and Mom gave Tim a banana to eat. Tim ran out with Michael and they got to soccer on time, thanks to Michael's dad and Tim's mom.")

Next Carla drops in on Alex, who has completed his story about his trip to Texas. His writing style can be classified at the early level of the writing stage. His story follows a sequential pattern that begins with leaving the house and ends when he gets out of the car that night. He includes time details ("8:30 in the afternoon"), elaborations ("I ate a Big Mac. That's my favorite thing"), transitional phrases and words (*after we finished, then, at last*), good word choices (*scrambled, journey*), and figurative language ("the moon was glowing with fog and the stars were shining like a light"). His writing provides evidence that he understands simple editing techniques (uses caret to add words; draws a line through text that he no longer needs). Carla prompts Alex to add more detail to his closing sentence (see Figure 6.14).

In the classroom, Shane's teacher Judy drops by and invites him to read his story (see Figure 6.15). She observes the influence of book language ("One dark stormy night") and the natural sequence of events that lead up to his story's ending. Judy uses the story to focus Shane's attention on new problem-solving activity with the chunk *ck:* "Can you find the word *brick* in your story?" When Shane locates the word *brik,* she says, "Yes, you're right. That's the way the word sounds,

Alex The big raid to texis.
I lefed my halse at
8:30 in the after nun.
On the Way We stoped
at macdonols I ate a
big mac (tat) thats my
favorit. thing after We wer
finishd we (skradold) bak...
in the car. Then it
Wos nit tam. the moon
Was (glowing) glowing with (fog).
and the stars war (shining)
like a lite. ~~wx~~ rit then
I fil aslep ~~then we fingl~~ at last
the Jerny is over.
and I got out of the car

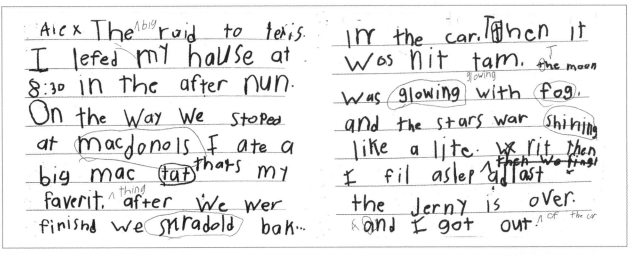

Figure 6.14 Alex's first-grade writing about a personal experience. ("*The Big Ride to Texas.* I left my house at 8:30 in the afternoon. On the way we stopped at McDonald's. I ate a Big Mac. That's my favorite thing. After we were finished we scrambled back in the car. Then it was nighttime. The moon was glowing with fog and the stars were shining like a light. Right then I fell asleep. At last the journey is over and I got out of there.")

but take a good look at the end of the word. Something doesn't look quite right. Can you find it?"

Shane looks carefully at the word and exclaims, "That should be a *ck,* not a *k*!"

Then Judy says, "Read your story again and see if you can find another word that ends like *brick*."

Shane rereads the story, locates the word *back,* and comments, "That should be a *ck* too." Having observed that Shane is ready to move into further revision and editing, Judy instructs Shane to read over his story and circle the words that he will need to work on.

> One dark stormy
> night I heard
> a Lad nos and
> I Looked Ait sid
> and I sow a
> (motr) I het the
> (motr) weth a
> (Brik) and He
> fal dan and I
> wet (Bak) to sleep
> and the motr
> (desg perd)

Figure 6.15 Shane's first-grade writing of a story. ("One dark stormy night I heard a loud noise and I looked outside and I saw a monster. I hit the monster with a brick and he fell down and I went back to sleep and the monster disappeared.")

Revising and Editing

Although some simple editing techniques can be introduced when writing aloud, the teacher must not overwhelm the children with too much attention to them. Instead, she needs to keep her primary focus on the composition process. Even solving words is a temporary detour from the fluent construction of the message. Later, when revising and editing processes are introduced to the group, the focus of instruction shifts to include more attention to overt revisions and the specific editing techniques that result in publishable work.

A Lesson with Early Writers

As children acquire more knowledge about the writing process, they exhibit a higher degree of control over their own work, applying independent strategies that were once demonstrated in a group setting. Their writing reflects revising and editing techniques that are necessary if their work is to be published. The children are behaving like writers who have a message to share with an audience.

As the children write, their teacher, Carla, moves among them and makes occasional comments about their work. She records strategies used by individual students and identifies common areas that would make productive mini-lessons for the group. She allows time during each writing session to meet with at least two children for an individual conference.

Today Carla stops by Karrisa's desk and asks her to read her story (see the second draft in Figure 6.16), which she has been working on for the past two days. Afterward, Carla asks, "Is there anything else you would like to add?"

Karrisa says, "I decided in my story I would not hit the people with my bommyknocker, even though they didn't find me any cats!" She continues, "I didn't want to be mean like the giant in the book." Karrisa is creating stories that link her personal and textual experiences.

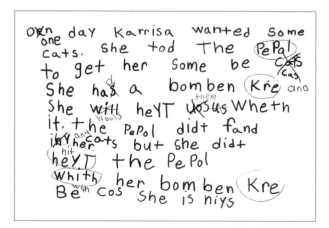

Figure 6.16 Karrisa's second draft.

Then Carla comments on Karrisa's independent editing skills. Although Karrisa shows progress in many areas, she needs support in using this knowledge more consistently and flexibly. Looking at Karrisa's story Carla observes the following:

- She is beginning to edit as she writes (she has crossed out the word *oen* and changed it to *one*).
- She shows some evidence of monitoring structure (she has changed the verb tense of the word *has* to *had*).
- She is aware of some of her misspellings (she has circled *pepol, whith,* and *kre*).
- She is starting to use periods with more consistency (all four sentences end with periods).
- She is somewhat aware that a sentence should begin with a capital letter (the second sentence begins with a capital letter).

During the follow-up conference, Carla praises Karrisa for her editing skills and focuses on helping her polish her work for publication. She encourages Karrisa to use available resources to correct her spellings for known words. She notes that Karrisa has written several of these words correctly in previous stories. Figure 6.17 is the published version of this story.

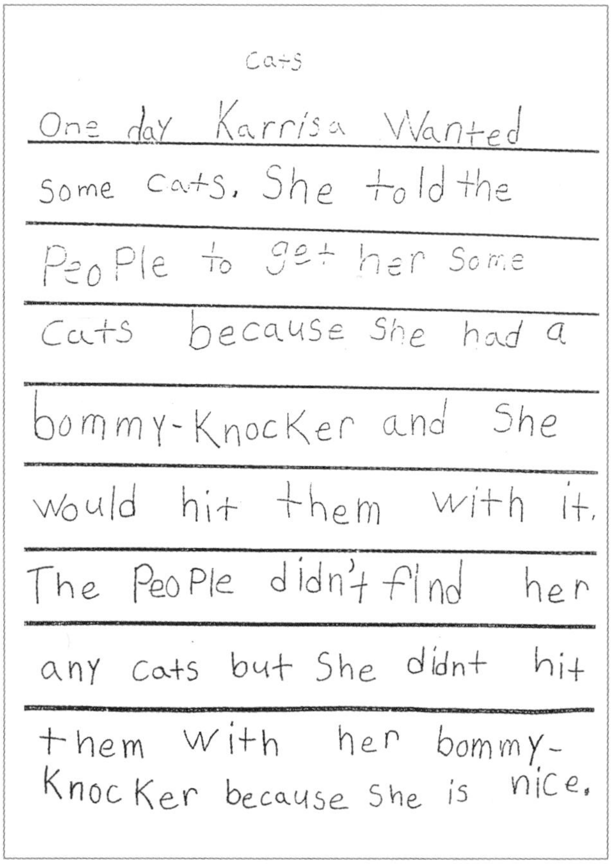
Cats
One day Karrisa Wanted some cats. She told the PeoPle to get her Some cats because She had a bommy-KnocKer and She would hit them with it. The PeoPle didn't find her any cats but She didnt hit them with her bommy-Knocker because She is nice.

Figure 6.17 Karrisa's published story.

A Comparison of First- and Third-Grade Writing Samples

The writing sample in Figure 6.18 is the first draft of a mystery story written by Tamarisk, a third grader. Comparing Tamarisk's work with Karrisa's, we see that both students are using their knowledge of text characteristics to create stories. Tamarisk has a more sophisticated style influenced by her more-varied experiences with texts. Her story is structured as a play with roles for herself and her friend Doris. Karrisa's story reveals her awareness that stories must adhere to a conventional set of rules that require a problem and a solution. In social interactions with a more knowledgeable person, both girls have acquired an understanding about written language that has carried over to their independent work. It is important for the teacher to recognize the individual needs of her students and design conferences that address not only their current knowledge but also their potential level of development. Appendix E examines the writing development of Laterica during the first ten weeks of her early literacy program. The transitions between lessons and the influence of group-assisted writing activities on her independent writing are highlighted.

A Lesson with Fluent Writers

Rhonda's third-grade class is beginning a unit on persuasive writing. During language and reading workshops, the students have acquired multiple experiences with persuasive texts, which will provide the foundation for writing in this mode. Rhonda is familiar with the writing continuum (see Appendix D-10), and she understands what students should know to produce well-written opinion pieces that persuade an audience to their point of view. Also, she knows that students will need focused instruction over a period of time, including revisiting the objectives and transferring their knowledge and skills to different contexts and for different purposes. At the end of the unit of study, the students will have achieved mastery in their ability to

- present an argument or an opinion with several sequenced pieces of evidence in an attempt to persuade the reader to accept the writer's point of view,
- write an introduction that establishes a personal position on the topic,

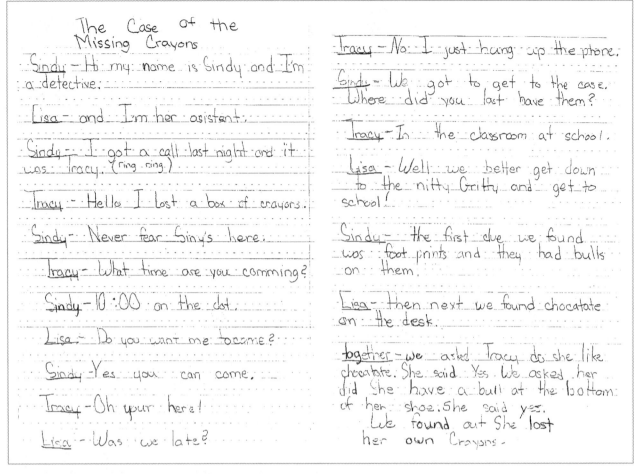

The Case of the
Missing Crayons
Sindy — Hi my name is Sindy and I'm
a detective.

Lisa — and I'm her asistant.

Sindy — I got a call last night and it
was Tracy. (ring ring)

Tracy — Hello I lost a box of crayons.

Sindy — Never fear Siny's here.

Tracy — What time are you comming?

Sindy — 10:00 on the dot.

Lisa — Do you want me tocome?

Sindy — Yes you can come.

Tracy — Oh your here!

Lisa — Was we late?

Tracy — No I just hung up the phone.

Sindy — We got to get to the case.
Where did you last have them?

Tracy — In the classroom at school.

Lisa — Well we better get down
to the nitty Gritty and get to
school!

Sindy — the first clue we found
was foot prints and they had bulls
on them.

Lisa — then next we found chocatate
on the desk.

together — we asked Tracy do she like
chocatate. She said Yes. We asked her
did she have a bull at the bottom
of her shoe. She said yes.
We found out She lost
her own Crayons.

Figure 6.18 Third-grade sample.

- use organizational structures that group related ideas to support the writer's purpose,
- identify an important problem and provide reasons that are supported by facts and details to describe the problem,
- link opinion and reason by using words and phrases, and
- provide a concluding statement.

Today, Rhonda's instructional goal is for the students to learn how to write a persuasive letter that identifies a problem, presents evidence (or details) about why it is a problem, and attempts to persuade the audience to do something about the problem. Rhonda uses clear and explicit language to introduce the instructional goal and set the purpose for the lesson.

Rhonda: Boys and girls, when we write persuasive texts, we want to make sure that our audience understands the problem we are writing about. We need to present our argument clearly and thoroughly. We need to share how we feel about the problem, but we need to do more than that. We also need to explain why the problem is serious. We have to give reasons or examples that support our argument. Today, we'll look at two examples of persuasive letters, and we'll talk about which one is more convincing and why.

Next, Rhonda displays the two examples on the interactive whiteboard and prompts the children to listen carefully as she reads each letter aloud. She explains, "The letters were written by students to persuade the principal to purchase more playground equipment for the school. As I read each letter, you should be thinking about which one is more convincing and why." She reads the first letter:

When I look out at the school playground, I am not very excited to play there. I see that the equipment is old, and there is not enough of it. Some of the equipment is not much fun for third-grade kids. Please, Principal Whitley: It's time for new playground equipment!

Then she reads the second example:

> What I see on our school playground is a big disappointment to any kid who loves to swing, climb, or slide. One big problem is that there is not enough playground equipment. There are only two swings, so if kids want to swing, they will have to stand in a long line waiting on a turn. Even worse, some of the equipment looks like it was bought for kindergarten kids. The monkey bars are so low that our feet almost touch the ground, and there are these bouncy little things that older kids don't play on. The slide isn't very fast because it has so many dents in it, and the seesaw gives you splinters. Kids need physical exercise, but our playground doesn't provide many opportunities for this! Admit it, Principal Whitley: It is time for new playground equipment!

Next, Rhonda engages the students in a brief discussion about their observations. She begins, "How did each writer feel about the playground?" Several students respond with "not very excited" and "disappointed"—words used by the authors to express their emotions about the playground. When prompted, the students unanimously agree that the second letter does a better job of explaining the problem. Rhonda extends the students' thinking by highlighting specific details used (or not used) by the two authors to present their arguments.

Rhonda: When I read the first letter, I know how the writer feels. The writer says, "I am not very excited." I also understand what the problem is—the need for new playground equipment. But I don't really get any sense of how serious the problem is. There are no details or examples to support the problem. The writer just says there isn't enough equipment and what they do have is old. When I read the second letter, however, I can see the problem in my mind. I can visualize the two swings and a line of kids waiting for a turn. I can see the kids' feet on the ground as they try to play on the monkey bars, and I can see the dented slide and an old wooden seesaw. And I totally empathize, or connect, with the writer's point of view. I really understand why the playground equipment is a disappointment. I would feel disappointed, too, if I were a student at that school.

Now Rhonda wants the class to have some guided practice in coming up with some persuasive details to a problem. She reminds them, "Persuasive writing is about getting other people to understand and support your opinion. To do so, you will need to provide convincing reasons for them to accept your belief." She continues, "A graphic organizer can help us to prepare our argument so that it clearly states our position and provides supporting details. We can use a graphic organizer to help us format our writing." She displays the graphic organizer on the interactive whiteboard and introduces a topic that she knows is important to the children. She writes in the Introduction box, "Our classroom library needs to be updated." Then she guides the class to meet in small groups to discuss four important reasons to support this argument. As the students interact, they record this information on the graphic organizer (see sample in Figure 6.19). After this group activity, the students return to their seats and use the graphic organizer to help them draft a persuasive piece. As they write, Rhonda circulates among the class and confers with individual students.

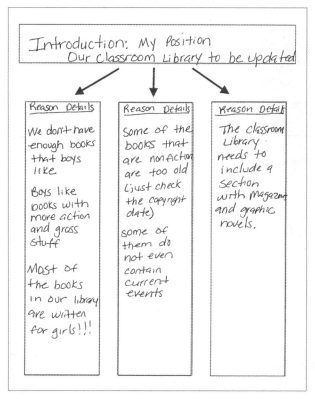

Figure 6.19 An example of one student's graphic organizer.

In subsequent lessons, Rhonda will create opportunities for students to expand their knowledge of persuasive texts, including how to (1) make use of transitional words and phrases, (2) use graphic organizers to focus on particular text structures (such as problem/solution and cause/effect), (3) distinguish between fact and opinion, (4) craft good leads to grab the reader's attention, and (5) write a strong concluding or summary statement. In assisted situations, Rhonda provides clear models and examples to illustrate key principles, followed by one-on-one writing conferences that zoom in on the personal needs of the individual student.

The Structure of Writing Conferences

The influence of the teacher in shaping children's writing development is clear. In the previous examples, the children were at different places in their writing development. This implies that teachers must be able to respond to the unique needs of children based on their current and potential levels of development. Writing conferences provide a natural context for differentiating instruction and personalizing feedback, therefore maximizing learning (see Anderson 2000; Calkins 1994). In this final section, we have two goals: (1) to provide more details for managing and implementing writing conferences and (2) to provide examples of prompts for different types of writing conferences.

Managing Writing Conferences

In writing workshop, teachers must be experts at creating multiple opportunities for conducting conferences with students. Typically, the writing workshop includes three types of conferences (see Dorn and Soffos 2001a):

1. Teacher-Scheduled Conferences: The teacher schedules daily writing conferences with individual children to provide tailored support and to collect ongoing data on their writing development. This type of conference is generally three to five minutes long, allowing the teacher to meet with approximately six children during a twenty-five-to-thirty-minute independent writing block.

2. Student-Scheduled Conferences: The student requests a conference if he feels a need for immediate assistance. Some students will ask for a conference to brainstorm ideas; others will request the teacher's support to edit and revise. As students become more independent and strategic, they are encouraged to seek assistance from peers before requesting a teacher conference.

3. Teacher Drop-In Conferences: The teacher conducts several drop-in conferences as the children are writing independently. The purpose is to ensure that the children are prepared to work independently for approximately twenty minutes while the teacher conducts the teacher-scheduled conferences. Drop-in conferences occur as needed throughout the independent writing component. With emergent and early writers, the teacher may need to devote more time to drop-in conferences in order to provide ongoing observation and scaffolding.

For writing conferences to be most effective, teachers should keep good documentation of students' learning. During teacher-scheduled conferences, the teacher records the type of conference, the student's progress, and next steps. For student-scheduled conferences, the teacher notes how often the student seeks a conference, as well as the student's specific needs. This information provides evidence of areas where the student needs more scaffolding. For example, if a student consistently seeks help in drafting his ideas, it is possible that the student does not understand the drafting task. During drop-in conferences, the teacher uses a clipboard with sticky labels to record anecdotal notes of each student's strengths and needs. These ongoing assessments of the student's independent writing provide the teacher with valuable data to planning instruction during assisted situations.

Elements of a Writing Conference

The ultimate goal of every conference is to have each child value writing as an important means of communication. Thus every conference begins with a sincere response to the child's written message. Then during the conference, the teacher adjusts her support to accommodate the child's understanding of the task at hand. The teacher uses instructional language to validate old knowledge and activate new learning.

A conference is a prime teaching time for lifting the child's learning to a higher level. To maximize this opportunity there are three parts of a conference: beginning, middle, and ending. Let's look at how Felecia, a second-grade teacher, structured Daren's writing conference to teach him about adding details.

To begin the conference, Felecia puts Daren in charge with her prompt, "How is your writing going? Read your story to me."

The middle part of the conference is where the teacher provides scaffolding within the child's zone of proximal development. This part of the conference is defined as the "teachable moment"—the place where the teacher uses the student's text to instruct him about a specific writing technique or strategy. As Felecia listens to Daren's story, she looks for the teachable moment and decides that Daren would benefit as a writer if he understood more about the importance of adding details to his message. She provides a clear explanation of this technique; then she guides Daren to locate specific places in his writing where details would help his reader visualize his message.

Felecia: When good writers are writing about something they have experienced, they try to bring their readers right into the experience with them. To do that, they need to create a vivid picture of where they are and what is happening. Can you think of some specific places you went and things you did that you could describe in detail for your readers?

Once the instructional goal has been established, Felecia's role shifts from teaching to scaffolding with Daren doing most of the talking. The teacher is an active listener, using prompts such as "Can you explain that again? I just want to be sure I understand" or "That's an interesting detail. What can you do to be sure you don't forget to include

that in your story?" In response, the student puts his thoughts into spoken words—a metacognitive process that helps him clarify his thinking and establish a plan for writing.

At the conclusion of the conference, the teacher prompts the student to articulate his plan for carrying out the writing in the teacher's absence. This can vary from asking the children to continue on with the writing, to doing some more research, to publishing the writing, to starting a new piece. In this example, Felecia concludes the conference this way:

Felecia: You saw some interesting places and had some very exciting things happen to you on your trip. You will want to add those details to your story. What can you do to help yourself remember them?

Daren: I think I should list them over here (*pointing to his planning page*) so I won't forget to add them.

Felecia: Yes, that would be helpful. Then you can refer to your list to ensure that you have included these details in your writing. Let me know if you need my help.

Types of Writing Conferences

During writing workshop, teachers design instructional opportunities for children to learn about the writing process. The teacher uses clear models and explicit language to mentor children into the qualities of good writing. She models her own thinking in front of the children, and she invites them to participate with her in the development of the written piece. During these interactions, the children learn that writing develops through a constructive process, including talking with others about ideas, drafting ideas on paper, organizing ideas using text maps and writing guides, revising the message, editing for grammatical and spelling errors, and reflecting on the process. These processes are shaped through assisted writing lessons and personalized through scaffolding language during writing conferences. In Figure 6.20, we present some language prompts for teachers to use in scaffolding young writers.

Prompts for Acknowledging the Writer

- How are you doing today as a writer?
- What do you need my help with today?
- What would you like to work on today?
- How's your writing going?

Prompts for Expanding and Elaborating the Message

- What do you mean by that?
- Can you say more?
- Could you explain this to me?
- Is there anything else you would like to add?
- Please help me understand this part.
- Is there any one way to say this that might help your reader understand it better?

Prompts for Applying the Process

- Have you planned out your draft?
- What's the focus of your writing?
- How you will organize your ideas?
- What kinds of revisions have you made?
- Have you edited your work for spelling?
- Which piece would you like to publish?
- What is your favorite piece in your portfolio? Why?

Prompts for Applying Strategies

- What have you tried so far?
- Is there something else you can try to help yourself?
- Why is this easy for you to do?
- What is making this so difficult for you?
- What do you need to work on now?
- How can you improve this part?
- What do you know that can help you here?

Prompts for Reflective Analysis

- I noticed an earlier place where you used varied sentences. Can you find another place to do this?
- Have you ever encountered a problem like this before? When? How did you go about helping yourself there?

Prompts for Reflective Assessment

- Which pieces would you like to publish?
- What is your least reflective piece? Can you improve it?
- What are you now able to do as a writer that you couldn't do before?
- How has your writing changed?
- What is it about this topic that interests you?
- Let's compare this piece with another piece.
- What would you like to tell someone about your writing?

Figure 6.20 Language prompts for scaffolding.

Closing Thoughts

In this chapter, we have focused on the link between assisted writing and independent writing and emphasized the power of scaffolding for lifting children's writing to a higher level. Here are some closing thoughts to keep in mind:

- Teaching leads development (Vygotsky 1978); therefore, teachers must be astute observers of children's writing behaviors to maximize the benefits from a writing conference.

- If the child does not respond to a writing conference, it is possible that the task is too difficult. Remember the goal of a writing conference is to help the child integrate new learning into existing knowledge. If the gap between the old learning and the new learning is too wide, the conference may degenerate into teaching items instead of prompting for strategies.

chapter seven

LETTERS, SOUNDS, AND WORD STUDY

A child cannot learn to read without attending to letters and sounds. Phonics is the relationship between the letters in written words and the sounds in spoken words. Phonics instruction is happening if letters, not just sounds, are involved in the teaching activity. For example, when a teacher demonstrates that *g* represents the sound heard at the beginning of *go, goat,* and *Gary,* she is teaching phonics. And, during an interactive writing lesson, when the teacher explains that the *an* pattern from *ran* can be found in other words, such as *man, can,* and *fan,* he is teaching phonics. At the upper levels, when a teacher models how to draw lines between an unknown multisyllabic word, then blend the parts together, she is teaching phonics. In each case, the instruction is systematic and well planned, and includes specific materials and teaching procedures.

A word study curriculum is designed to ensure that students acquire the skills and strategies they need for automatic word recognition. However, as illustrated in the previous examples, the teaching for an emergent reader will look different from the teaching for a transitional reader. Word study is based on a developmental continuum that moves from simple to complex and emphasizes strategies for learning how words work. In a balanced literacy program, teachers examine students' reading and writing for evidence of how they solve unknown words and then use this information to plan constructive word study activities (Dorn and Soffos 2011a; Gunning 2001).

Word study lessons can occur in whole or small groups; however, for the struggling reader, the small-group format is essential. The ultimate goal of word study is for students to acquire the knowledge, skills, and strategies to solve unknown words as they read and write whole text. An apprenticeship approach to word study includes three components:

- Clear Models and Explicit Language: The teacher provides an explicit demonstration of the process to be learned.
- Guided Practice and Scaffolding: The teacher provides an opportunity for students to apply the new learning with guidance and adjustable scaffolding.
- Transfer to Independent Reading and Writing: The teacher provides an opportunity for students to apply the new learning to independent reading or writing.

In previous chapters, we presented numerous examples of how teachers use word study activities during reading and writing. For instance, during assisted writing, children use ABC charts, magnetic letters, and marker boards to learn about letters, sounds, and words. While writing independently, children analyze the sequence of sounds within words and apply strategies for noting relationships between spelling patterns. To complement this learning, the teacher addresses phonetic skills during group and individual conferences. The teacher also prompts the children to find, predict, confirm, and search for visual information while reading. All these activities occur within the context of meaningful reading and writing. In the process, children learn how to transfer their knowledge about letters, sounds, and words across varied and changing circumstances.

In this chapter, we explore additional ways that knowledge of letters, sounds, and words are developed through word study lessons. Learning about words is a strategic process, rather than recall or drill. Thus we structure learning opportunities that focus on categorization, comparison, integration, and analogy. At the same time, we provide children with varied experiences that promote automatic and flexible control of letters, patterns, and words. Although this information is presented in isolation, students are expected to transfer the knowledge and strategies while problem solving within whole text.

Learning About Letters and Sounds

Research on beginning reading indicates that letter knowledge is a strong predictor of children's success in reading. However, letter learning is not a memorization task but a systematic process whereby children learn how to analyze features of letters. When children write letters, they attend to the distinctive differences between similar forms. For example, a simple curve distinguishes the *c* from *o*, and if it is ignored, the two letters will be confused. Letter learning progresses through a perceptual continuum, beginning with a primitive classification of similarities, progressing to an analytical comparison of differences, and resulting in the automatic, unconscious recognition of letters (Dorn and Soffos 2001b).

As children develop letter knowledge, the teacher provides them with opportunities to learn a sound for that letter and how to construct the letter shape. Teachers use language prompts that describe the sequential movement of the letters. For example, "over, around, and open" describes the path of movement for forming the letter *c*, whereas "over, around, and close" describes the path of movement for forming the letter *o*. (See Dorn and Soffos 2001a.) The process of learning letters, sounds, and their formations concurrently provides children with feedback for checking and confirming each sensory system. In a balanced literacy program, teachers present opportunities for children to transfer their knowledge of letters and words to meaningful reading and writing experiences.

As children become more automatic with their letter knowledge, they begin to notice how letters come together in left-to-right sequence to represent whole words. In the process, they learn that many words contain predictable and recurring spelling patterns. They attend to larger chunks (blends, clusters, inflectional endings, word families, prefixes, suffixes, root words) within words, and they note relationships between chunks of letters and clusters of sound.

Chunking words is a strategy for breaking larger words into smaller parts, thus promoting faster recognition of unknown words. This process is more efficient than the slow and laborious process of sounding out words letter by letter. For example, if the unknown word is *stack,* and the child knows the words *stop* and *back,* he can use these known parts to decode the unknown word. This strategy enables children to solve unknown words with greater speed, thus freeing their attention to focus on comprehending the message.

Rimes are very useful for helping children develop spelling knowledge: nearly five hundred primary-grade-level words can be derived from a set of only thirty-five rime patterns (Wylie and Durrell 1970; see Figure 7.1). Figure 7.2 provides a few examples of how students can blend the onset and rime patterns of two known words to learn a new word.

Rime	Examples	Rime	Examples
-ack	back, black, sack	-ight	light, sight, right
-ail	mail, pail, tail	-ill	hill, mill, will
-ain	rain, brain, pain	-in	bin, pin, win
-ake	bake, lake, make	-ine	fine, mine, wine
-ame	came, game, name	-ing	bring, king, sing
-an	can, pan, ran	-ink	rink, sink, drink
-ank	bank, sank, thank	-ip	drip, chip, lip
-ap	cap, lap, nap	-it	fit, hit, quit
-ash	cash, flash, crash	-ock	clock, knock, rock
-at	sat, hat, bat	-op	chop, hop, pop
-ate	gate, hate, plate	-ore	more, sore, store
-aw	draw, saw, straw	-ot	dot, hot, shot
-ay	day, hay, play	-uck	luck, stuck, duck
-eat	meat, neat, seat	-ug	bug, rug, mug
-ell	sell, bell, tell	-ump	jump, stump, bump
-est	best, rest, test	-unk	bunk, junk, chunk
-ice	mice, nice, slice		
-ick	quick, sick, lick		
-ide	ride, side, hide		

Figure 7.1 Thirty-five most frequently occurring rimes in beginning reading.

Onset of Known Word	Rime of Known Word	New Word
ball	sack	back
by	tall	ball
by	red	bed
book	pig	big
bat	cut	but
cat	man	can
do	may	day
from	might	fright
got	save	gave
good	hot	got
no	came	name
see	went	sent
she	back	shack
she	line	shine
she	name	shame
stop	jump	stump
stop	sick	stick
the	sing	thing
the	bat	that
to	cake	take
we	day	way
who	then	when

Figure 7.2 Using onset and rime patterns to learn a new word.

The ultimate benefit of word study is that children become better readers and writers. When proficient readers try to unlock unknown words, they apply some quick problem-solving strategies based on their understanding of language and their knowledge of sound-symbol relationships and how words work. They can select and use these strategies quickly because they have practiced them many times and can be flexible as they encounter unfamiliar words. For word study to be effective, teachers should ask three questions:

1. What does the reader already know about words?
2. What does the reader need to know about words?
3. Where is the reader's learning on a word study continuum?

The Word Study Continuum

In a balanced literacy program, there is no scope and sequence for learning particular letters and sounds; rather, the learning is guided by the knowledge that children bring to the task. The teacher designs instructional activities that are geared to validate old knowledge and activate new learning. As the children become more competent in certain areas, the teacher ups the ante. It is important for teachers to recognize the progression of complexity within word learning and to plan instruction accordingly.

Letter Categories

One of the earliest things children learn about literacy is a category for letters (Adams 1996). The singing of the "Alphabet Song" and chanting the alphabet in sequence is used to reinforce letter categories by giving children the letter name. An alphabet chart can also be used to give children a strong picture association with the corresponding letter.

Letter Discrimination

Children must learn how to discriminate letters quickly and effortlessly. Letter-discrimination tasks allow them to develop letter knowledge based on the physical characteristics, or shape, of the letter. Instructional activities are structured to where the children are guided to notice distinguishable features, or attributes, such as letters with sticks, letters with circles, letters with sticks and circles, and so on. Children who exhibit scribble writing in their independent writing are the ones who need explicit instruction in this area.

Letter Name Identification

Letter names are designed to connect the physical shape of the letter with the letter name. Children need to be able to recognize individual letters quickly and confidently. Research shows that when children know letter names, it is easier for them to attach letter sounds to them. Children are also firming up their knowledge of letter names through guided reading and writing activities.

Letter Name Identification assessments allow teachers to see how many letter names children have acquired. When analyzing letter knowledge, it is important to note the following:

- How quickly does the child recognize the letters of the alphabet? (Note, if the child responds correctly but is slow in responding, he may need a little more practice with letter name activities.)
- Does the child get a letter name correct, yet call two other letters that same letter name? If so, he will need more practice with attending to letter features.
- If a child gets very few letters correct on the Letter ID assessment, which letters were they? Were these letters in his name? Were the letters predominantly stick letters? Circle letters? What type of letters is he paying attention to visually? This will guide the teacher in where to start the instruction.

Sound-Symbol Relationships

Children must obtain knowledge of letters in several ways in order to become fast, fluent, and flexible with letters. Remember, automaticity is the goal. A good way to achieve automaticity is for the teacher to design sound/symbol instruction so that it is multimodal. The purpose is for the children to know the letter in several ways, including the name of the letter, the letter formation, the features of the letter, the sound it makes, and how the letter looks embedded within the word. When children are self–regulated with this knowledge, it frees up the brain's attention for comprehension and fluency.

In the word study continuum of sound/symbol relationships the following sequence is widely accepted:

- **Start with consonants and short vowels** so that many CVC (consonant-vowel-consonant) words can be generated, such as *hat, hit, sit, cat.*
- **Build to more advanced phonetic elements**. After consonants and short vowels are known, instructions should move to more complex patterns such as the following:
  - ➢ Blends (*r*-family blends, *s*-family blends, *l*-family blends)
  - ➢ Digraphs (*ch, sh, th, wh*)
  - ➢ Final *e* (*a_e, e_e, i_e, o_e, u_e*)
  - ➢ Long vowels with multiple spelling patterns (*ai, ay, ea, ee, oa, ow,* and so on)

- ➢ Variant vowels (*oo, au, aw*)
- ➢ Dipthongs (*ou, ow, oi, oy*)
- ➢ Structural analysis: contractions, compound words
- ➢ Silent letters (*kn*)
- ➢ Inflectional endings (*-ed, -s, -ing*)
- ➢ Prefixes and suffixes
- **Extend to multisyllabic words.** At this stage, word analysis and synthesis is addressed. In addition, more advance structural analysis is covered, such as more complex compound words, affixes, and so on.

As you can see, the above continuum progresses from simple to complex. Teachers can design instruction around these elements to help children understand how words "work" (see Figure 7.3). This system is further internalized as children are actively engaged in authentic reading and writing activities that increase in complexity over time.

Word Study for Letter, Sound, and Word Knowledge

The teacher designs word study lessons that help readers learn about letters, sounds, spelling patterns, and words. Although word study lessons are implemented with the whole class, it is essential for struggling readers to receive tailored word study instruction during their guided reading or assisted writing small-group lesson. The ultimate goal of word study is for students to apply strategies for solving unknown words within texts while maintaining their focus on the message. Therefore, the teacher sets a purpose for unlocking words within text. For instance, if the word study lesson focuses on onset and rime patterns within words, the teacher prompts the students to apply this strategy when encountering an unknown word in text.

Here is an example of how this might look during a guided reading lesson. Before the lesson, the teacher has determined that the students need to attend to the endings within words. She has noted that when they encounter an unknown word in text, they tend to sound out the individual letters in the rime pattern, which is interfering with their meaning-making process. Therefore, the word study lesson includes four steps: (1) select two known words and use magnetic

Reading Level	Grade Level	Orthographic and Phonological Knowledge
Emergent	K	Concepts of print: concept of letter, concept of word, and so on
Emergent	K	Alphabet recognition
Emergent	K	Letter discrimination
Emergent	K	Letter name identification
Emergent/Early	K/1	Consonants and short vowels (*a,e,i,o,u* CVC pattern)
Emergent	K	Phonological awareness: listening, rhyming, syllables, and so on
Early	1	Phonemic awareness
Early	1	Final *e* pattern (*a_e, e_e, i_e, o_e, u_e*)
Early	1	Consonant clusters (*br, cl, st, str*)
Early	1	Blends (*l*-family, *s*-family, *r*-family)
Early	1	Variant vowels (*oo, au, aw*)
Transitional	1	Dipthongs (*ou, ow, oi, oy*)
Transitional	1	Long-vowel digraphs (*ai, ay, ea, ee, oa, ow*)
Transitional	1	Silent letters (*kn*)
Transitional	1	Structural analysis: verb endings, plurals, contractions, compound words
Transitional	2	Multisyllabic decoding Six syllable spelling patterns • Closed: syllables end in a consonant. (*rabbit, napkin*) • Open: syllables end in a vowel (*tiger, pilot*) • Vowel-silent *e* (VCe): syllables generally represent long-vowel sounds (*compete, decide*) • Vowel Team: Vowel sounds spelled with vowel digraphs such as *ai, ay, ea, ee, oa, ow, oo, oi, oy, ou, ie,* and *ei*. • R-Controlled: When a vowel is followed by *r*, the letter *r* affects the sound of the vowel. The vowel and the *r* appear in the same syllable (*bird, turtle*). • Consonant + *le*: Usually when *le* appears at the end of a word and is preceded by a consonant, the consonant + *le* form the final syllable (*table, little*).
Transitional	2	More advanced structural analysis: compound words, affixes
Transitional	2	Greek and Latin roots

Figure 7.3 An alignment of orthographic and phonological knowledge in learning to read.

letters to model how to break each word apart at the onset and rime pattern; (2) guide the students to build a known word with magnetic letters on their lapboards, prompt them to break the word apart at the onset and rime pattern, and provide a second or third example for additional guided practice; (3) inform the students that when they encounter an unknown word in their reading, they should say the first letter, then look for the rime pattern in the word; and (4) if a student needs more scaffolding during the reading, use a sliding card to uncover the onset and rime pattern in sequence while prompting the student to blend the two parts into a whole word. The teacher understands that the goal of the word study lesson is achieved when the students are able to transfer their knowledge and strategies to the actual reading while keeping their focus on comprehending the message.

Multiple Ways of Learning About Print

As children progress through the word study continuum, it is important that lessons be designed to be interactive and multimodal. In this section, we share example lessons from various parts of the continuum to provide a glimpse of how instruction changes over time. First, we begin with a lesson where the focus is on letter learning, plus learning a new high-frequency word. In this lesson for emergent to early readers, Carla gradually increases the task difficulty through language prompts and scaffolding techniques. She prompts the children to think about how to categorize, associate, link, and generalize information. The lesson begins with a simple letter-sorting activity and ends when the children record a new word in their dictionary.

Sorting Letters and Learning a New Word

Carla, an intervention specialist, calls a small group of kindergarten children to a carpeted area of the room, where they sit in a small circle around her. Each child has a dry erase board with three sets of lowercase letters *t*, *s*, and *o*, placed in the upper-left-hand corner. Carla tells the children, "Look on your board at all the letters that are over to the side. I want you to find all the *t*s and pull them to the middle of your board. Be sure to say the name of the letter as you pull it over." Since the children are already familiar with these letters, Carla knows this simple task will elicit fluent, quick responses. When the children have finished sorting the letters, Carla prompts them to check their work: "I want you to check it really good. Look at the other letters and make sure there are no *t*s left."

Next Carla directs their attention to the formation of the letter. She says, "Now let's trace over the letter *t* and say how we make it. Watch me first." Carla uses explicit language to describe her movement pattern ("Down, across") and matches her words with the action of creating the *t* form. "Now," she says, "what is that letter?"

The children respond, "*T*." When Carla is certain that the children understand her intentions, she instructs them to go to the side of their boards and write the letter *t*. She reminds them, "Be sure to say how you make it as you write it." As the children write the *t*, Carla observes them carefully to be sure they are using the correct movement pattern and that they check and confirm their work. She wants the children to know the letter in several ways:

- the letter name
- the movement pattern for forming the letter
- the sound of the letter
- the feel of the sound in the mouth
- the way the letter looks in a word

Therefore, her next interaction focuses on guiding the children to associate letters with sounds. Through explicit language and coaching, Carla helps the children acquire some special cues for the letter-sound relationship. She uses the *t* letter-sound book and the ABC chart. First she asks, "What letter is on the cover of the book?" Then she prompts them to relate the letter to the picture cue: "What is the picture on the cover?"

"Tiger!" the children say. Carla goes on to link this information with the ABC chart:

Carla: Billy, go find a *t* on our ABC chart. What is the picture on the chart that starts with a *t*?
Billy: Tiger.
Carla: So we have *tiger* on the cover of the book and a tiger on our chart. Why do you think they put a picture of a tiger there?
Kevin: Because *tiger* starts with *t*.

Next Carla guides the children to use still other senses to reinforce and extend this information. She says, "Let's all say *tiger*; let your mouth feel the *t* sound." Carla says the word, stressing the beginning sound. As the children repeat the word, she encourages them to articulate their knowledge: "Where do you feel the *t*?"

Several children comment, "The top of my mouth." Voices murmur throughout the group as the children practice this new learning.

Now Carla links the *t* sound with other words that start that way. Together, she and the children look through the pictures of colorful objects in the *t* book and name each object: turtle, tiger, teeth, television. From time to time, Carla asks, "Now, what letter is that? Can you find it? Check to be sure the word starts with a *t*."

Carla: How are all the words alike in this book?
Tanisha: They all start with *t*.
Carla: Do we know anyone whose name starts with a *t*?
Several children: Tanisha!

Carla moves on, prompting the children to notice relationships between upper- and lowercase letter forms. She directs their attention to a large pocket chart that contains all the children's names, which have been cut apart into individual letters. She says, "Tanisha, bring the *T* from your name and let's see how it is different from the *t* in your book." Tanisha goes to the pocket chart, returns with the *T,* and points to the appropriate letters as she says, "This is a capital *T* and this is a little *t.*"

Next Carla directs the children's attention to the large ABC chart and the alphabetical placement of the *t* on the chart: "I want you to look at the ABC chart and tell me where the *t* is. Is it at the beginning or near the end of the alphabet?"

"Near the end," the children respond.

Carla: Let's look at our class ABC book and put Tanisha's name in the book. Where do we need to open the book to—the beginning or the end?
Several children: The end.
Carla: Why?
Kevin: Because the *t* is near the end of the alphabet.
Carla: Tanisha, can you find the *t* page and write your name in the book? (*Tanisha quickly does so.*)

Carla's final interaction focuses on learning a new word that starts with the letter *t.* She signals her intentions by saying, "Now I am going to teach you an important word that starts with the letter *t.* The word is *to.*" Carla models how to make the word *to* on her magnetic board. After she makes the word, she reads it and checks it with her finger.

Then she tells the children to take a good look at the word and find the letters they need to make the word on their board. The children quickly search for the *t* and the *o* and make the word *to.* Carla emphasizes the importance of speed: "Okay, I want you to make it fast. Push the word over to the side and write the word real fast. What is the word you are writing?" When the children respond correctly, Carla asks a series of reinforcing questions: "What letter does it begin with? What are other words that begin like *to?*" Then she has the children record the new word in their dictionary.

Carla: Now, we need to put the word *to* in our personal dictionaries. Where do you need to turn—at the beginning or the end?
Nick: Near the end.
Carla: Quickly, everyone find your *t* page. What are you going to write on the *t* page?
Several children: *To.*

Carla ends the lesson by asking the children to reflect on their learning: "Everybody, I want you to think a moment and tell me one thing you learned about the letter *t* today."

Quickly, the children begin to articulate their new learning:

Laterica: Tanisha starts with *t,* but it is a capital *T.*
Kevin: *To* starts with *t.*
Tanisha: *T* is at the end of the alphabet.
Billy: *T* is at the top of our mouth.
Nick: We have three words on the word wall that start with *t.*

Figure 7.4 A student records a high-frequency word in his personal dictionary during a word study lesson.

Learning About Blends

In the next example, Nancy, a first-grade teacher, presents a lesson on blends to a small group of early readers. Nancy has gathered the children's dry erase boards, letter baskets, and the appropriate letter cards for the lesson. She begins the lesson by displaying several picture cards that begin with an *s*-family blend in a pocket chart. She shows the children each picture card and engages them in naming the object while listening for the blend at the beginning of the word. She asks the children to name each picture again and explains that each picture begins with an *s*-family blend. She then models the *s*-family blend sound by pointing to each picture and placing the two letters that make up the blend underneath the picture card. The children line up the letter cards *s, k, p, t,* and *m* on their desks, pull down each card, and say the letter name. Nancy instructs the children to find two letters for the beginning of the word *spin*. She then prompts, "Run your finger underneath the letters as you say the *s*-family blend. Now push the letters back up to the top of your desk." Nancy repeats the task with three examples.

To make the lesson multimodal, Nancy instructs the children to pull down the *s*-blends and say a word that starts with those letters. She prompts, "Pull down the letters *sw* and say a word that starts like that."

The children say, "*Swim, sweater, swing, sweet.*" As the lesson proceeds, Nancy instructs the children to practice writing specific *s*-blend words on their dry erase boards. Finally, Nancy prompts the children to find words with the *s*-pattern blends in a familiar guided reading book. The children read the sentence in context and frame the word with the *s*-family blend.

At the end of the lesson, Nancy creates an anchor chart, where she writes the *s*-family blends in large letters. She then prompts the children to brainstorm words with *s*-family blends, and the children underline the *s*-family blend in each word on the anchor chart. Nancy then hangs the chart in the class for easy reference in case children need it for reading or writing.

Manipulating Onset and Rime Patterns to Make New Words

Robin, a first-grade teacher, meets with a small group of students before their guided reading lesson. The students have acquired a bank of known words, including blends, digraphs, and rime patterns, and they understand the principle of onset and rime for solving unknown words. Robin believes the students could benefit from using a manipulation strategy for learning new words. She selects two familiar words with known rime patterns and models the manipulation strategy with magnetic letters on a large board. She explains, "Today, I will show you how you can use parts of words that you already know to solve unknown words." She describes her actions as she constructs the word *stop* in the left-hand corner and the word *jump* in the right-hand corner.

Robin: I will break out the first part of *stop* and pull it to the middle of my board. Then I'll break out the last part of *jump*. Now I'll add the two parts together and I have a new word. Who can tell me the new word?

Students: *Stump*!

Robin: Yes, you used word parts that you know to help you figure out an unknown word. Let's try it together one more time; then you can try it by yourself.

When Robin is confident the students understand the manipulation strategy, she gives them two new examples. The students use magnetic letters to build the familiar words; then they break out the onset and rime patterns and assemble the parts to create the new word. As they work independently, Robin circulates among them and provides support as needed. At the end of the word study lesson, she reminds them to use what they know about words to help them solve unknown words as they are reading and writing.

Using Open-Syllable Patterns to Solve Words

Max, a second-grade teacher, introduces his students to the principle of the open-syllable spelling pattern. He begins his instruction by holding up picture cards with examples of words that have open-syllable patterns and explains that the words all end in a long-vowel sound. Then Max distributes letter cards to each student. He wants the lesson to be hands-on and interactive. Max also knows the value of instructing children by starting with known information and moving into their zone of proximal development. Therefore, Max asks the students to make some very easy words, such as *be* and *he* with their letter cards. He asks them if the vowel sound at the end of each word is long or short. All students reply that the vowel sound is long. Max wants to ensure that each student understands the principle of the open-syllable spelling pattern as a generative strategy that can be applied to other words. As the students quickly generate words, Max explains that these words are also examples of open-syllable spelling patterns. Next, the principle is transferred to two-syllable words. Max writes new words, such as *lady* and *silent* on the board. Then he and the students clap the syllables in each word and discuss where to divide it into syllables. Next, Max instructs the students to locate the open syllable in each word. Max reminds them that an open-syllable pattern has a long-vowel sound.

Finally, Max engages the children in a word sort, which entails sorting words with open- and closed-syllable spelling patterns. (Note: Max has previously taught his students about closed-syllable spelling patterns.) Max places category cards in the pocket chart to represent the syllable spelling patterns for the words that he has preselected for the sort (see Figure 7.5). He then gives each student a word to categorize in the pocket chart. This activity requires the children to reflect on their learning and articulate why they put their word card in the category they chose.

Max: At the top of the pocket chart I have placed three category cards. They are closed/open, open/closed, and open/open. I want you to take a look at your word card and analyze your word to see which category it fits into.

Next, each student analyzes his or her word. As Max calls the students up to the pocket chart, they place their word card in a category and explain to the other children why they placed it there. The students then discusses whether this is the correct category. If for some reason it is not, they help find the correct category to which it belongs.

Max: Harrison, what word do you have?
Harrison: I have the word *robot*.
Max: Where does the word *robot* belong on our pocket chart?
Harrison: It belongs in the open/closed category.
Max: Tell us why.
Harrison: I placed it there because the first syllable is *ro* and it is open. It ends in a vowel, so it is most likely long. The second syllable is *bot*. It ends in a consonant. It has a short-vowel sound. I put them together in chunks, *ro-bot*. It is the word *robot*.

Max continues the sort until all the words have been discussed.

Closed/Open	Open/Closed	Open/Open
Funny	Robot	Gravy
Happy	Program	Shiny
	Total	Shaky
	Siren	Shady
	Iris	

Figure 7.5 Open-syllable pocket chart.

The lesson closes as Max invites children to find multisyllabic words in their familiar guided reading text. They practice together by analyzing each word and reading it in chunks, or syllables. They then put it in context again by reading it fluently together.

Using Chunking Strategy to Solve Multisyllabic Words

As students learn about words, they acquire a toolbox of patterns that can be used to solve multisyllabic words with efficiency. Good readers understand that multisyllabic words consist of smaller chunks, including prefixes, suffixes, inflectional endings, root words, blends, and such. If a student is having difficulty with solving multisyllabic words, the teacher provides explicit instruction in this area.

In this example, Dana, a third-grade teacher, has observed that her struggling readers do not apply their knowledge of spelling patterns to help them solve large words. Today, her word study lesson focuses on how to use familiar chunks to decode multisyllabic words, and she has selected four words (*perpendicular, uninterrupted, precipitation, misunderstanding*) to illustrate this principle. Dana begins her lesson by modeling how to use visual chunks to decode the word *perpendicular*. She writes the word on a large chart tablet and thinks aloud.

Dana: This is a word that I don't know, but I can use chunks inside the word to help me solve it. I'll draw lines between the parts I know; then I'll blend these chunks together to help me read the word.

As Dana draws a line between the parts, *per- pen-dic- u- lar,* she pronounces each chunk in isolation. Then she rereads the parts again, this time blending them together. "The new word is *perpendicular,*" she says. "I used my knowledge of spelling chunks to help me solve it, and this strategy will help you when you are reading multisyllabic words in your books."

Dana models the chunking strategy with the second exemplar word, *uninterrupted.* After the demonstration, she gives each student a sentence strip with the new word *precipitation* recorded on the strip.

Dana: This is an important word, and you need to be able to read it quickly so that you can keep your mind focused on understanding the message. Looking for chunks you know within the word can help you read it more quickly. Please draw a line between the five chunks you know in the word.

The students draw lines in *pre- ci- i- ta -tion,* and Dana prompts each student to read it in chunks, then read the word as a whole. The students apply the strategy to a second word, *misunderstanding.* At the end of the word study lesson, Dana reminds the students to use the chunking strategy when they encounter unknown words in their reading.

Learning About Words in Whole-Group Lessons

Teachers use sorting activities to help children acquire effective strategies for perceiving and remembering visual information. Using known sources as a cue, children develop classification strategies for organizing visual information into related groups. Through repeated practice, children internalize specific knowledge about printed language. As children become more competent, the teacher adjusts her level of support to accommodate this higher-level understanding.

A Few Examples from the Classroom

In kindergarten, teachers promote letter recognition through picture-sorting activities in which children organize known pictures under a key letter. Before the lesson, Dave displays four letter cards (*b, c, d, f*)

in a large pocket chart. The children are familiar with these letters, and each card contains a picture cue. To begin the lesson, Dave guides the children in a shared reading: they chant, "*B, b, bat, C, c, cat, D, d, dog, F, f, fish.*" Then Dave holds up separate pictures of common objects that begin with one of the four letters in the chart. He prompts the children to identify the beginning letter by slightly stressing the initial sound: "What can you hear at the beginning of *fork*?"

"*F!*" the children respond.

Dave then asks a child to come to the chart and place the picture under the appropriate letter. This instructional conversation continues until all the cards have been placed in the appropriate pockets.

As children become more competent, this early skill is replaced by more complex strategies: sorting words according to multiple criteria, for example. Word-sorting activities are designed to help children acquire inner control (or automaticity) of orthographic patterns. This knowledge provides the reader with a ready storehouse of visual information that promotes fast, fluent responses during reading.

In this example, Carla randomly distributes a small pile of word tiles, approximately twenty words per child. She instructs the children, "Now you know many ways in which words are alike and different. I want you to look through your words and group them together in any way you want to." She encourages the children to articulate some ways that words can be classified: "What are some ways that we group the words together?" As the children call out various categories, Carla records their responses on a flipchart:

- words that start the same
- words that end the same
- rhyming words
- one-, two-, and three-syllable words
- words in the class dictionary
- words that end in *ed, ing,* and *er*

As the children organize their words, Carla observes the classifications they choose. The children extend their personal groupings by exchanging word tiles with other group members. For instance, Nick's category is words from his dictionary, and he recruits help from the other children in his group. He exclaims, "Hey, I know *they*! I need *they*! Who has *they*?" Laterica quickly scans her word pile and without comment picks up the word *they* and throws it into Nick's pile. Carla notes that Laterica has organized nine words into three categories: words that include the *at* chunk, words that start with *s*, and words with two letters. Laterica seems somewhat puzzled about how to manage the nine remaining words in her pile, which do not fit her other categories. Looking at Billy's pile, she sees a word that she needs. Pointing to the word *she*, Laterica says, "I'll give you these words for that word." And so the children bargain with one another as categories are established, negotiated, and expanded. Occasionally, Carla leans over and coaches a child to notice a new relationship.

Next Carla invites all the children to describe how they organized their words. As the lesson comes to an end, Carla picks up the small pile of remaining words and says, "Listen as I read these words and see if they fit anybody's categories." This activity comes to a quick close as the children say no to all the words, with the exception of *my*, which is put into Laterica's two-word category.

A Few More Thoughts About Word Sorts

Word-sorting activities are guided by the knowledge that the children bring to the task. Therefore, once the children have had numerous word study mini-lessons and have acquired a number of known words, they develop classification strategies for organizing words into related groups. They later apply this strategy in reading and writing when they activate their knowledge of familiar spelling patterns to figure out unfamiliar words. Organizing words, or word sorting, is performed in whole-class and small-group settings. It may also be done individually in a literacy center after the children understand the process. The above example with Carla and her children was an open sort, in which the children select the categories. Teachers may also have children engage in a closed sort. In a closed sort, the teacher asks the children to find words with specific features. For example, she might instruct the children to look through their pile of words and find all of the words with the *ing* pattern. Lists are then created and generalizations are drawn as children discover sound, letter, or meaning patterns.

In both types of word sorts, the teacher asks the children to articulate some ways in which they classified their words. It is important that the teacher con-

nect the new learning to how it can be used in authentic reading and writing experiences to decode and encode unfamiliar words. Here are some other types of word-sorting activities to include in instruction:

- Speed: Key words are placed as category heads and children sort words they have seen before.
- Blind: Key words are placed as category heads and children sort words they have not seen before.
- Buddy: Children work with a partner to sort words into appropriate categories.
- Writing: Children write words in appropriate categories.
- Common feature: Common features are placed as category heads, and children sort words and discuss similar meanings.
- Meaning: Children build automaticity by sorting words into appropriate categories as quickly as possible by their meanings.
- Pattern: Children work to sort words into appropriate categories by various patterns.
- Sound: Children sort words into appropriate categories by sounds.
- Six basic syllable spelling patterns
  - Closed: Syllables end in a consonant (*rabbit, napkin*).
  - Open: Syllables end in a vowel (*tiger, pilot*).
  - Vowel-silent *e* (VCe): Syllables generally represent long-vowel sounds (*compete, decide*).
  - Vowel team: Vowel sounds spelled with vowel digraphs such as *ai, ay, ea, ee, oa, ow, oo, oi, oy, ou, ie*, and *ei*.
  - R-controlled: When a vowel is followed by *r*, the letter *r* affects the sound of the vowel. The vowel and the *r* appear in the same syllable (*bird, turtle*).
  - Consonant + *le*: Usually when *le* appears at the end of a word and is preceded by a consonant, the consonant + *le* form the final syllable (*table, little*).

Activities for Promoting Familiarity with Frequently Encountered Words

Children must acquire a ready storehouse of common words. As the children encounter these words in authentic reading and writing, the teacher looks for memorable opportunities to focus their attention on the visual features.

In selecting appropriate words for word study, the teacher examines the children's reading materials and lists the most commonly occurring words. The children should know these words instantly and thus be able to focus on the real task of reading, which is to construct meaning. If children experience difficulty with these words, their reading fluency will be disrupted.

It is important to select words for word study that the children have already encountered in text or have already written in a story. However, children need repeated encounters with a word before it ceases to be a partially known word and enters their long-term memory. The textual experience is an entry point. The teacher can use the partially known information as a foundation for further visual analysis. Thus the teacher plans activities that enable the children to gain fast and unconscious control of important commonly occurring words. After such a word study lesson, the teacher is careful to bring the children back to meaningful text. For instance, she might

- encourage the children to locate and read the word in the story,
- have the children look for the word in other texts, or
- have the children locate the word in a story they are writing.

Some ways in which classroom teachers can help children learn frequently encountered words are by:

- writing the words on narrow strips taped to the children's desks for easy reference;
- recording the words in personal dictionaries;
- recording the words in large class dictionaries;
- filing the words in alphabetized word banks; and
- classifying the words on wall charts according to particular criteria (first letters, ending letters, number of letters, and so on).

In addition, the teacher can provide the children with opportunities to practice word development on their own. We discuss this in more detail in Chapter 8, but some independent activities might include

- playing speed games with word cards;
- circling words in familiar poems (which have been laminated);
- constructing words with magnetic letters;
- categorizing letter cards, word tiles, or other manipulatives, according to teacher- or self-generated classification systems; and

- practicing writing the words quickly in a variety of places and with different media.

Change Over Time in Learning About Words

For this lesson, Carla, an intervention teacher, has displayed the letters *e, y, b, o, b,* and *t* across the top of the children's magnetic boards. Again, these are known letters, so she expects the children to respond quickly: "I want you to bring your letters down really fast and tell me the names of each letter. Ready? Go! Fast!" Afterward, the children push the letters back to the top of the board.

Her next instructional move is to use two of the letters to make a known word: "Make the word *be.* You know this word, so you should be able to make it really fast." Carla knows the children must gain automatic control of some frequently encountered words, which they can then use to monitor their reading and writing. She wants these words to enter their long-term memory so that they'll be able to concentrate on more important reading tasks.

The children build the word rapidly and then check it with their fingers. Carla prompts them to reflect on their actions: "Were you fast? Did you check it to be sure you are right?" The children confirm their actions, and Carla moves on: "Now, bring down two letters and make the word *by*—right underneath *be.* How are they alike?" The children make the two words and explain, "They both start with *b.*" Carla uses this experience to activate old knowledge, coaching the children to think of other words that start with *b.* The children respond with various *b* words from previous experiences.

Carla then prompts the children to new learning: "Now I want you to take two more letters and make the word *to.* Put the word *to* right under your other two words. After you finish, read all three words. Be sure to check your work." As the children read all three words, Carla asks, "Which word starts differently?" In unison, the children respond with the word *to.* Next Carla instructs the children to turn their magnetic boards around to the dry erase side. She says, "Pick one word that you can write really fast and write it." Carla concludes the lesson by encouraging the children to record the words in their personal dictionaries.

Working with Known Words

The instructional interactions in this lesson are designed to emphasize letter-sound cues and fluency with known words. In preparation, Carla has organized the letters *b, t, e, h, e, h, e,* and *e* across the top of the children's magnetic boards. She instructs, "Quickly pull your letters down and say their names." Then she says, "Use the letters and make three words you know." The children quickly make *be, the,* and *he,* in various orders. Carla has the children read their words. Then, activating new learning, she asks, "Which word starts like *balloon*?"

Billy responds, "*Be.*"

Next she asks, "Do you know other words that start like *balloon* and *be*?" The children call out various responses: *Billy, bike, and bananas.* Then Carla says, "Take a good look at the words you made. Tell me how your words are the same."

Laterica comments, "They all end with *e.*"

Carla knows that the children must gain automatic control of frequently encountered words. So she prompts the children, "Turn your board over and get ready to write fast." Then she calls out the words *be* and *he,* which the children write fluently. Next she says, "Now write the word *the.*" She observes that the children show no hesitancy in shifting their attention from similar patterns (*be* and *he*) to a new pattern (*the*).

Next Carla links the children's knowledge about *the* to a new situation: "If you add the word *the* to our dictionaries, what key word will help us with the first letters?" This is an easy question, because the *th* chunk is displayed on the ABC chart, which is read every day during shared reading.

"Thirty!" Laterica and Nick exclaim with confidence.

Carla proceeds, guiding the children to associate the letters with other sensory information: "Everybody say *thirty.* Where is your tongue?"

The children repeat the word and say, "Touching my teeth—at the top of my mouth."

Carla continues to prompt the children to new cognitive activity: "Where would you find *thirty* in your dictionary—in the beginning, middle, or end?"

"At the end," the children respond with confidence.

"Now quickly," Carla says, "I want you to find the pages in your dictionaries where you can write the words *he* and *be.* You know where to look. I won't help

you unless you need me." The children independently find the correct pages and record the new words.

Simple Analogies with Onset and Rime

In the next lesson, Carla ups the ante. Instead of giving the children words to make, she prompts them to make their own words from a selection of magnetic letters. She has displayed *a, c, a, l, n, t, a,* and *l* at the top of the children's magnetic boards. Quickly, the children pull down the appropriate letters and construct three known words: *can, all,* and *at.*

Now Carla guides the children to manipulate onset and rime to make a new word: "Borrow the *c* from *can* and put it in front of *at.* What is the new word?" Carla watches the children to ensure that they understand what she's said. Without hesitation, the children move the appropriate letter and respond with the correct word, *cat.*

Then Billy points to the rime (*an*) that remains on his board from *can* and comments, "There's a new word, *an.*"

Carla acknowledges Billy's response and guides the children further: "Now take the *c* from *cat* and put it in front of *all.* Quickly, what is your new word?"

"Call," the children say.

Next Carla prompts the children to practice the same simple analogies in a different context. She says, "Turn your board over and write the word *at.*" Since this is a known word, the children write the word quickly. "What word did you write?" Carla asks. The children say *at,* establishing auditory support for the rime. Then Carla directs the children's attention to the letter *f* and the identifying picture on the ABC chart: "Now borrow something from *fish* and put it in front of *at.* What is the new word?"

The children quickly add an *f* to the word *at* and respond, "*Fat!*"

Then Carla prompts the children to articulate what they've done. She asks, "What did you do to make your new words?"

Several voices respond, "Put a new letter in front of the word."

Since the children have demonstrated that they understand the concept of changing onsets to construct new words, Carla prompts them to provide their own examples: "Who can think of a letter that we can put in front of *all* to make a new word?" Several children respond with appropriate letters for making new words: *ball, hall,* and *tall.*

Now Carla shifts the lesson emphasis to recording information in the class dictionary. Her goal is to promote fast and flexible use of the dictionary: "Look on the *a* page. Where is it?"

"First," the children say.

"*F* page?" Carla asks.

"Middle!" the children say.

Next Carla throws out a word cue: "Where will we put the word *all*? What page?"

"A page at the beginning," the children respond quickly.

"Okay," says Carla. "Find the *c* page." She wants to guide the children to apply the analogy strategy in a new context. The children quickly flip to the *c* page in their personal dictionaries. "Now listen. Borrow the *c* from *can* and put it in front of *all*. Write the new word in your dictionary." All the children record the word *call*. Carla prompts them to create one more word and then asks the children to read the new words.

More Analogies with Onset and Rime

Now that the children understand the concept of analogies for making new words, Carla places a larger selection of magnetic letters—*b, h, e, c, t, a, u, p, m, e, r, p, j*—randomly at the top of the children's lapboards. She begins the lesson by prompting the children to make two familiar words, *jump* and *be*. Then she says, "Borrow the *b* from *be*. Now take away the ending chunk from *jump*. Make a new word." The children quickly construct the new word, *bump*.

Carla: Push all the letters to the top of the board. Now pull down the letters you need to make *old*. Make it fast! Check it. Now make *cat*. You can make it fast, because you know that word really well. Now borrow something from *cat*. Put it in front of *old*. Make a new word. What is it?

As the children move the letters around, Carla carefully observes their behavior and is prepared to increase her support if needed. Without hesitation, the children construct the new word *cold*. After constructing the word, Nick comments, "If you put an *f* in front of it, you have *fold*." Clearly Nick is able to generate new examples from old experiences.

Carla continues to increase the complexity of the task: "Now make *her*." The children quickly pull down the necessary letters to construct the new word. Carla prompts the children to use their knowledge in a new activity: "What could you borrow from *her* and add to the end of *cold* to make a new word?"

"*Er*," the children say.

"That's right!" says Carla. "What is your new word?"

The children add the *er* chunk to the end of *cold* and respond, "Colder!"

Carla ends the lesson by encouraging the children to articulate what they have done: "Tell me what you did to make new words." The children give several explanations that reflect their understanding of the analogy strategy for constructing new words.

Closing Thoughts

This chapter presents ways in which teachers can help young children acquire phonetic knowledge. Although the lessons take place in isolation, they originate from contact with meaningful texts. In a literacy apprenticeship, the teacher structures lessons that provide children with flexible opportunities to apply word-level strategies across repeated and varied circumstances. It is important to link new learning to old learning: the knowledge children already have about letters, sounds, spelling patterns, and words creates a personal foundation for noticing new relationships and forming generalizations about how written language works. The teacher plays a critical role, coaching the children through guided participation and scaffolded instruction.

chapter eight

ORGANIZING FOR INDEPENDENCE AND TRANSFER

Children need opportunities to work both with and without assistance during a typical classroom day. An important principle of apprenticeship learning is the role of routines in promoting literacy development. Teachers must create well-organized learning environments encompassing predictable routines that promote children's independence. It is important for children to participate in planning, rehearsing, and organizing the learning structure of the classroom. In doing so, they acquire important organizational skills that are directly linked to the development of self-regulation. In this chapter, we discuss how teachers organize their classrooms to activate their students' learning across whole-group, small-group, one-to-one, and independent contexts. In the process, students learn how to transfer their knowledge, skills, and strategies from one setting to another.

In *Shaping Literate Minds,* Dorn and Soffos (2001b) describe the relationship between instructional settings, the degree of teacher assistance in each context, and the role of transfer. Let's apply this theory to Dave and his second-grade students. During the past few weeks, Dave has introduced various text features (such as table of contents, index, headings) and provided the children with ample opportunities to transfer this learning across multiple settings. In each case, the new learning was first introduced in a whole-group setting with a high degree of teacher assistance, including explicit demonstrations and thinking aloud. Dave understands that shared reading of an enlarged text creates an ideal setting for scaffolding his students to acquire new learning while engaging them in a motivating experience. Today during shared reading, his instructional goal is for his students to understand how authors of expository texts use photographs with labels to help their readers comprehend the text information. After the shared reading experience, Dave meets with children in guided reading groups, where he introduces a nonfiction text that includes text features from previous learning, plus photographs with labels. Finally, the students are expected to independently transfer the new learning to a new situation. Here, he instructs the students to use the classroom library to locate other nonfiction texts that use real photographs with labels to explain the text content. From this theory, the goal of instruction is twofold: (1) to comprehend the particular text; and (2) to transfer the knowledge, skills, and strategies to new texts. This is higher-level thinking.

If a student is unable to transfer his learning to an unassisted setting, the teacher should consider five instructional influences (Meichenbaum and Biemiller 1998):

1. The examples (models) in the assisted settings were inadequate; therefore the student did not see the connection between the models and the task to be performed.
2. The student may not have been actively engaged and challenged during the assisted situations.
3. The teacher did not provide appropriate prompts for scaffolding the student's strategic activity.
4. The literacy task in the assisted situations was too dissimilar to the independent work, and the student failed to see the relationship.
5. The student's misconception of the concept (based on stubborn background knowledge) may have muddied the learning, and the teacher failed to intervene appropriately to prevent the interference.

Organizing the Environment

A well-organized learning environment is necessary for scaffolding students' learning and promoting transfer across multiple settings. For example, Vicki has organized the spaces in her third-grade classroom for whole-group, small-group, individual, and collaborative learning. At the front of the room is a large U-shaped carpeted area for whole-group instruction: word study lessons, shared reading, read-aloud, and explicit mini-lessons. This open space is outlined on two sides by the classroom library, represented by low shelves with colorful book bins, with the third side drawn by a long, comfortable sofa for independent reading. The children's desks form a backdrop for the open space while also providing Vicki with a bird's-eye view of the children as they work on their literacy activities. To one side of the room is a writing table with a nearby shelf containing a variety of writing resources, including dictionaries, a thesaurus, mentor texts, writing checklists, and an assortment of publishing materials. In a corner at the back of the room, Vicki has created a private space for meeting with children in guided reading groups. Across the room is a cozy corner with comfortable chairs arranged to accommodate the conversational moves of literature discussion groups (Figure 8.1). Around the perimeter of the room are various literacy spaces where children can work independently or collaboratively on projects. Vicki uses a Reading Workshop Option Board (see Figure 8.2, as well as Dorn and Soffos 2005) to assign children to meaningful and relevant projects, such as working in the classroom library, conducting research projects, or engaging in book discussions. The room is not large, but it gives the appearance of openness because of the careful arrangement of spaces.

Figure 8.2 During reading workshop, teachers use a Reading Workshop Option Board with a variety of meaningful activities for independent and collaborative projects. Photo used with permission from Dorn, L., and C. Soffos, 2005. *Teaching for Deep Comprehension: A Reading Workshop Approach.* Portland, ME: Stenhouse.

Harriet is a reading specialist who provides supplemental small-group interventions to struggling readers. Like Vicki, she understands the importance of predictable environments and structured routines for developing self-regulated learners. She believes her role is to help her students acquire strategies for monitoring and regulating their literacy behaviors, including the ability to use resources for assisting their learning. At the beginning of the year, Harriet coaches the children in self-management techniques: retrieving and storing their own materials, using resources for checking on their learning, recognizing the signals for moving into new instructional activities, and understanding the how and why of particular routines. Harriet models the expected behavior, uses explicit language to describe her actions, and guides the children through rehearsals of the expected routines. Thus the children have conceptual models of acceptable standards that they can use as benchmarks

Figure 8.1 Space is arranged to allow children to make eye contact with one another as they discuss books during literature discussion groups.

for evaluating their own performances in certain areas. When children internalize the concept of acceptable standards for particular classroom behavior, they have a scaffold that frees their minds to focus on the real issues of learning.

Classroom Library

The classroom library is a social and intellectual hub where students meet to collaborate on literacy projects or select books for independent reading. Therefore, it is essential that the students understand how to use the classroom library. To promote seamlessness across the school, many teachers have developed a schoolwide classification system for organizing their classroom libraries, and students use this information as they progress through the grades. During mini-lessons, teachers model how to find books according to conventional features (such as genre, authors, awards, chapter books, and holidays) and provide opportunities for students to apply this knowledge independently during reading workshop. Also, teachers encourage students to develop new classification schemes (funny books, books for girls, books for boys, favorite books, and so on) and to label bins with these personal categories. In addition to paper copies, classroom libraries include e-readers, and students are motivated to read their favorite books and magazines on these digital tools. In some classrooms, at the beginning of the school year, the classroom library remains under construction for several weeks as the children work together to file the books, create new categories, and learn how to use the library as a resource for their learning. In Leanne Bongers's fourth-grade classroom, the children are actively engaged in constructing the classroom library (see Figure 8.3).

Figures 8.3a & b Children take an active role in building the classroom library. Books are filed in book bins with labels.

Organizing for an Integrated Workshop Framework

The ultimate goal of an integrated workshop framework is to enable students to generalize their knowledge and strategies for different purposes and across multiple settings. A workshop framework allows teachers to develop grade-level content in a whole-group setting, follow up with differentiated instruction in a small-group or one-on-one context, conclude with a debriefing session and teacher assessment, and finally, create opportunities for students to transfer their learning to varied contexts. This theory is the basis of a successful integrated workshop.

Since no schedules are the same, we present two examples. First, we share how teachers can implement an integrated workshop that includes reading, writing, language, and content (science and social studies) blocks across the school day. This four-hour framework provides a structure for aligning the curriculum and differentiating the instruction to meet students' needs. Next, we share an example for implementing a two-hour language arts framework that includes whole-group lessons, guided reading groups, and writing workshop. Technology and research should be embedded naturally into all workshop structures.

An Integrated Workshop Block

Here is a typical schedule of an integrated workshop framework (see Figure 8.4). The schedule is approximately four hours long, with more than 50 percent of this time spent in a whole-group setting. As the teacher works with the entire class, she mingles among the students to provide scaffolding to meet their individual needs. In small groups, the teacher prompts the children to apply their knowledge and strategies to reading and writing. For independent work, the teacher uses the Reading Workshop Option Board (see Figure 8.2) to assign individual children to the tasks that most appropriately meet their strengths and needs. Below we illustrate the relationship of whole-group instruction to small-group and independent work.

- Word study, spelling, or vocabulary (approximately 15–20 minutes).

  The teacher provides clear demonstrations, explicit teaching, and guided practice to ensure that students learn about words. Then she prepares specific word-solving tasks that align with the whole-group lesson for independent work.

- Language studies (approximately 30–40 minutes). Within a whole-group setting, the teacher delivers instruction through interactive read-aloud and language investigations around units of study: literary units (genre or author studies), expository units (nonfiction, content studies, procedural texts), and persuasive units. She uses mentor texts, text maps, anchor charts, and reader response logs as instructional tools for teaching the functions of the language system, including grammatical structures, text conventions, vocabulary, and crafting techniques. During independent work, the children use the classroom library, plus digital tools, to work on language projects related to the unit of study.

- Writing workshop mini-lesson (approximately 15 minutes).

  During this whole-group lesson, the teacher provides explicit demonstrations and clear models to help students acquire important knowledge about the writing process.

- Writing workshop independent writing (approximately 25–30 minutes).

Workshop Framework for Integrating Curriculum and Differentiating Instruction

Morning Block and Approximate Times	Afternoon Block and Approximate Times
Word Study – Whole Group *(15–20 minutes)* • Phonics • Spelling • Vocabulary	**Reading Workshop – Differentiated Framework** *(90 minutes)* • Whole-Group Reading Lesson • Small-Group Instruction: Guided Reading, Assisted Writing, Literature Discussion • Teacher Conferences (individual) • Independent and Collaborative Work in Centers or Option Board • Whole-Group Debriefing
Language Studies – Differentiated Framework *(30–40 minutes)* • Whole-Group Read-Aloud or Language Lesson • Units of Study (Genre, Text, Content) • Language Investigations (using grammar and conventions in context) • Collaborative Projects	**Content Workshop – Differentiated Framework** *(45–60 minutes)* • Whole-Group Content Lesson • Collaborative Research Projects • Whole-Group Debriefing
Writing Workshop – Differentiated Framework *(45 minutes)* • Whole-Group Writing Lesson • Teacher Conferences (Small Group or Individual) • Whole-Group Debriefing	

Figure 8.4 Four-hour integrated workshop schedule.

The children write independently, and the teacher conducts individual or small-group writing conferences. Each student's writing portfolio will contain multiple pieces of writing from other workshop experiences, and the student will decide which piece to work on during writing workshop. For example, the student might choose to work on a PowerPoint presentation begun in language workshop, to draft a scientific report from notes taken during content workshop, or to start a new story for a book to be published. Teachers should keep in mind that children are writing across the school day, and the independent writing block provides a context for integrating writing opportunities.

- Writing workshop debriefing (approximately 5–10 minutes).

During this whole-group meeting, the teacher convenes the class and prompts students to share a piece of writing or discuss a strategy they used to improve their work.

- Reading workshop mini-lesson (approximately 15 minutes).

In a whole-group setting, the teacher provides a well-crafted lesson that highlights an important skill, procedure, or reading strategy. She instructs the children to transfer this knowledge to independent tasks; for example, they might ask them to find descriptive words in a familiar book and record these words in their reader response log.

- Reading workshop reading groups (approximately 60 minutes).

The teacher meets with small groups for guided reading or literature discussions. In this personal context, she is able to provide more tailored support to meet student needs. Generally, the teacher meets with three groups daily for approximately fifteen to twenty minutes each.

- Reading workshop debriefing (approximately 10 minutes).

During this whole-group meeting, the children bring reading logs and share the evidence of independent work. The teacher uses this setting to assess the students' learning.

- Content workshop lesson (approximately 30–45 minutes).

This whole-group lesson focuses on specific grade-level content knowledge in science and social studies. The teacher provides a clear explanation of the content to be learned and provides the appropriate scaffolding to ensure the students' understanding. After the whole-group lesson, the students engage in collaborative or independent work, and the teacher mingles among the class to support as needed. The content workshop emphasizes the research cycle while also helping students apply problem-solving strategies when they are reading content information.

- Debriefing content lesson (approximately 10–15 minutes).

This whole-group meeting brings the class together to discuss learning, including the students' progress on their research projects.

A Language Arts Block

Now we present an example of a first-grade classroom schedule that is based on a two-and-a-half-hour language arts block (see Figure 8.5). The day begins with fifteen minutes of independent reading and teacher assessment. As the children read from their independent book boxes, the teacher takes a running record on approximately four children each day. This literacy component serves two purposes: (1) the children engage in volume reading, allowing them to build their vocabulary and content knowledge while practicing fluency and reading strategies as they read for meaning, and (2) the teacher is able to collect reading data on all children and to monitor their independent reading development. After this component, the teacher engages the students in three whole-group lessons: shared reading, read-aloud, and word study. Next, the teacher meets with three guided reading groups for approximately twenty minutes per group. When the students are not with the teacher, they are engaged in appropriate activities at literacy centers. During their center time, the intervention specialist provides an additional reading or writing group for students who are struggling in reading. During the last thirty minutes of the language arts block, the students participate in writing workshop, which includes a ten-minute whole-group lesson and twenty minutes of independent writing and teacher conferences, and concludes with a five-minute debriefing session on strategies used during writing.

Workshop Framework for Integrating Curriculum and Differentiating Instruction

One-Hour Block (Whole Group)	One-Hour-and-30-Minute Block
Independent Reading and Teacher Assessment *(15 minutes)* • Familiar or easy books for emergent to early readers • Easy new books for transitional readers • Teacher assessment and reading conferences **Shared Reading** *(15 minutes)* • Big Books • Poetry **Interactive Read Aloud** *(10 minutes)* • Listening Comprehension • Comprehension Charts	**Reading Block** *(60 minutes)* **Teacher selects the most appropriate small group** • Guided reading groups • Assisted writing groups • Literature discussion groups For struggling readers, the teacher meets daily with this group and the intervention specialist also meets with this group during their center time. **Literacy Centers** *(15–20 minutes at each center for 2 rotations)* Grade-level and above students work in center activities for approximately 40 minutes. Struggling readers will meet in literacy center for 15 minutes daily.
Word Study – Whole Group *(20 minutes)* • Phonics • Spelling • Vocabulary	**Writing Workshop –** *(35 minutes)* • Whole-Group Writing Lesson (10 minutes) • 20 minutes of independent writing; teacher conferences (drop in or individual) • Whole-Group Debriefing (5 minutes)

Figure 8.5 Two-and-a-half-hour language arts schedule.

Teachers can adjust these schedules to meet the demands of their school. However, the goal is to create a structure that promotes integration and transfer across multiple blocks while ensuring that struggling readers receive an additional layer of instruction to allow them to catch up with their peers as quickly as possible.

Meeting Student Needs in Small Groups

Guided reading requires that children be placed in groups at their instructional level. These groups must be small enough for the teacher to be able to observe each child's reading strategies, because these observations allow her to extend the children's cognitive development. A teacher monitoring a whole class or large reading group often misses these opportunities.

Assisted writing groups complement guided reading groups. If a student is struggling in reading, an assisted writing group can have a positive effect on reading development. Many teachers like to meet with

guided reading groups three days a week and assisted writing groups on alternate days.

During literature discussion groups, children read and discuss texts that are clustered around units of study. These groups are most appropriate for children at the transitional reading level. The format includes strategy-based mini-lessons, previewing and surveying strategies, silent reading, book discussions, and writing about reading (see Dorn and Soffos 2005).

A typical classroom will include readers at various points along the reading continuum; therefore, it is essential for teachers to offer small-group instruction to meet the unique needs of all learners.

Organizing Materials for Small-Group Instruction

Any teacher arranging a work area for small-group instruction will want to make sure there is easy access to materials. Some teachers have a bookshelf near their guided reading table on which to store their book sets in baskets or boxes labeled according to the reading levels. Others place the guided reading books for each reading group in a basket labeled for that particular group.

Some teachers take reading records on notebook paper attached to a clipboard. These records are later placed in individual student portfolios. Other teachers organize notebook binders with tabbed sections for each student's reading records. Running record forms and blank notebook paper are worthy tools as the teacher records and analyzes her observations.

Many teachers conduct their assisted writing sessions in the same area used for guided reading. The chart paper for writing can be placed on an easel at the front of the room (see Figure 8.6). All of the materials (markers, alphabet charts, chalkboards, dictionaries, and so on) can be stored nearby in a portable cubby or tub.

Practices for storing and distributing magnetic letters and letter cards vary widely. Some teachers use inexpensive plastic tubs to sort letters for each child. Many teachers use letter cards and sort them in laminated library envelopes. Others use a fishing-tackle box or similar kind of segmented container (see Figure 8.7). Still other teachers find it easier just to pass out small slips of scrap paper and have the children write on them the letters they will need for the day's activities.

Distribution of magnetic letters or letter cards needs to be efficient. Simple techniques such as choosing a different child to pass out the materials can save valuable learning time while also demonstrating shared responsibility in classroom management.

Sharing Materials

Finding enough books of various difficulty levels for guided reading can be a problem in some schools. A schoolwide book room is a good way to share materials. A number of schools are using an electronic system to easily scan and track sets in and out of the shared book room. A simple way to organize the book room is to place sets of leveled texts in separate gallon-size zipper storage bags, label them, attach a pocket with a library card or scan number, and place them in baskets labeled by text level. The text sets could also be sorted into color-coded fiction and nonfiction tubs or into genre units.

Literacy Centers

A literacy center (also called a literacy corner) is an area of the classroom where children interact with specially designed activities, read, or write independently during the fifteen-or-twenty-minute rotations the teacher is working with small groups for guided reading, literature discussion, or assisted writing. The teacher creates an assignment board to rotate students from one center to another (see Figure 8.8 for an example). Since the board is a permanent classroom fixture, it needs to be made of heavy cardboard or some other durable material. It also needs to accommodate ever-changing groups, as the children develop their individual reading and writing skills. On the board, the children's names are attached with Velcro, so the teacher can move a

Figure 8.6 Teachers organize their materials for assisted writing.

Figure 8.7 Letter cards are stored in a plastic container and used during whole-group word study lesson.

name from group to group very easily. In technology-based classrooms, an assignment board can be created and saved on an interactive whiteboard , allowing the teacher the same flexibility to rotate groups and activities. Each literacy center is usually identified by an icon that represents the literacy task; these icons are also attached with Velcro for easy movement.

Children must have opportunities to work independently on literacy tasks that are within their control. Toward this goal, teachers create specially designed activities at literacy centers that promote automaticity and transfer. This theory implies that students understand the expectations associated with the particular literacy center, plus they must be able to monitor, regulate, and assess their own independent performance according to the standard. A team of primary-grade teachers at Washington School for Comprehensive Literacy in Sheboygan, Wisconsin, developed rubrics to help their students understand behavioral expectations for working independently in a center. The rubrics used a three-point rating scale for analyzing the quality of a cupcake (a concrete object) and applying these same qualities to the student's

Figure 8.8 Example of rotation board for corner assignments.

independent behavior in the literacy center. The rubrics were written on anchor charts hanging in the room, and the teachers referred to these assessment tools during the debriefing component of reading workshop (see Figure 8.9).

Children are assigned to a literacy center based on the teacher's observations of things they need to practice. Each center includes a writing opportunity, such as writing about how a problem was solved, responding to a text, composing a story, or conducting a research project. The centers include a range of opportunities, and teachers should use their judgment about the most appropriate centers for meeting student needs. It is important to remember that all center activities are an extension of instruction that has occurred during the various workshops.

The following are typical literacy centers in the early grades: name center, letter and word work center, shared reading center, independent reading center, listening center, writing center, and research center. You will notice that some centers are more appropriate for specific grade levels. For example, the name center is designed for kindergarten students, whereas the research center includes a range of grade-level experiences. As children acquire more strategies and skills in particular areas, many center activities are discontinued, and children select literacy options from the Reading Workshop Option Board (page 116).

Name Center

Children's names provide a personal scaffold for learning how words work. The activities in this center are most appropriate for kindergarten and beginning first-grade readers.

Materials

chart with the children's names and pictures (Underline the first letter of each name.)
shoe bag
pocket chart
basket with the children's first names written on sentence strips
magnetic tape
basket containing a picture of each child
magnetic letters
paper and crayons
large sheet of butcher paper

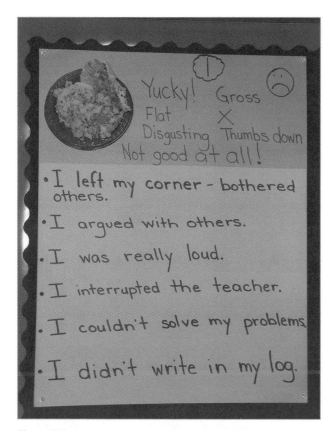

Figure 8.9a

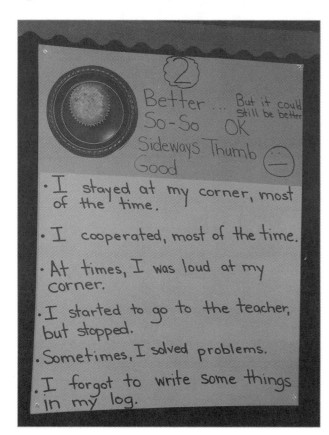

Figure 8.9b

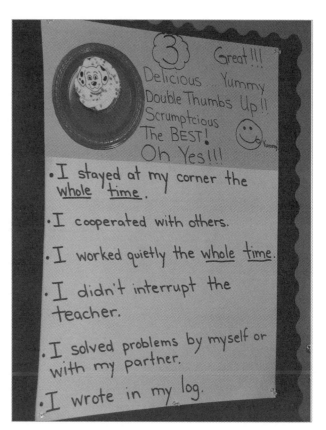

Figure 8.9c Anchor charts with a three-point rating scale provide children with a tool for regulating and assessing their independent behaviors in a literacy corner.

Design Considerations

1. Hang the name/picture chart on the wall beside the file cabinet that will be used for making names with magnetic letters.
2. Hang a pocket chart down low.
3. Create a basket of the children's names written on sentence strips with a small piece of magnetic tape placed on the back of each one.
4. Arrange a small table with a sheet of butcher paper and a large marker.
5. Have other paper and markers nearby.

Sample Activities

- Have children use a shoe bag to sort names according to beginning letters (see Figure 8.10).
- Have children sort the sentence strip names by beginning letter.
- Have children sort the names by number of syllables.

Figure 8.10 A child sorts children's names according to beginning letter.

Figure 8.11 Children can match the name with the picture at the name center.

- Create other labels to focus on specific letters. For example, names beginning with *s*, names with *s* as the last letter, names that have more than one *s*, names that have no *s*'s, names that begin with *sh*, and names that begin with *st*.
- Create picture labels so that the children can sort names by the sound they begin with (for example, *dog*, *sun*, and *fish*, or none of these sounds).
- Provide magnetic letters for name making. Have the children place a name card on the file cabinet and make their name under the model. This task can be made more supportive by placing the letters needed for a name under the name rather than having the children select from an abundance of letters.
- Label the pocket chart "girls" and "boys." Place the children's pictures under the correct columns. Have children match the names with the pictures. (See Figure 8.11.)
- Allow the children to use the name chart to draw pictures of their friends and label the pictures with the names.
- Use the butcher paper to create a sign-in chart. (See Figure 8.12.) The children can sign in every day by responding yes or no to a question such as the following:

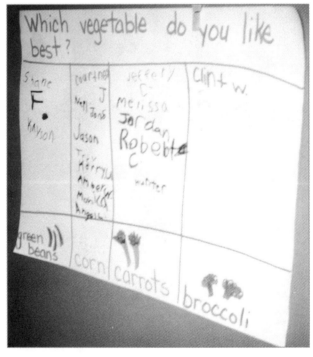

Figure 8.12 Children can use a sign-in sheet to vote on important issues.

- Have you ever given a dog a bath?
- Do you have buttons on today?
- Would you let a piglet suck your fingers?
- Have you ever been to a farm?

By signing under the appropriate number:
- How many letters are in your first name?
- How many people live in your house?
- How old are you?

By signing under the appropriate picture:
- My eyes are (blue, green, hazel, brown, black).
- My favorite color is . . .
- My costume is scary.
- My costume is friendly.

Letter and Word Work Center

This center provides opportunities for students to build automaticity with letters, sounds, high-frequency words, and spelling patterns. Many activities are designed to incorporate multisensory systems (visual, auditory, motor) in learning about print. All activities are carefully planned to align with children's reading and writing levels.

Materials

four sets of uppercase magnetic letters
eight sets of lowercase magnetic letters
six magnetic boards, cookie sheets, or pizza pans
letter cards of alphabet letters typed in different print styles, or fonts, in various font sizes
clothespins, clothesline, letter cards, and picture cards for sorting
task cards for letter sorts
picture cards for sorting letter sounds
one pocket chart
assorted pointers (Chopsticks work well.)
one set of large alphabet letter cards (three- or four-inch size)
little letter books highlighting objects that begin with a certain letter
alphabet books of all types
spiral notebooks with blank paper for creating individual alphabet books
chart paper to create an alphabet writing wall
sponge-tip paint roller
stamp sponge for writing letters on chalkboard
paintbrush and water for writing letters on chalkboard
large chalk for writing letters on chalkboard
alphabet stencils
tactile letters: sandpaper, sponge, plastic, foam, and letter tiles

alphabet puzzles
alphabet sound games such as Sound Concentration
copies of alphabet pictures for pasting in individual alphabet books
paper, crayons, and scissors for name/sound activity
picture cards with corresponding words written on the back for making words
word cards for word pattern sorts
reading log with section designated for word study activities at center
iPads with ABC charts uploaded to them

Design Consideration

1. You will need an area that has metal surfaces for sorting magnetic letters—for example, sides of a filing cabinet or other storage cabinets, the front of a metal desk, or a magnetic board. If metal surfaces are hard to find, you can purchase and use metal cookie, or pizza, sheets.

2. Baskets or plastic tubs are excellent for storing magnetic letters. However, for some activities, you may want a set of magnetic letters that are already sorted. In that case, a plastic fishing-tackle box works well. It is also handy for the small letter cards that are used in sorting.

3. Use four-by-six-inch index cards and write the sorting and word-building tasks on them. You can place a magnetic strip (available in craft departments) on the back. This will make them ready to place on the metal surface. Another idea is to attach the magnetic strip to the back of a clothespin and place the clothespin on the metal surface; the task cards can then be clipped into the clothespins.

4. A four-by-six-inch plastic index-card box is a good tool for storing task cards.

5. Use baskets to store all the alphabet books together and all the letter books together. Baskets can also be used to store the alphabet books written by the children.

Sample Activities for Letter Recognition

- Have students chant the alphabet chart by pointing to and saying the name of each letter and naming the object; for example, *Aa apple; Bb ball; Cc cat.* (See Figure 8.13.)

Figure 8.13 Two children engage in shared reading of individual ABC charts.

- Have students read alphabet books and name the letters and the pictures in the book.
- Have students read the ABC chart from iPad (see Figure 8.14).

Figure 8.14 A child reads the ABC chart from an iPad.

- Make an environmental-print wall and have students read the wall and name the letters and words they recognize (see Figure 8.15).
- Give students a list of known letters and have them practice writing these letters on a dry erase board.
- Have students use highlighter tape to locate a known letter several times in a book or poem.
- Have students use highlighter tape to find a particular sound/symbol relationship in a poem or book.
- Have students sort picture cards by sound/symbol relationships.

Figure 8.15 Make an environmental-print wall and have children name the letters and words they recognize.

- Provide a stack of picture cards and instruct students to build or write the words using the sound/symbol relationship being focused on, such as blends, digraphs, and prefixes.

Sample Activities for Sorting Letters

- Attribute sorts can be done using only uppercase letters, only lowercase letters, or both together. Some examples of attribute sorts include letters with sticks; letters with straight sticks; letters with slanted sticks; letters with straight and slanted sticks; letters with circles; letters with open circles; letters with closed circles; letters with sticks and circles; letters with sticks, circles, or sticks and circles; tall or small letters; letters that look alike; and letters that look different as uppercase letters than they do as lowercase letters (see Figure 8.16).
- Begin with an easy sort, such as one by color. Display the task cards: red, blue, green, yellow, and so on. Use various letters in many different colors. Instruct the children to sort the magnetic letters according to similar color. Another way to

Figure 8.16 Sorting letters by attributes.

sort by color would be to use one letter formation in many different colors.

- Display the following task cards: circle, circle and stick, and stick. Instruct the children to sort the magnetic letters according to similar features. For example, *b, d* = circle and stick; *o, c* = circle; *l, I* = stick.
- Have students attend to more specific features. For example, open circle (*u, n, c*), closed circle (*o, D, Q*), straight stick (*l, t*), slanted stick (*v, w*), straight and slanted stick (*Y, k*).
- Finally, put away the magnetic letters and replace them with other letter forms to sort: a bowl of alphabet cereal, for example, which can be eaten after sorting.
- Letter cards with letters in a variety of print styles can also be sorted. Use one letter typed in a variety of fonts. Clip a model of each letter font on the sorting surface. Don't use too many different styles at any one time!

Sample Activities for Writing Letters

- Children need ample opportunities to practice the formation of the letter movements that make each letter distinctive. A large piece of butcher paper provides incentive for novice learners to practice their developing knowledge of the alphabet. They can use markers and write BIG! Or they can write tiny.
- Provide a model for the children to copy by clipping a large alphabet card to the wall.
- A dry erase board makes a good writing wall. Children love to use colored markers, without the confines of lines on the board, to practice letter formation.
- Stamp sponges can be filled with water and used to write disappearing letters on the chalkboard. A cup of water and a large paintbrush may also be used.
- Paint sponges are fun to use on the writing wall. They dry quickly!

Word-Building Center

This center provides children with opportunities to develop automaticity with some high-frequency words and to practice word-solving strategies on unknown words.

- Provide picture cards and magnetic letters to make the words. Scaffold the task by placing the exact letters needed for each word directly underneath the picture. Make the activity self-checking by writing the word on the back of the picture.
- Provide word cards and a mixture of magnetic letters. The children construct the word directly underneath the word card.
- String a clothesline with word cards representing several rime patterns. For example, *cat, read, pig*. Instruct the child to read the word card in the basket and clip it to the word that has the same pattern. When they have finished, they can make the first word out of magnetic letters and practice manipulating the onset to make other words (see Figure 8.17).

Figure 8.17 Word-building activities must be structured to support the level of the learner.

- Provide a word card with two words written on it, with one written directly underneath the second. Instruct the child to make a new word by using the first part of the top word and the ending chunk of the second word. For example: *he* and *cat* are written on the card. The child chooses the magnetic letters needed to build the word *hat*. Finally, the child can write the new words on a sheet of paper and draw pictures to go with them (see Figure 8.18).

Figure 8.18 An onset-rime activity.

- Choose three rime patterns, such as *at, ed, ig*. Make five or six cards of each rime pattern. Fill a muffin tin with all of the *at* cards in one cup, the *ed* cards in a second cup, and the *ig* cards in a third cup. Instruct the children to take the patterns out of the cups and add a magnetic letter or letters to the beginning of each card to make words (see Figure 8.19).
- Provide a word card. Instruct the children to build the word out of magnetic letters and use more magnetic letters to add the *ing* ending to the word. Finally, they are to take a separate sheet of paper and use the new word in a sentence. For example: word card—*go*; new word—*going*. This can be done with other word endings as they are learned in assisted instruction with the teacher.

Sample Activities for Learning About Patterns

- Display category heads to represent common features, and have students sort words under the

Figure 8.19 Practicing word endings.

appropriate category and write words with similar meanings.
- Have students sort word cards into meaning categories.
- Have students sort words into spelling patterns.
- Have students sort words into sound categories.
- Display key words to represent category heads, and have students sort words they haven't seen before.
- Have students sort words into logical categories as quickly as possible.
- Provide word cards and a mixture of magnetic letters, and instruct the students to construct the word directly underneath the word card.

Shared Reading Center

The purpose of the shared reading center is to provide children with opportunities to read familiar materials. In the process, they learn to apply reading strategies within context, practice fluent reading, and notice new details about the print code. Interactive whiteboards have many tools to support learning such as the highlighting feature and the window-shade feature that students can use to highlight rhyming words or to cover up certain words so they can ask their partner to make a prediction.

Materials

- enlarged copies of poems, songs, and chants written on chart paper
- two sets of sentence strips written in two different colors to match each poem
- large notebook rings for storing the sentence strips
- one set of word cards written on different-colored construction or index paper for each poem
- gallon-size zipper storage bags for storing the word cards
- enlarged copies of chants and stories written using rebus pictures and environmental print to create interactive charts
- clothesline, clothes rack, or other place to store the rhymes on hangers with clothespins
- interactive whiteboards with files of poems, songs, and chants
- one or more pocket charts
- copies of rhymes glued on eight-by-eleven-inch brown envelopes
- eight-by-eleven-inch colored copies of the poems cut into sentence strips and placed in the envelopes
- eight-by-eleven-inch colored copies of the poems cut into word cards, placed into a zipper storage bag, and put into the envelopes
- enlarged copy of the alphabet chart
- large pointer and small pointers
- colored transparency windows
- several different sizes of focus frames
- highlighter tape
- skinny sticky notes

Design Considerations

1. You will need a place to store the copies of the enlarged poems. Hanging them on clothes hangers using clothespins and then hanging them on a clothes rack works well. You may also use a clothesline if you have the space.
2. Use a hook or a nail in the wall to create a place to display individual poems as the children pull them off the rack for rereading.
3. If you have the space and an overhead projector, place it on the floor and shine it onto a wall. The children can then use the transparency poems and literacy tools for rereading, predicting, or highlighting certain elements.
4. Hang the pocket chart(s) on the wall at an appropriate height for the children to use the text and word cards.
5. Make individual text-matching activities by duplicating three copies of a rhyme on three different colors of paper (for example, white, yellow, and pink). Paste one copy on the outside of an eight-by-eleven-inch brown envelope (white). Cut one copy into sentence strips (yellow). Cut the last copy into word cards (pink) and store in a zipper storage bag. Place the sentence strips and the bag of word cards into the envelope.
6. Store the envelopes of poems in an appropriate container. The children can select a poem and take it to their desk for text and word matching.

Sample Activities

- Have children reread enlarged poems, songs, or chants using a large pointer (see Figure 8.20).
- Have children match pictures to sentences (see Figure 8.21).

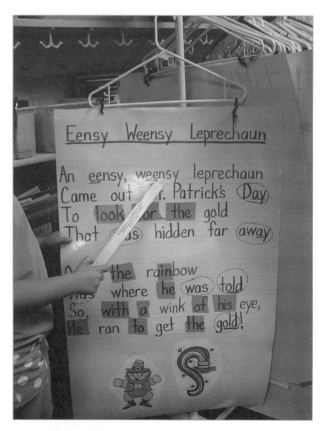

Figure 8.20 A child reads an enlarged copy of a song using a pointer.

Figure 8.21 Children match picture cards to sentences.

- Have children reread poems on the interactive whiteboard using assorted pointers.
- Have children use sticky notes to cover up certain words and then ask their buddies to make predictions.
- Have children locate rhyming words and mark them with highlighter tape.
- Have children use the focus frames to locate the words that they know and record them on a piece of paper.
- Have children reassemble a poem in the pocket chart using sentence strips. (One set of sentence strips can be placed in the pocket chart as a model if you like.)
- Have children match word cards on top of the sentence strips.
- Have children reread interactive rebus charts with a pointer and match word cards to the pictures using clothespins.

Independent Reading Center

This center provides children with opportunities to apply reading strategies, increase vocabulary knowledge, practice fluency, and increase reading volume.

Materials

individualized book boxes for each child with familiar guided reading books at each child's instructional level

book sets organized into different levels if there are not enough guided reading books to create individualized sets

a system for allowing children to check out books for home

library books organized by topic

Big Books

laundry basket for storing Big Books

pointers for reading Big Books

can for storing the pointers

class-published stories and Big Books

individual poetry notebooks

comfortable area with carpet or beanbag chairs

an assortment of stuffed animals to read to

clipboards with story maps or blank paper for story retelling

reading log (second/third grade) or traveling log (first grade)

Design Considerations

1. Use small baskets to store books and have the students label them by genre during the first twenty days of school as nonfiction and fiction is discussed.

2. Keep a clipboard or notebook in the book corner with a page for each child. Have the child write the title of the book and the date when it is checked out. Cross it out upon return. Another idea is to have the child write the name of the text on a sticky note with his or her name and stick it on a checkout chart. Then, remove the note when the book is returned.

3. Arrange a comfortable area, preferably on the carpet. Include soft pillows or furniture.

4. A laundry basket of Big Books can be stored underneath the Big Book stand. Pointers can be stored in a metal can.

5. Clipboards with story-retelling activities can be stored in a large basket or other suitable containers.

6. Place read-aloud books and mentor texts in a book box or in a spotlighted section for children to reread during independent reading time.

Sample Activities

- Read, read, read—familiar guided reading texts, library books, class texts, poems, and Big Books.
- Read to a friend or a stuffed animal.
- Use pointers to track text in Big Books.
- Use story maps to plot narrative text.
- Use blank paper to record written story retellings or facts from expository text.

Writing Center

The writing center is critical to building independence in literacy. This is a place where students can write in response to their own experiences, a book they have just read, or a school event; write a letter to the editor; or continue to work on a writing project they started during writing workshop. It is important that they experience many types of genres. Here are some of the genres you might want to include:

- journal
- personal narrative
- realistic fiction
- informational report
- procedural
- biography
- research report
- book review
- persuasive text

Materials

an abundance of assorted paper

old calendars, checkbooks, receipt books, and greeting cards

various writing instruments: pencils, pens, markers

a collection of interesting pictures to use as story starters

date stamp

individual student journals

writing portfolios

small alphabet charts and blend charts

picture dictionaries

thesaurus

books of words

children's personal dictionaries or spelling books

stapler

scissors

tape

samples from a wallpaper book for book covers

a shoe bag or other type of sorting container to serve as mailboxes

clipboards for writing around the room

revising and editing checklist

writing checklists and writing rubrics

text maps

iPad

Design Considerations

1. This corner can be stationed near the teacher, because the children usually work quietly.
2. You will need to arrange a small table and some chairs with the supplies nearby.
3. Continually collect the writing supplies.
4. Label everything.
5. Display children's writing.
6. Genre features can be highlighted on a display in the writing center.
7. Featured author displays with excerpts from books can demonstrate how writers use language in their texts.

Sample Activities

- Glue a picture onto a sheet of paper and write a story about it.
- Use a greeting card to write a note to a friend.
- Fill out a check and send it in a letter to a friend.
- Fill in a monthly calendar with activities you would like to do. Write a letter to your mother and tell her about them.
- Fill out a change-of-address form and write a note to a friend telling her how much you'll miss her.
- Use an iPad to make a book (see Figure 8.22).
- Develop a topic list.
- Use the revision and editing checklists to improve your writing.
- Use a category card with pictures/words to write about a favorite topic (see Figure 8.23 of a category card for football).
- Examine the language in your text. Use what you know about powerful words and a thesaurus to enhance your writing.
- Record in your reading log how the author used language in this text. Create your own example of this style of writing.

Figure 8.22 Teachers can download apps for the iPad that students can use to create and illustrate a book.

Figure 8.23 A student uses a category card as a resource when writing a story about football.

Listening Center

This center provides opportunities for children to practice fluency, build background knowledge, and interact with favorite authors on tape.

Materials

- CD players
- headphones
- computers
- e-books
- baskets of books with tapes
- file folders with graphic organizers or retelling maps
- instructions posted on a chart with how to operate the equipment

Design Considerations

1. This corner should be located away from the teacher's small-group area, because it tends to be a bit noisy.
2. Most teachers find it helpful to code the "play" and "stop" buttons with green and red tape for easy use by the students.
3. CDs and books can be sorted into gallon-sized zipper storage bags. A star can be marked on the side of the CD that needs to face up in the CD player.
4. Students bring independent reading logs (second and third grade) or travel logs (first grade) to the listening corner. Narrative retelling maps or expository graphic organizers may also be used at this corner and glued into the reading or travel logs.

Research Center

The research center is a place where the integrated curriculum truly comes together. It is a place where the students get to read, write, listen, learn, and extend their understandings of topics that are going on in the classroom. Below are a few examples of activities that link social studies and science.

Materials

- computer or iPad
- reference materials such as dictionaries and thesauri
- informational text around the research topic
- folder of various graphic organizers
- knowledge binders with articles and related materials (see Chapter 2)
- card pockets for organizing information into topic categories (see Figure 8.24)
- paper and cards for note taking
- anchor chart and sticky notes for classifying information for science project (see Figure 8.25)
- multimedia formats of information around various topics
- writing tools of various kinds

Figure 8.24 A student uses card pockets to organize his notes into topic categories for writing a research report.

Figure 8.25 Students place sticky notes on an anchor chart to classify information for a science project.

Design Considerations

1. Use small baskets to store books around units of study.
2. Have computer access for further research on a topic.
3. Have large graphic organizers posted in the center or anchor charts on which students can post newly found information.
4. This station can be located away from the teacher, as students sometimes work collaboratively on research projects.
5. Arrange the furniture in the center for collaborative work and independent work, so that students can learn multiple ways of gathering information.

Activities

Pose a Question
Purpose: Identify problems and potential solutions for an issue or scenario

Example: Why is the ground polluted with paper?

- Post the following questions in the center; have students write responses in journals:
  o What do you think about when you see the playground polluted with cans, paper, and debris?
  o Why is the ground polluted with paper?
  o What would happen if no one picked the trash up?
- Next, post the following scenario:
  o You want to play baseball on the playground with your friends, but debris and the cans could cause someone to be injured. Besides, the park is not a pretty sight. What could you do to solve this problem and make the playground a better place?
- Have students work collaboratively to identify the problem and come up with a solution for the playground problem.

Problem	Solution

Visualize Experience
Purpose: Use sensory experiences to activate and build conceptual understandings
Example:

- Ask students to work independently and use the resource materials such as the computer, texts, videos, and other materials in the center to enhance their knowledge of landslides and earthquakes.
- Give each student working in the center a graphic organizer.
- Tell them to observe, or carefully watch, everything that happens, because they will be writing down what they have seen.
- Post reminder questions around the center to scaffold students' learning, such as, What do buildings do? What do the trees look like? What sounds do you hear? Are people frightened? Why?
- Then ask students to compare and contrast earthquakes and landslides.
- Ask students to write about Earth's changes, comparing earthquakes and landslides.
- Note that it may take several days for students to complete the research center project.

Earth's Changes	Sight	Sound	Smell	Taste	Touch
Earthquakes					
Landslides					

Concept Connections

Purpose: Synthesize and extend understandings of a central topic or theme

Example:

- Have students independently research to refine and synthesize their understanding of matter.
- Have students identify common characteristics, nonexamples, definitions, and other words that relate to the topic of matter. Ask students to record responses on their graphic organizers.
- Have students share the information they learned in the research center in the science lesson to extend the discussion.

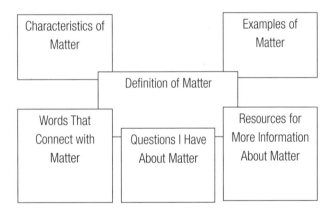

Closing Thoughts

An apprenticeship classroom should be structured so that children can work in their assisted and unassisted learning zones, including whole group, small group, one-on-one, and independently. In a well-organized classroom, children learn self-management techniques for regulating their learning across multiple settings. When established routines are in place, children can focus their attention on the literacy task at hand. In the next two chapters, we discuss how teachers create learning environments for accelerating the literacy development of their students.

chapter nine

HIGH-QUALITY LITERACY CLASSROOMS

There is a preponderance of research on effective literacy practices. With all this knowledge, we should feel confident that all children will become successful readers and writers, yet we know that is not the case. What would it take to ensure that every child reaches his or her highest potential in reading? What would it take to ensure that every teacher is successful with teaching every student—regardless of background, socioeconomic status, race, or ethnicity—to learn to read?

First, we believe that teachers must understand how to design responsive teaching that is grounded in sensitive observations of their students' learning over time. This means that instruction is not static, but rather is finely tuned to match the continual shifts that occur in the student's learning. And we believe that collaboration among teachers is one of the most important factors in ensuring student success, particularly for students who are struggling in literacy. Finally, we believe that schools must create apprenticeship-type settings where teachers can refine the craft of teaching through peer observations and professional dialogue.

In the concluding three chapters, we bring these core beliefs together. First, we share the stories of two exemplary teachers who are implementing research-based practices in their elementary-grade classrooms. Next, we look at the practices of an exemplary reading specialist as she provides supplementary intervention to a group of struggling readers at two points in time. Last, we share examples from several schools where teams of literacy educators collaborate on teaching and learning issues.

In this chapter, we begin by looking inside a third-grade classroom where the teacher uses a four-hour workshop framework to integrate instruction across reading, writing, language, and content areas (see Figure 8.4). Then we conclude with a look inside a first-grade classroom where the teacher uses a two-and-a-half-hour language arts block to organize instruction across reading and writing areas (see Figure 8.5). In both classrooms, a balance of whole-group, small-group, and one-to-one instruction allows for differentiation and responsive teaching.

A Look Inside a Third-Grade Classroom

Sheena, a third-grade teacher, recognizes that each student in her classroom develops on an individual time line. She has several students who are reading below grade level, and she understands the urgency of reading proficiency by the end of third grade. Therefore, she has two instructional goals:

1. to expose all students to a challenging, high-quality curriculum; and
2. to differentiate her instruction for the students who lack the reading skills and strategies to access the grade-level content.

Sheena believes an integrated curriculum within a workshop framework offers the perfect approach for meeting these goals. Within this structure, she provides opportunities for her students to transfer their knowledge, skills, and strategies across the school day, and she is ready with scaffolding prompts to facilitate the transfer process. The integrated approach works because

1. it allows for whole-group, small-group, and individual interactions;
2. it promotes social learning and collaboration among students;
3. it enables students to develop conceptual knowledge as they generalize their learning from one context to another;

4. it fosters deeper comprehension through units of study that are carried across the curriculum; and

5. it creates a natural context for differentiating instruction.

Sheena's theory of instruction is grounded in the seven principles of apprenticeship learning (see Figure 2.1). Gradual release of responsibility is evident in her teaching, and her instruction is continually adjusted to accommodate the changes in her students' learning.

Word Study

The literacy day begins with a twenty-minute whole-group word study lesson that focuses on word analysis skills and vocabulary development. Sheena knows that her third-grade students must be able to identify and comprehend the meaning of common prefixes and use this information in decoding unknown words within texts. She understands that a well-designed word study lesson includes six procedures: (1) review of existing knowledge; (2) application to new information, including clear examples; (3) guided practice with teacher scaffolding; (4) collaborative work in pairs or small groups; (5) writing about learning; and (6) summarizing learning, including implications for transfer.

Sheena begins her lesson by reviewing what the students already know about prefixes from a previous lesson on the *re-* and *un-* prefixes. She directs their attention to the anchor chart titled "Prefixes" that is hanging on the wall. During the previous lesson, Sheena had written the definition for *prefix* at the top of the anchor chart. She wants the children to memorize this definition, so she prompts them to read it with her. They chant, "A prefix is a word element placed in front of the root word, which changes the meaning of the word." Then she points to the words *relearn*, *recycle*, *uncover*, and *uncommon* and instructs the students to read the words and identify the prefixes. Sheena reminds her students that they should use what they already know about prefixes to help them comprehend a message during their reading. She engages them in a brief discussion with her prompts: "When would you need to relearn something? What does it mean to recycle something? What is something that you can uncover? What does it mean to be uncommon?"

Next, Sheena introduces the new prefixes *dis-*, *mis-*, and *pre-*. She writes several words on the white-board, circles the prefixes, and explains the meaning of each. She then uses the word bank on her white-board with several prefix words in it. She asks students to turn to their neighbor and talk about the prefixes in each word and what each word means. As the students interact with one another, Sheena listens to their discussions and provides scaffolding as needed.

Now Sheena assigns the students to work in heterogeneous pairs to collaborate on a sorting activity with prefixes and base words. They turn to a clean page in the Language Study section of their reading log and write three headings: (1) Not or Opposite of—for prefix *dis-*; (2) Wrongly—for prefix *mis-*; and (3) Earlier or Before for prefix *pre-*. The children talk about the word meanings and agree on the appropriate column for each word. Last, they select two words from each column that they will later use in sentences as an activity in the word study center (see Figure 9.1).

Not or Opposite of	Wrongly	Earlier or Before
Disadvantage	Misguide	Precaution
Disapprove	Mishandle	Precook
Disagree	Mislead	Predate
Discomfort	Mistrust	Prehistoric
Discontent		Preset
Disarm		Pretest

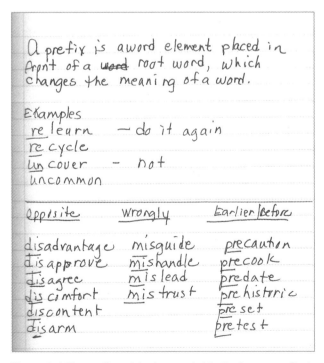

Figure 9.1 The prefix activity is recorded in the Language Study section of the student's reader response log.

As the lesson concludes, Sheena convenes the students for a whole-group debriefing. She begins, "Who can tell us what we learned today about prefixes?" She listens attentively as students share their learning. Then she adds the new prefixes to the class anchor chart and calls on several students to record the words from their reading log under the appropriate column. Her final words to the students focus on the rationale for today's lesson: "Now how will this help you when you are reading?" The students respond correctly, but Sheena knows that the true test of their learning will occur as they problem-solve within texts, and she will be prepared to scaffold them as needed.

Language Studies

The language studies block provides a structure for increasing students' listening (receptive) and speaking (expressive) comprehension through read-alouds, which include rich, interactive discussions in response to the text and co-constructed text maps for analyzing information. Sheena understands that oral language is the foundation on which written language is built and that during interactive read-alouds, her students are developing vocabulary and content knowledge that is essential for their independent reading. She designs her units of study based on state and national standards, and she ensures that her students are exposed to a variety of texts, including literary texts (fiction, literary nonfiction, and poetry) and informational texts (expository, persuasive, and procedural). During the language studies block, Sheena is able to address the functions of language at multiple levels, including genre characteristics, text features, sentence structures, and word usage (see Dorn and Soffos 2005).

Today, Sheena is introducing the students to the genre of fables. This three-week unit of study will be integrated into the reading and writing workshops. She knows that her readers will understand and comprehend texts at deeper levels when they are familiar with how texts are organized.

To prepare for the genre study, Sheena has read aloud a variety of fables to the students to familiarize them with the genre. She has also collected numerous fables at different reading levels to use for multiple purposes: more challenging texts for read-aloud and mentor texts, instructional-level texts for guided reading and literature discussion groups, and easier and familiar texts for independent reading. She will use graphic organizers and anchor charts to engage the students in analyzing the read-aloud texts for important features.

To begin the lesson, Sheena writes the word *genre* on an anchor chart. She asks the students, "Who can explain what the word *genre* means?"

Amy responds, "A kind of something," and Sheena confirms her answer. Then she asks, "How many of you like to watch action movies?" Several students raise their hands. She continues, "How many of you prefer comedies?" Again, several students raise their hands. Sheena then explains that comedies and action movies are genres, or types of movies. She also explains that all action movies share certain characteristics, and that all comedies have some features in common too. She explains that as readers and writers we must pay close attention to the genre to help us comprehend better. She also explains that recognizing the genre will help us anticipate what will happen next or what we will learn.

Next, Sheena displays on her whiteboard a concept-web graphic organizer. In the middle, she has written the word *Fables*. Sheena then takes her collection of familiar fables and discusses with the students how they are organized. She asks them to think about how they would define what a fable is. Sheena makes the task interactive by asking the students to turn and talk to a classmate and jot down any features of a fable they know. She then brings the students together and asks them to share their ideas. Finally, she records their responses on the group web. She reinforces the concept that all fables have certain common features. She tells students that they will be returning to the concept web after they learn more about the genre.

To move the students to a deeper understanding of the genre, Sheena provides guided practice by reading aloud a mentor text for the fable "The Tortoise and the Hare." After the reading, the students add more information to the concept web. Sheena discusses how writers use literary devices to activate the reader's imagination, and explains that many writers use personification to make their writing unique and interesting. She pulls out several books of Aesop's fables from the fables genre basket. She tells the students that these fables are filled with personification. She then gives the students an opportunity to practice identifying personification.

When it is time for independent reading, Sheena asks students to select a fable from the basket. She provides sticky notes for students to look for features of a fable that are listed on the anchor chart. She also posts the following questions for students to choose to respond to in their reader response log:

- What human trait does each animal character show?
- Compare and contrast the characters. How are they alike? How are they different?
- What is the moral of the story?
- Which character learns something from the other character? What is it?
- Which character has the flaw? What is it?

Writing Workshop Mini-Lesson

Writing workshop begins with a mini-lesson that is approximately ten minutes long. To prepare students to write their own fables down the road, Sheena has chosen to focus on character flaws. The students have just discussed the features of a fable during their language studies, so Sheena thinks this is the perfect time for them to make the connection to writing.

The lesson begins with Sheena writing the word *flaw* on the board. She asks the students to name some synonyms for the word based on their earlier discussion from the mentor text, "The Tortoise and the Hare." The students call out the following words: *shortcoming, imperfection,* and *weakness.* Sheena writes these words on the board. Next, Sheena shares one of her own flaws so that students can relate to the meaning. She shares the story of how she is sometimes very messy and disorganized, which makes her life difficult at times.

Next, Sheena divides the class into small groups and instructs them to think of traits or character flaws that could create problems for one or more characters in a story. As they work together, Sheena creates an anchor chart with two columns: one labeled "Character Flaws" and one labeled "Problems." Then she invites the students to share their lists of traits and potential problems that each flaw could create, and adds this information to the anchor chart. Sheena closes the mini-lesson by reminding the students that when they write their own fables, they can refer to the list of flaws on the anchor chart to develop their characters and plot.

Writing Workshop Independent Writing

During the independent writing block, the students are allowed to select a piece of writing from their portfolio to work on. Sheena knows that they will have several opportunities to write a fable during the unit of study; therefore she does not insist that all students begin a fable today. It is more important for students to make choices about their writing pieces, as long as they understand that particular pieces of writing are required by a certain date. As the students write, Sheena conducts one-on-one or small-group conferences. (See Chapter 6 for types of conferences.)

Writing Workshop Debriefing

During the last five minutes of the writing workshop, Sheena reconvenes the class for a whole-group meeting. She prompts students to share a piece of writing or to discuss a strategy they used to improve their work.

Reading Workshop Mini-Lesson

After writing workshop, Sheena transitions her students into reading workshop. The workshop begins with a fifteen-minute mini-lesson that highlights a comprehension strategy: today's lesson focuses on making inferences. Sheena knows the importance of starting with a familiar concept when teaching an abstract strategy, such as inferring. She says, "I'm going to tell you a short story, and I want you to listen for clues to figure out what happened." She begins, "Robins have built a nest in a tree beside Harrison's window, and the mother has been sitting on the nest for weeks. This morning, when Harrison left for school, he heard little chirping noises coming from the nest in the tree." Sheena prompts, "What do you think happened? What clues did you use to help you figure it out?" She asks students to turn to a partner and share their thinking. Then Sheena explains, "You just made an inference. An inference is when you use one or two clues or pieces of evidence to state a fact."

Next, to guide practice, Sheena displays on her whiteboard a picture of a boy standing in front of some spring flowers and blossoming bushes, holding a tissue and looking like he is about to sneeze. Sheena prompts her class to make an inference about the picture. She asks them to tell what kinds of information in the photo helped them make an inference about why the boy is sneezing.

Now that the students have the concept of what an inference is, Sheena moves the strategy to text. She displays the story "The Tortoise and the Hare" on her whiteboard. She highlights an excerpt, the students read the passage together, and Sheena encourages them to make inferences about the traits, feelings, and relationships of the characters in the passage and to identify the clues that support the inferences. As they work through the passage, they use the highlighter tools and other resources to annotate the text. As the lesson concludes, Sheena prepares the students for their independent reading during reading workshop. She instructs them to identify one or two places in a book they are reading where they made inferences, and to write about the thinking in their reader response log. Finally, she reminds the students to bring the book and response log to the debriefing session at the conclusion of reading workshop.

Reading Workshop—Reading Groups

The small-group component of reading workshop is approximately sixty minutes long. When students are not meeting with Sheena, they are working on individual or collaborative projects in reading, writing, and research areas. During this time, the school's reading specialist comes into the room to provide a guided reading lesson to a small group of struggling readers. (Sheena will also meet with the children in a guided reading group.)

As the students work, Sheena begins calling reading groups for small-group instruction. She has one group participating in a guided reading group and three groups participating in literature discussion groups (LDG) (see Dorn and Soffos 2005). The LDG groups are not static; from time to time Sheena changes the groups based on interest levels and other important needs. All groups are reading fables as part of the third-grade unit of study.

The LDG framework is designed to promote deeper comprehension through units of study. The students have learned about fables during language and writing workshops. Now in reading workshop, they are reading and discussing books within the fable unit. The LDG follows a predictable five-step format, which takes place over three to four days (see Dorn and Soffos 2005; Henderson and Dorn 2011):

1. Day 1: Previewing and selecting books within the genre unit. Sheena believes that choice is an important factor in reading motivation, but she knows that beginning readers need teacher guidance to select books they can read with minimal assistance. Therefore, she uses a "managed choice" format, which includes six procedures: (1) she preselects three or four books within a unit; (2) she presents a brief book talk on each book; (3) she reminds the students of how good readers preview books (a strategic activity that was previously taught during a mini-lesson); (4) the students use previewing strategies, such as reading the front and inside flaps and back cover; reading the first page or lead paragraph; and looking at illustrations, figures, or other visual features; (5) the students rank each book in order of reading preference; and (6) she prompts the students to explain their rationale for each book choice.

2. Setting a purpose for reading and using a reader response log. After the books are selected, Sheena provides a book orientation for the first choice. She reminds the students to use comprehension strategies to help themselves when reading and to flag places where they encounter difficulty. She gives them a purpose for reading, and she explains that while they are reading, they should use their reader response log as a resource to, for instance, write questions, take notes, make comments, sketch ideas, and record vocabulary. She reminds them to bring their reader response logs to the book discussion the next day.

3. Independent silent reading. Next, Sheena instructs the students to find a comfortable spot in the room and begin reading silently. During this component, she meets with the next reading group.

4. Day 2: Teacher conferences. During reading workshop, Sheena conducts one-on-one reading conferences with each student. The reading conference is generally three to five minutes and is highly personalized to meet the unique needs of the individual. Sheena uses this personal experience to accomplish four goals: (1) interact with the student about the message to ensure that the student is comprehending the text, (2) assess the student's oral fluency by having him read aloud a short selection in the text, (3) address a significant area in decoding or vocabulary, and (4) prepare the student to engage in the upcoming book discussion.

5. Book discussion and conversational moves. An important goal of the LDG is to promote deep comprehension through interactive dialogue and conversational moves (norms) that keep the discussion in motion. Before the first book discussion, Sheena introduces the students to conversational norms, such as agreeing or disagreeing with each other, expressing confusion when puzzled, seeking or giving clarification, comparing ideas, and offering evidence. Generally, she introduces one or two moves at a time, records these on an anchor chart, and engages the students in practicing the language during the book discussion. For example, she might model, "Does anyone agree with Jaylon?" or "Can anyone provide evidence for what Brittany just said?" Sheena and her students co-construct an anchor chart titled "Our Literature Discussion Guidelines," which is used as a resource for mediating interactive and thoughtful book discussions (see Figure 9.2).

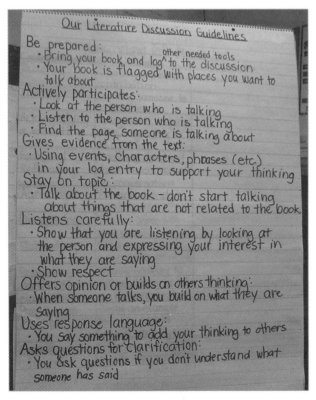

Figure 9.2 Anchor chart of "Our Literature Discussion Guidelines."

6. Independent writing about reading. In LDG, the students use a reader response log for writing about their reading (see Figures 2.6a and 2.6b; also see Dorn and Soffos 2005). The first section, "My

Thinking," is where students write personal reactions to the text, questions for the author, summaries or retellings, and a variety of other thoughtful responses. The second section, "Language Study," is the place where students can record particular language from books they are reading, such as interesting phrases, transitional words, figurative language, strong verbs, and good leads. This section can also be used during the word study component. For example, earlier in the day, Sheena instructed the students to use this section to record their learning about prefixes. The third section, "Text Studies," is used for literary definitions, text and genre maps, lists of mentor texts, and other related information. After the book discussion, Sheena instructs the students to write independently in their reader response log while she meets with another group of students.

Reading Workshop Debriefing

The debriefing component pulls together the minilesson and independent work, thus bringing the reading workshop to closure. The students bring their reading logs, plus a book where they used inferences to comprehend the text at a deeper level. As Sheena calls on a few students to share examples, she assesses their knowledge of this comprehending strategy.

Content Workshop

Sheena recognizes that her students must transfer their reading strategies and skills into content workshop. This is true evidence of an integrated curriculum. In science, during the past two weeks, the students have been studying the solar system, and today they are focusing on the sun. Sheena has gathered many books on the solar system and the sun in particular. She has entered several YouTube and Internet sites into her whiteboard to make learning come alive for her students. In addition, she has set up projects in the research section of the room and identified reader response activities to deepen comprehension from the science textbook.

Sheena introduces the science big idea that most of Earth's living things depend on the sun to survive. She asks, "What words come to mind when you think about the sun?" As students share their words, Sheena writes them on chart paper and guides the students to discuss how each word is related to the sun. Next, she displays the first section about the sun on the whiteboard. She and the students read the passage together and stop at critical points in the text to discuss key concepts. Sheena begins an anchor chart on the sun (see Figure 9.3).

Page	Main Idea	Supporting Details
298	The sun is a star.	Not a planet, a medium sized star, but looks big to us because it's the closest one
300	The sun is the center of our solar-system.	Also called heliocentric system, all planets circle sun and are held by sun's gravity

Figure 9.3 Anchor chart on the sun.

As the whole-group lesson concludes, Sheena assigns the students to small groups to collaborate on the following tasks:

- Why do you think Ptolemy and other astronomers believed Earth was the center of the solar system? Write about your thinking in your reader response log and share.
- How are the sun and Earth alike? How are they different? Write about your thinking in your reader response log and share.
- Why are spacecraft sent into space to collect information about the sun? Write about your thinking in your reader response log and share.
- Look at the poster in the research center. Describe and explain the aurora borealis to someone who has never seen this light display. Use details from the picture to support your answer.

Debriefing Content Lesson

During the last ten minutes of the content workshop, Sheena pulls the small groups together for a whole-class discussion. She invites a few students to share their work while encouraging others to ask questions and provide feedback. She keeps a record of which students contribute each day, ensuring that each student has an opportunity to share across the week. She uses the last few minutes to clarify any confusion and prepare the students for the next day's work.

Sheena's Theory of Instruction

Sheena believes that children learn best when the curriculum is integrated. Her theory guides her instructional planning. She uses her state standards, as well as the Common Core State Standards (NGA/CCSSO 2010), to create units of study in science and social studies that enable her students to develop deeper understandings in essential areas. When concepts are new, she begins with a common, everyday experience; then she introduces the new information, thus moving the learning from the concrete to the abstract. Her theory is grounded in a sociocognitive approach, including opportunities for children to collaborate on projects and learn together. She incorporates modeling and scaffolding techniques into her teaching demonstrations, and views assessment and instruction as reciprocal processes. Sheena holds a theory of responsive teaching, and she is meeting the needs of all her students through an integrated workshop framework.

A Look Inside a First-Grade Classroom

In this final section, we look inside a first-grade classroom that uses a two-and-a-half-hour language workshop for delivering literacy instruction (see Figure 8.5 schedule). Angela collaborates with Carla, the intervention specialist (see Chapter 10), in meeting the diverse needs of her struggling readers.

Whole-Group Shared Reading

Angela calls her class of emergent to early readers together and begins the morning with shared reading. Instead of following a prescribed scope and sequence for teaching concepts about print and letter-sound relationships, Angela plans each day's lesson to respond to the strengths and needs of the children. She realizes the importance of designing instruction aimed at their learning zones. The activities she chooses validate old knowledge and activate new learning.

Today, as soon as the children are gathered on the carpet in the shared reading corner, Angela introduces a familiar nursery rhyme: "I have a rhyme today about a little boy named Jack." The children guess "Little Jack Horner" and "Jack and Jill," but Angela has selected "Jack Be Nimble." After reciting the rhyme aloud, she shows the children a large, colorful copy of the poem. Using a chopstick for a pointer, she points to each word as the children read with her. As they reread the poem, Angela's voice pauses and drops off at certain points so the children can make predictions based on the pattern.

Next Angela invites Marty to come up and use the pointer as she asks important questions that direct the children's attention to concepts about print:

- Where do I begin reading?
- Which way do I go?
- Where do I go after that?

After Marty successfully demonstrates his knowledge of these print conventions, Angela displays the poem on the whiteboard. On this copy, she has left out Jack's name. Some of the children immediately comment on this. "That's right," says Angela. "I wonder whose name I could put in Jack's place." The children perk up as Angela writes Landon's name in the blank space in the poem. Angela guides the children in a shared reading of the poem with Landon's name; then she calls on Landon to demonstrate some more print concepts. She gives him a "magic highlighter paddle." (This is a small white wooden paddle that Angela uses to focus the children's attention on specific visual aspects of the text; she has several paddles of various sizes to accommodate letters, chunks, words, and phrases.) She tells Landon, "Find your name in the poem and pull it out with the magic paddle." Landon places the paddle against the poem on the wall, and as he slowly pulls it away, he pulls his name out of the text. The children lean forward, fascinated, as Landon moves the paddle back toward the wall and replaces his name in the poem. Then Angela hands Landon a chopstick to use as a pointer and asks him to point to the words as the children read the rhyme together.

"I've got a rhyme about a star," Angela says next. Some children squeal with delight as their predictions of "Star Light, Star Bright" are confirmed. Angela goes through the same steps, reciting the poem orally before introducing the print, pointer, and print-concepts questions. However, this time Angela has the children locate several words in the poem that they can use to monitor their reading. Angela uses a focus frame (a colored transparency with a "window" cut out of it) to direct the children's attention to particular words in the text. The frame colors over the entire poem, and only the word or letter shows through the window in black print. Today Angela has one child locate the known word *I* in several places.

Next, Angela has the children apply their knowledge of rhyme and searching strategies by prompting them to locate two words that rhyme—*light* and *bright*. Angela takes the learning to a new level of visual analysis by asking the children to tell her how the two words are alike.

Next, Angela points to the picture of a monkey on the alphabet chart and writes the word *day* on the whiteboard. She says, "Can you find a word in our poem that starts like *monkey* and rhymes with *day*?"

The children exclaim, "May!" Angela asks Alissa to use the focus frame to locate the word *may* in the poem. After Alissa successfully frames the word, Angela writes it on the whiteboard underneath the word *day*. She prompts the children to articulate their analysis: "How did you know that this word was *may*?"

Chaddrick responds, "Because it starts with an *m* and rhymes with *day*." Angela uses precise language to confirm how using what they know about two words can help them learn a new word. A second, fluent rereading of the poem follows these quick, focused activities.

The children respond eagerly as Angela pulls out a chart with a poem printed on it in large black letters with large spaces. As Angela points to each word, the children join in the reading. It is clear they have read the poem before.

When the poem has been read and enjoyed several times, Angela passes out sentence strips on which she has printed the lines of the poem. She assembles a second set of sentence strips in the pocket chart and has the children search their sentence strips for each line of the poem. Several children need the model of the poem for support to match the lines of the text visually. They eagerly place their sentence strips on top of the model in the pocket chart to rebuild the poem. As each child adds a sentence, he or she uses the pointer and rereads the sentence. Some children need Angela to guide their hands to match the print to their spoken words.

Now Angela increases the difficulty of the task by passing out individual word cards to each child. The children eagerly compare their cards with the text displayed in the pocket chart. They reread the text before adding each word so that they can predict the next word needed.

Finally, Angela announces, "It's rhythm-and-rhyme time. Who can tell me two words in our poem that rhyme?" The children respond with *day* and *play*. Angela directs the children to reread the poem and find the two words. When they locate *day* and *play*, Angela pulls these word cards out of the poem and inserts them in a second pocket chart. She asks the children to tell her how the words are alike. The children respond that both words have the letters *ay*. She praises them for their careful observation and highlights the *ay* pattern as she explains that this chunk can help them think about some other words that they want to read and write.

To demonstrate how to use a knowledge of beginning sounds and ending patterns to read new words, Angela quickly writes the words *day* and *play* on the dry erase board and underlines the *ay* chunk. Then she says, "If you know *day* and *play*, that can help you figure out my new word." Angela writes the word *may* on the board. The children shout out the word. Angela prompts the children to articulate their knowledge: "How did you know that my new word was *may*?" The children point out the ending pattern. Angela then guides them through one more example of the *ay* pattern, reminding them that using words that they know can help them when they get to a new word that they want to read and write. The poem is reread fluently one more time.

After a little stretching exercise, the children move on to a final shared reading activity. Today Angela introduces a new Big Book called *Where Do Monsters Live?* (Williams 1994). She has chosen the book because it has a very predictable, repetitive sentence pattern; pictures that support the sentence pattern; and an excellent text layout (consistent print placement, large type, and adequate spaces). In addition, its subject appeals to the children.

Angela guides the children to make predictions from the pictures and story line: "The title of our book is *Where Do Monsters Live?* I wonder where they might live."

Several voices chime in with a common prediction: "Under the bed!" Angela validates their response; then she invites the children to look at and discuss the pictures in the story. The children laugh with enjoyment at one they say is "a polka-dotted monster!" Although the text identifies the monster as "spotted," Angela chooses to ignore the children's substitution because (1) it is meaningful and (2) it presents an opportunity to direct the children's attention to first-letter cues. After the prediscussion, Angela turns to the page with the monster and comments, "On this page, you called the monster polka-dotted. Could we also call him a spotted monster?" The children say yes. Then Angela lets the children hear the beginning sound in the word *spotted*, stressing the *s*: "What can you hear at the beginning of *spotted*?" The children exclaim, "*S*!" "Yes," says Angela. "Who can find the word *spotted* in our story?" Sarah comes to the chart and locates the word. As she frames it with the framing card, she comments, "That's like in my name." Angela then asks whether anyone can find the word *a* on the first page. She invites Kimberly to locate it in the text. Next, Angela prompts the children to search the page to find it in another place. Brittany locates a capital *A*. Angela praises the children and reminds them, "Words you know can help you keep your place when you are reading."

Angela points to each word as she reads the book aloud, thus modeling the relationship between spoken and written language. The children quickly pick up the structural pattern and join in the reading. Angela pauses at appropriate points to allow the children to predict a word from the rhyming patterns of the language and from the picture cues. A second reading of the text follows the first, with even greater participation by the children. Through repeated readings of the text, the children are able to make predictions faster and apply reading strategies.

At the end of the shared reading session, Angela tells the children to check the assignment board and go to the designated literacy centers (see Chapter 8). Before she calls her first guided reading group, she glances quickly around the room to ensure that all children are on task.

Small-Group Guided Reading

Walking to the guided reading corner of the room, Angela is pleased to see that the children are reading familiar books from their individual book boxes, texts they have previously read during their guided reading lessons. Angela has carefully selected these books to build on the children's current knowledge and to promote the acquisition of successful reading strategies. The five children in this group of early readers are at the same instructional level, as determined by Angela's observations of their reading and writing behavior during shared reading, familiar reading, interactive writing, and independent writing.

As the children read, Angela observes their behavior, asks questions that promote problem solving, and takes running records on one or two children. She carries a composition notebook with the children's names written on plastic tabs that extend beyond the sides of the pages—a simple record-keeping tool that lets her maintain ongoing documentation on which to base her assessment of the children's progress over time.

After checking that the other children are working productively in the literacy corners, Angela tells the guided reading group that she is going to introduce a new book. The book she has selected, *The Cake That Mack Ate* (Robart 1986), includes opportunities for the children to practice old learning (in the zone of actual level) and to work with new learning (in the zone of proximal development). It is a cumulative, repetitive book about all the ingredients that went into the cake that Mack ate.

Angela begins by talking about the main idea of the story and guiding the children to discuss the pictures. She skillfully uses some of the vocabulary and phrases the children will encounter in the story—*who, this is the,* and *that went into the cake that Mack ate.* Next, Angela prompts the children to predict the letters they will see in the words *ate* and *that.* The children successfully locate and frame each word. Finally, Angela guides the children to reflect on the strategies that good readers use when they come to an unknown word. The children suggest a variety of things to do—rereading, making the sound for the first letter, looking at the picture, thinking about what would happen in the story, and sounding out the word. Angela confirms these suggestions and restates the behavior she wants to see them using when they read.

The children begin reading the story in whispers while Angela moves around the circle and listens in. She guides and prompts the children to use particular strategies to help them figure out unknown words. She notices that Brittany is having trouble with the word *planted:*

Brittany: (*Reading*) "This is the farmer who . . ." (*Hesitating*)

Angela: Why did you stop?

Brittany: (*Monitoring by rereading up to the unknown word*) "This is the farmer who . . ." (*Stopping*)

Angela: Is there a part of the word that you know?

Brittany: (*Sounding the letters*) Pl—pl—.

Angela: Think about what the farmer is going to do with the seeds. Go back and reread, and think of what would make sense and start with those letters.

Brittany: "This is the farmer who planted the seed that grew into the corn that went into the cake that Mack ate."

After this first reading, Angela gives the children an opportunity to reread. Rather than focus on specific words, she chooses a teaching point that will help the children apply the checking and confirming strategies that are part of an effective processing system. Several children, Brittany among them, are not initiating effective responses to unknown words without prompting. They need repeated practice with successful strategies to develop a conceptual understanding of the significance of problem solving. Angela therefore decides to direct the children's attention explicitly to the importance of predicting and confirming textual information based on accumulating visual cues. She uses the cloze procedure on a sentence from the text to guide the children through the process of using first letters to initiate a fast response, looking at the rest of the word to collect more information, and confirming these sources with the meaning of the text. (See Chapter 3 for more on how to do the cloze procedure.)

After the guided reading lesson, *The Cake That Mack Ate* goes into the children's book boxes. During the next guided reading lesson, Angela will take a running record on one or two children's reading of this book. Now she signals that it is time to change literacy centers and guided reading groups. Angela's schedule allows her to see two guided reading groups each day for approximately twenty minutes each. (Chapter 8 discusses daily schedules in detail.) After the children in the second guided reading group have completed their lesson, Angela announces that it is time to rotate literacy centers once again.

Small-Group Assisted Writing

Angela's first assisted writing group is made up of children whose writing abilities have moved beyond very basic interactive writing. The children are fairly adept at hearing sounds in words and applying the basic print concepts. They are now ready to hear sounds in sequence and use words they know to write other words by simple analogy. Angela therefore provides opportunities to apply these new problem-solving processes. She is also aware that the children are able to compose longer texts with more details and logical sequences. Today Angela and the children co-construct a story based on a personal experience that has happened to Angela. The result is a clear, well-formed story that activates the children's imagination and communicates Angela's distress: "I got mad when I had to take out the trash in the rain. I tripped over the curb and spilled the trash can in the street. I was soaking wet and muddy after I picked it all up."

Next Angela helps the children learn about simple analogies:

Angela: Let's go back and reread our story so far.
Children: "I got . . . (*rereading and predicting the word* mad) mad."
Angela: Mad. Do you know another word that can help you think about the word *mad*?
Several children: *Dad!*
Angela: Write *dad* on your boards. (*They write the word on their dry erase boards.*) Now erase the *d*. What is the chunk you have left?
Rose: *Ad.*
Angela: Now put an *m* in front of the *ad* chunk. What new word did you make?

Children: *Mad.*
Angela: Let's try it with one more word. What letter do you need to change *mad* into *sad*? (*The children quickly erase the* m *and add an* s.) Say and check it with your finger to be sure you are right.
Children: (*Confirming the word*) *Sad.*
Angela: Now what is the word in our story?
All: (*Rereading*) "I got . . . mad."
Angela: Rose, come write the word in the story. I want everyone else to erase your board and then write the word *mad* quickly and check it.

Angela continues to guide the children to record the story. Throughout the process, she models important behavior, such as saying words slowly, making multiple attempts on the whiteboard, using word analogies, and rereading the text after each problem-solving attempt. She uses two additional examples in keeping with her focus on teaching the children a strategy for word analysis: *will, bill, spill* and *get, bet, wet.* At the end of this interactive writing lesson, the children fluently reread the story.

Small-Group Writing Aloud

Before sitting down to work with her next group, Angela checks that the literacy-center rotation went smoothly and that the other children are working appropriately. This group of children is in a transitional stage of spelling development. Angela needs to coach them to think about the visual spelling patterns in the words they want to write.

During the lesson, Angela will also guide the children to compose longer and more descriptive texts. She began this yesterday by composing her own story in front of the group and modeling revising and editing skills using the whiteboard. The children helped her, and at the end of yesterday's lesson Angela asked them each to select one piece of their own writing to be revised and edited.

Today Ariana's work is displayed on the whiteboard. It is a piece of nonfiction about animals. First, Ariana reads her piece, and Angela praises her for writing a good story about penguins. Then Angela points out a list of questions designed to prompt Ariana to clarify meaning and add descriptive details:

1. Did I tell the name of the animal?
2. Did I tell where the animal lives?

3. Did I describe what the animal looks like?
4. Did I tell what the animal eats?
5. Did I tell one or two other important or interesting facts about the animal?

She includes all the children in the group in the process: "Let's look at the checklist and see if Ariana has included all the information that we need when we write about animals." Angela then invites Ariana to reread the story. Ariana immediately exclaims, "I forgot to tell what kind of animal a penguin is." Angela shows the group how to make additions to a story:

Angela: Where should you add that in your story?
Ariana: It needs to be at the beginning.
Angela: Let me show you what we can do when we want to add a sentence. We use this little mark called a caret. (*She draws a caret.*) Now you can write the sentence right here. (*Ariana adds the sentence to the beginning of her story by writing on the whiteboard.*)

Angela asks Ariana to reread the first two sentences of her story. Then she continues guiding the revising process, asking the group to read the story and check for any other sentences that tell how the penguins look. They find two such sentences at the end of Ariana's story, and Angela tells Ariana to circle them.

Angela: Would it make sense to move those two sentences to the beginning of the story with the other sentence that tells how the penguins look?
Children: Yes!
(*Angela draws an arrow on the whiteboard.*)
Angela: We can do that by drawing an arrow from those sentences to where we want them to be moved.

Ariana next decides she wants to add some other interesting facts about penguins. Since there isn't enough room on the page, Angela shows her how to draw a star on the story at the place where she wants to insert the new sentence, draw the same star on another piece of paper, and add the new information (see Figure 9.4).

Angela concludes the lesson by having the children reread the entire story together. She praises Ariana for including so many fascinating facts about

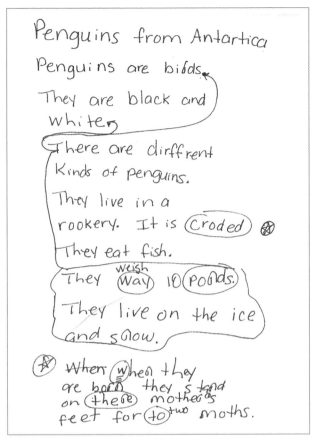

Figure 9.4 Ariana's story draft.

Figure 9.5 Ariana's final draft.

penguins. The children are now ready to revise their own stories about animals.

Tomorrow Angela will use Ariana's story again, this time to edit for spelling and punctuation. The final draft (Figure 9.5) is bound into a large book titled *Animal Facts,* which is placed in the reading corner.

Independent Writing and Teacher Conferences

After Angela finishes the writing aloud, she pulls the children together as a whole group and they begin writing in their journals. During this writing block, Angela supports the children in three ways:

1. She circulates among them and observes how they are doing. She makes sure that everyone is on task and prepared to begin a new text or continue working on a piece already in progress. If anyone appears to need extra support, she coaches in appropriate ways.

2. She selects two or three children each day for focused conferences. This allows her to meet individually with all the children within a two-week period. These personal conferences are in addition to daily observations of and drop-in support for all the children.

3. She circulates among the children one last time and observes where they are in their writing. She occasionally stops by a child's desk and makes a relevant comment about his or her work.

Today Angela calls Chaddrick to the conference table. Chaddrick is an early writer at the phonetic spelling stage. He has control over a few frequently encountered words, can articulate words slowly, and can hear most consonant sounds in sequence. Angela is working to help Chaddrick make an important transition in his writing: to use visual information from a word he knows to write other words. She is also helping him acquire important strategies for remembering how words look.

The ultimate goal of every conference is for the child to value writing as an important means of communication. Thus, every conference begins with a sincere response to the message. Then, during the conference, Angela adjusts her support to accommodate Chaddrick's understanding of the task at hand. She uses instructional language to validate old knowledge and activate new learning. Today Chaddrick is eager to compose a new story, which he immediately does. With excitement he tells Angela, "Me and my friend are going to play football."

After Angela reacts to the message, she supports Chaddrick as he records his story in his journal. "How are you going to start it?" she asks. Chaddrick says the word *me* and fluently writes it down. When he hesitates on the word *and,* Angela prompts, "Try it out on the practice page." Chaddrick writes it quickly, says, "Oh, yeah," and then adds the word to his story. After he finishes writing his story, Angela praises him for his correct letter-sound associations by placing a light checkmark above them on his paper. Then she prompts him to reread his story and draw a picture to support the text (see Figure 9.6). As Angela walks away, she comments, "Tomorrow, you might like to write about the football game. Then you can make it into a longer story and put it into the class book."

Circulating among the other writers, Angela observes them and makes appropriate responses according to the children's strengths and needs. Then she returns to the conference table and calls for Nick to bring his story over for revising and editing. Nick's story is about his friend's bicycle wreck and the trip to the hospital. Angela's goal in this conference is to prepare the story for publication. First she prompts

Figure 9.6 Chaddrick's story.

Nick to reread the story for clarity of message. Then she asks him to circle the spellings of words he will need to check. As Nick reads his story, he corrects the spellings for *went, friend,* and *stamp;* inserts the phrase *on the ground* to expand meaning; ads the word *and* to connect two thoughts; and tries out the spelling for the word *hospital* (see Figure 9.7). Angela coaches Nick to think about how words look and then to use the dictionary to check his work. At the end of the conference, Angela suggests that Nick rewrite his story and put it in the class publication box.

Now Angela calls Tranisha to the conference table. Tranisha brings a story she began yesterday, which was based on her sister's trip to the nurse to get a shot. Thus far, Tranisha has written the first three sentences of her story: "One day my sister was sick. My mom took her to the nurse. The nurse got her a shot and she got a sore."

As she does in all her conferences, Angela invites Tranisha to read her story, then reacts to it: "Ohhh, that must have hurt!" In conversation, Angela coaches

Tranisha to add details to her story: "What happened after your sister got the shot?" As Tranisha begins to expand on the event, Angela encourages her to record her thoughts on paper so that other people can read her story. As she talks, Tranisha adds two new details to her text, which now has a humorous ending: "And we went home and my sister said, '"You need a shot. No, I don't. You need another."' (See Figure 9.8.)

This concludes the individual conferences, and Angela now conducts a few drop-in conferences with several other children. There are twenty children in the class, and Angela recognizes their diverse needs. They are working at different points in their writing. They are using a variety of resources: ABC charts, picture dictionaries, and "word strips" of frequently encountered words taped to their desks. They are also using a variety of writing materials: unlined and lined paper, pencils and felt-tip markers, composition notebooks, and bound journals. Angela instructs her emergent and early writers to use unlined paper, so that the lines do not restrict their writing forms. As the children be-

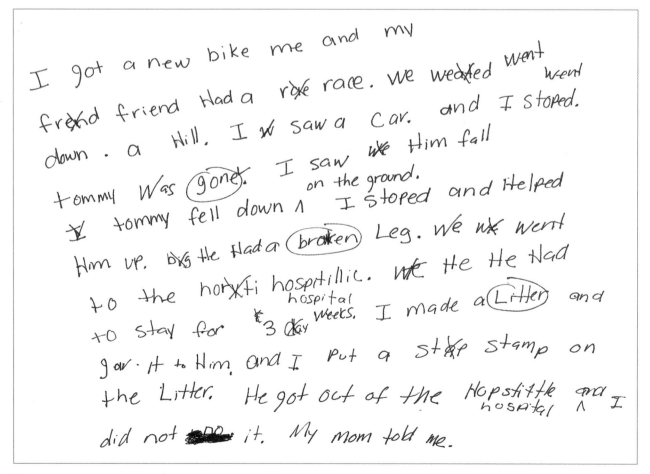

Figure 9.7 Nick's writing sample.

One day my Sister was
sikk my mom took her to
the nurse the nurse got her a
shot an She got a s m.
and we went home and my
Siste Say you ned asm.
tha no I don you ned antKer.

Figure 9.8 Tranisha's writing sample.

come more accomplished writers, Angela gives them lined tablets. Ariana's first draft was written on lined paper; other children, like Nick, choose to write their first draft on unlined paper. However, when a text is ready for publication, Angela encourages the children to rewrite it neatly on lined paper. Some children type the stories on the class computer. Although Angela believes it is important for the children to use a variety of writing materials, she insists that any published texts be presented in a format that frees the reader's attention to focus on meaning and enjoyment.

Word Study

Again, Angela signals that it is time for the children to put away their writing and prepare for the next literacy block—word study. During this time, Angela leads the whole class in instructional word-building activities designed to help learners identify words.

With the children seated at their desks, table monitors quickly pass out small letter cards for the consonants *b, c, d, m, r, s,* and *t* and the vowels *e* and *a*. Angela tells the children they will be making some words today that end in the chunk of letters *eam*. On the large magnetic board at the front of the room, she pulls three magnetic letters together to make the *eam* pattern. Then she prompts, "Look at the letters and say the chunk." Next she coaches, "Find the letters on your desk to make the *eam* chunk." After the children accomplish this task, she asks, "What letters

did you use? What sound did you make?" Angela now guides the children to apply this knowledge at a new level: "Find the letter that starts like *bike* and make the word *beam*." Quickly, the children pull down the *b* and place it in front of the chunk. When Angela is sure that all the children understand the significance of using first-letter cues to make a word, she goes to her magnetic board and pulls the *b* letter in front of the *eam* chunk. Then she asks the children to confirm their word with the one on the board.

Angela goes on to prompt the children to new constructive activity: "Change *beam* into the word *seam* by changing just one letter." Walking around the room, Angela notices that Christy has spelled it c-e-a-m. Angela increases her support:

Angela: That was a good try, Christy. The letter *c* does sometimes sound like the beginning of the word *seam*. But there is another letter that makes that sound. Look on the alphabet chart and find another letter that sounds like *seam*.

(*Christy finds the letter* s *on the alphabet chart.*)
Christy: S—sailboat.
Angela: Are you right? Say seam—sailboat.
Christy: Seam—sailboat. Yes, it's an *s*.
Angela: See if you can fix it.

Christy corrects the word. Angela calls Brittany to the magnetic board to build the word *seam* under the word *beam*. Then she instructs the children to make the word *team* before moving on to some words that have blends at the beginning. She coaches and scaffolds based on her observations of individual students. Some children need specific letter-cue prompts and closer supervision.

At the end of the lesson, Angela has the children articulate how all the words are alike by examining the letter pattern at the end of each word. Next she links the task to writing by directing the children's attention to the word *dream* on the board. She models how to add the *ing* chunk on the end of the word to make the word *dreaming*. She coaches, "Now, let's think of other words that have the *ing* chunk on the end of the word." The children raise their hands enthusiastically and begin to call out words: *jumping, climbing, reading, laughing*. As the children dictate the words, Angela lists them on the board. Then she asks, "What is the same in each word?"

The children exclaim, "The *ing* on the end."

Finally, Angela writes on the board, "I can hear you screaming." She says, "Find something about the last word that you know." Some children point out the *eam* chunk, and others point out the *ing* chunk. Angela then guides the children to read the sentence and use what they know about the word to help them. When they come to the new word, Angela articulates the *scr* pattern and the children fluently complete the word.

Angela's Theory of Instruction

In Angela's first-grade classroom, her students have numerous opportunities to read and write in their learning zones. She observes them and provides scaffolds commensurate with their needs. During small-group reading and writing activities, she provides instruction aimed at her students' potential levels of development. During independent activities in the literacy corners, she provides flexible opportunities for students to use their knowledge and practice their strategies on easy and familiar tasks.

Angela understands the importance of a well-organized and predictable classroom environment that builds on instructional routines for promoting children's independence. In line with literacy apprenticeship, Angela uses language for various purposes, including modeling, coaching, and scaffolding the children's learning. She promotes the children's conscious awareness of their problem-solving actions as she encourages them to articulate and reflect on their literate behavior. Through guided participation, Angela enables her children to accomplish tasks with her help that they would be unable to accomplish alone. And as the children become more competent learners, Angela will create new transitional moves that reflect their increasing control.

Closing Thoughts

In this chapter, we have shared a look inside the classrooms of two exemplary teachers with a strong theory of teaching and learning. In classrooms such as these, most children will become successful readers without supplemental help. However, a small population (less than 20 percent) will need more intensive intervention from a reading specialist, in addition to high-quality classroom instruction. In the next chapter, we look at how Carla, a reading specialist, provides reading and writing interventions to struggling readers in Angela's first-grade classroom.

chapter ten

SUPPLEMENTARY SUPPORT FOR STRUGGLING READERS

Most children will achieve reading proficiency with high-quality, differentiated classroom instruction. Indeed, classroom instruction is the first line of defense against reading failure. If the child is lagging behind his peers, the classroom teacher provides tailored support during small-group instruction and one-on-one conferences. However, we know that some children will need supplemental support from a reading specialist to close the literacy gap. For those children, it is crucial that the classroom teacher and intervention teacher plan together to promote instructional congruency. If this does not occur, poor readers may have difficulty transferring their knowledge, skills, and strategies from one context to another. Schools should implement a wraparound approach where struggling readers are immersed in congruent, high-quality instruction across multiple contexts that include varying degrees of teacher assistance (Dorn and Schubert 2008; see Figure 10.1). This approach is conceptualized in the Comprehensive Intervention Model, which includes a portfolio of small-group interventions that align with classroom instruction (see Dorn and Soffos 2011).

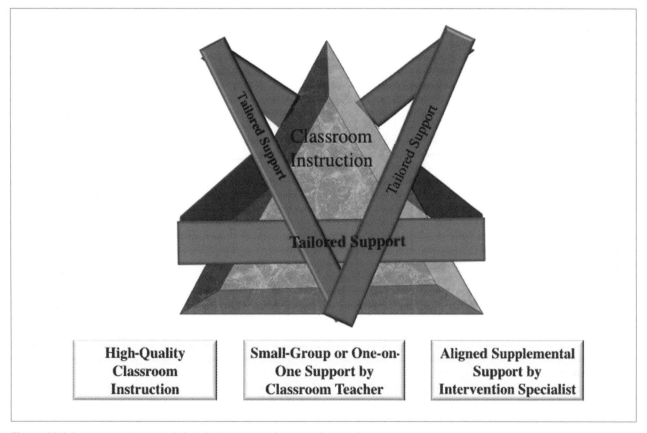

Figure 10.1 A wraparound approach for aligning support for struggling readers.

In previous chapters, we focused on the role of the classroom teacher in meeting the needs of struggling readers within the classroom setting. In this chapter, we describe the role of the intervention specialist for providing supplemental (and complementary) support to the most at-risk readers from the classroom. First, we describe two small-group interventions: interactive writing intervention and writing-aloud intervention. Then, we present an example of guided reading with the same group of students at two points in time.

Interactive Writing Intervention

The interactive writing intervention is similar to the interactive writing lesson of the classroom (see Chapter 5; also see Dorn and Soffos 2011). The intervention is organized to span two thirty-minute phases: a reading phase and a writing phase. During Phase 1, the children acquire valuable reading experiences that they will use during the writing phase, which occurs on the following day. The reciprocity of reading and writing is essential for accelerating reading development.

In this example, Carla provides an interactive writing intervention for thirty minutes daily to four beginning early readers. On Day 1, she focuses on three components: shared reading, reading of the ABC chart, and letter and word work. On Day 2, she focuses on four components: read-aloud, interactive writing, independent writing with teacher conferences, and follow-up discussion. To promote the transfer of reading to writing, she uses prompts such as, "What did you learn from reading today that will help you in writing?" Group activities are structured in a predictable format that promotes the children's independence.

The Reading Phase of Interactive Writing

When the children enter the room, they are familiar with the routine. Without hesitation, they come to the carpet to begin the shared reading component of their lesson. Carla, their intervention specialist, has designed a well-organized space to promote student engagement. Her teaching materials include an easel, a flipchart, several large laminated poems, a large alphabet chart, ABC books, and three or four pocket charts for manipulating rhyming words and matching sentence strips. In addition to these group materials, each child has a special place on the rug with a small basket of personal materials: a small ABC chart, a small magnetic dry erase board, one dry erase marker, one black felt-tip marker, a small container with magnetic letters, and a personal dictionary for recording frequently encountered words.

Carla directs the children to a pocket chart displaying a familiar poem, written on sentence strips, about a little turtle that lives in a box and catches different creatures. Carla chooses this particular poem, which is a favorite of the group's, because she knows the children enjoy its rhythm, rhyme, and opportunities for movement and because the text contains some supportive features that will build on their reading strengths. For example, the distinct placement of the word *he* at the beginning of most lines provides a nice visual anchor. The text also contains rhyming word patterns, which will help the children hear the language patterns before paying attention to the visual chunks.

Carla and the children begin reading this familiar poem expressively and fluently. The children's eyes follow the pointer as Carla explicitly demonstrates early behavior such as starting position, one-to-one matching, and return sweep. As the children read along, Carla observes their emotional response to the story as they engage in the movements being described and predict upcoming words based on the natural rhythm of the language.

After the reading, Carla calls Billy to the chart and asks him to point to the top starting position and the first return sweep. (Billy is inconsistent in his control of directional movement when writing his stories, but has no difficulty with correct movement when he reads.) Billy's successful performance gives Carla a chance to highlight his actions: "Billy, you pointed to the beginning of the story and followed the first line. Then you went to the beginning of the second line. Always going in this direction can also help you when you write."

Next Carla pulls out a framing window to focus the children's attention on a known word. She asks Laterica to come to the chart and locate the word *he*. (Laterica has written the word *he* several times in her journal, so Carla expects her to be able to locate the word with ease.) After Laterica frames the word, Carla validates her action: "You found that word really fast, didn't you?" Carla then passes out to each member of the group a word card with *he* written on it. She instructs the children to match the word card to the same word in the pocket chart. After the children position their word on the appropriate spot, Carla says, "Now I want you to write the word *he* on your boards. Be sure to say the word as you write it." The children quickly write the word *he* three times.

Now Carla prompts Tyler to come to the chart and locate an unknown word based on his knowledge of a known letter, *r*. She scaffolds the process with a language cue: "Now where in the poem did the little turtle climb?" "On the rocks," the children reply. Then she says to Tyler, "What can you hear at the beginning of the word *rocks*?" "*R*," Tyler responds. Carla then prompts, "Find a word in the poem that starts like *rocks*."

After Tyler locates the new word, Carla guides the children to think of other words that begin like *rocks*. She pulls out a simple letter book that contains several words, all starting with *r*. She says to the children, "Listen to the words as I read them. Can you hear how they all start the same?" Then Carla and the children read the letter book together, paying special attention to the beginning sound.

Next, Carla directs the children's attention to a large ABC chart. The familiar pictures on the chart are special cues they use to associate letter and sound relationships while reading and writing. As Carla leads the group in a shared reading of the ABC chart, she uses a large pointer to direct the children's attention to each letter (upper- and lowercase) and each picture cue. The children read the letters fluently, and Carla pauses at appropriate points to let them say the name of a letter or identify a picture.

This component sets the stage for letter and word work. In preparation, Carla has planned a lesson that will help the children acquire fluent and flexible control of letters, sounds, and words. Today, she tells the children to take a group of preselected magnetic letters (*h, m, w, e*) from their basket and place them at the top of their board. To promote fluency with known letters, she says, "Pull each letter down fast and say the name of the letter as you pull it down." Afterward Carla asks the children to push the letters back to the top of the board. Then she focuses the children's attention on letter-sound associations by asking them to pull down the letter that makes the beginning sound

of the word *hot*. The children quickly pull down the letter *h*. Next Carla asks, "Do you know any other words that start like *hot*?" The children call out several words: *happy*, *Halloween*, and *house*. Carla writes the responses on the board. Then she does the same thing with the words *mouse* and *wet*.

Next, Carla prompts the children to use a known word to form an unknown word. She says, "Make the word *he* from your letters. Check it after you make it to be sure you are right." The children quickly construct the word; then they run their finger under it as they say the word slowly. Tyler exclaims with delight that this word was in the poem they just read. Carla then directs the children's attention to the large magnetic board on the easel, where she constructs the word *he* with magnetic letters. With the other two letters over to the side of the board, Carla demonstrates how to remove the beginning letter *h* and to insert the letter *m* in front of the *e* to make the new word *me*. She uses clear and explicit language to describe the process. As the children construct the word *me*, Carla watches them carefully to ensure that they are confirming their actions by saying the word and checking it with their finger. Since this is a new word, Carla provides them with several opportunities to learn it. First, she asks the children to write the word *me* underneath the magnetic model. Her next prompts are designed to help the children acquire a strategy for memorizing the visual pattern: "Now I want you to shut your eyes and look at the word in your head. What is the word you are looking at?"

"*Me!*" the children say.

"Tell me how it looks," Carla prompts. In unison, the children repeat the names of the letters *m-e*. Then Carla says, "Now keep your eyes shut and write the word *me* in the air three times." After this she tells them to look at the pocket chart with the poem "Little Turtle": "Can anyone locate the new word *me*?" Continuing to model the analogy process, Carla returns to the first word *he* (since this is a more secure word for the children), removes the onset letter, and replaces it with a *w* to make the new word *we*.

Again returning to the known word *he*, Carla prompts the children to make *me* one last time. Now that the children are somewhat familiar with the word, Carla asks them to open their personal dictionaries to the *m* page with its special picture cue, a mailbox. As the children start flipping through the book, Carla increases her support: "Would you find the letter *m* at the beginning, middle, or end of your dictionary?"

Tyler exclaims, "In the middle!" The children quickly find the *m* page and record the word *me*.

Carla's final question highlights the relationship between the new word and the page where it is entered: "Why did we put the word *me* on the mailbox page?"

In unison, the children say, "Because they both start with *m*."

The Writing Phase of Interactive Writing Intervention

The next day's lesson begins with the interactive writing lesson. Each child has a dry erase board, an individual alphabet chart, and a black marker for making contributions on the writing chart. During interactive writing, Carla uses her knowledge of the children's strengths to help them focus on print concepts, sounds in words, letter knowledge, and fluency. Through these experiences, the children will gain control of emergent reading and writing behavior and be able to move on to more complex learning.

To begin the lesson, Carla tells the children about her meal at McDonald's the night before. She holds up a brown paper bag bearing the McDonald's logo and asks the children, "Guess where I went to eat last night?"

"McDonald's!" the children say.

Tyler asks, "What did you eat?"

"I ate a hamburger, french fries, Coke, and ice cream, Carla answers. "I ate so much that I got a tummy ache!" The children contribute similar experiences of their own.

Then Carla guides the children to help her compose a story: "Now I want you to help me write the story. Let's think about the most important thing and write about it. What can we say?" During guided participation, the children and Carla compose the story: "I ate at McDonald's and I ate too much. I got a tummy ache!" Carla takes the children through this brief rehearsal because their control of the oral composition will help them write it down. She also realizes that oral rehearsals will not be necessary for long, because the children are quickly learning how to plan, hold, and organize their thoughts into written creations. As they become more competent writers, Carla expects them to revise and correct their messages as they transcribe their thoughts to paper. But for now, the children in this emergent group require guided participation and scaffolding to teach them the process of moving from spoken ideas to written messages.

Next, Carla asks, "What is the first word in our story?"

Without hesitation, the children respond, "*I*." All the children know this word, so Carla instructs Billy to write it on the chart while everyone else writes it on their dry erase board. As Billy approaches the chart, Carla asks, "Where should we begin writing?" prompting him to notice the starting position (since he sometimes deviates from it during journal writing). As Billy locates the starting position and correctly writes the word *I* on the page, Carla instructs the children to reread and predict the next word, so that their thoughts don't get ahead of the words actually written—as often happens with young writers. As the children reread and anticipate the upcoming word, they begin to articulate it slowly and respond with the letters and sounds they can hear within the word. They all hear the beginning sound of the word *ate*. Carla tells them to locate the letter *a* on their individual ABC charts and asks Karrisa to write the known letter on the chart. Then Carla guides the children to slowly articulate the word again and listen to the next sound. They quickly notice the *t* sound. As each letter and sound is analyzed, a child comes up to the chart and writes the known letter with his or her marker. Laterica remarks that the word *ate* needs an *e* on the end of it. Carla reinforces the importance of visual attention to words: "Yes, it needs the *e* to make the word look right." After the word is recorded in the story, Carla prompts the children to reread to see what comes next. The next word in the story is *at*. Since this is a known word, the children do not need to articulate it slowly. Instead, Carla encourages the children to write the word "fast" on their boards, and she calls Tyler to the chart to record the word in the story. Rereading the story, the children realize that the next word is *McDonald*'s. Several of them say, "*M*," and Carla writes the entire word into the story with no further analysis.

The lesson continues like this, the children continually being prompted to go back and reread to predict the next word. Carla uses the lesson as an opportunity for them to practice slow articulation of sounds within words and to promote fluency with known words. Throughout, Carla prompts them to locate and practice letter formation, spacing between words, and punctuation at the end of the sentences. She encourages them to rehearse their attempts on the practice board before recording them on the chart.

After the story is completed, Carla guides the children in a shared reading of a large interactive writing checklist. This checklist includes important behaviors relevant to where the children are in their writing development. There are currently eight checkpoints to remind them to become better writers:

1. Did I start in the right place?
2. Did I leave spaces between the words to make it easier to read?
3. Did I say the words slowly and write the letters that made those sounds?
4. Did I use the alphabet chart to help me with letters and sounds?
5. Did I reread to help me know the next word to write?
6. Did I use your practice page to help me work on the hard parts?
7. Did my story make sense?
8. Did I use an *?* or *!* or . at the end of each sentence?

Carla and the children review the points one by one to check on their group composition. The checklist is a temporary scaffold to help children learn how to assess their own work in terms of appropriate benchmarks. A reduced copy of the checklist is placed in their writing journal.

Although the written text is short, the interaction between Carla and the children is very powerful. Carla's language is specific to the learning task. She observes the children closely and monitors her support to accommodate their understanding. When the children are writing the word *and* on the dry erase boards, Billy writes *ad;* Carla coaches him to say the word slowly and listen to the letter after the *a*. She also encourages him to "feel the letter in your mouth." With this gentle reminder, Billy is able to supply the missing letter and confirm the correct spelling. Tyler notices the word *my* inside the larger word *tummy.* He

is beginning to notice visual patterns within words. Karrisa comments, "If you take off the *y* and put in an *e,* you would have the word *me.*" Her strategies for analyzing words are becoming stronger. As the children gain competence in phonemic awareness, letter identification, directionality, spacing, and control over some frequently encountered words, Carla creates transitions that move them to a higher level of cognitive activity.

Independent Writing and Teacher Conferences

Carla now tells the children that it is time for them to write their own stories: "Talk with your neighbor about a story you would like to write about today." Laterica turns to Karrisa and says, "I saw a black cat when I came to school this morning."

Karrisa giggles and says, "Last night I saw a lion." Then she laughs. "I really didn't, but I want to write it anyway." After sharing their stories, the girls get up and walk to the writing table, where they gather their journals and begin to write.

Carla glances at Tyler, who appears to be deep in thought. She asks him, "What would you like to write about today?"

Tyler immediately responds, "Rosie walked over the table."

Carla smiles. "Oh, you want to write about *Rosie's Walk*?" She knows that *Rosie's Walk* (Hutchins 1971) does not include this particular detail, but she is pleased that Tyler is embellishing the story. Billy also rehearses a message based on a familiar story: "Ten little cows are rolling in the mud." Karrisa's, Billy's, and Tyler's stories reflect their previous experiences with book structures, patterns, or vocabulary phrases.

As the children begin to write, Carla circulates among them and talks with them about their stories and their problem solving. Each child has an ABC chart, a personal dictionary, and the writing checklist to use as resources. Carla observes the children's ability to articulate words slowly; write frequently encountered words fluently; attempt words on the practice page; use spaces between words; follow directional movement across the line and return sweep; reread to predict the next word; and use the ABC chart, writing checklist, and dictionary to help solve problems. She notes that the children are applying the teacher-modeled behavior from interactive writing to their independent work. (The children's stories are shown in Figures 10.2 through 10.5.)

As Carla holds conferences with the children, she focuses on these points:

- She responds to the message with interest and enjoyment.
- She records the story correctly underneath the children's writing.
- She praises the children for concepts of print that are relevant to the children's learning zones.
- She channels the children's attention to letter-sound associations by placing a light checkmark over the children's responses.
- She points to the story copy and asks the children to read it with their finger.

Figure 10.2 Laterica's independent writing. ("I see a black cat on a fence.")

Figure 10.3 Karissa's independent writing. ("Last night I saw a lion. The lion said, 'roar!'")

Figure 10.4 Billy's independent writing. ("Ten little cows are rolling in the mud.")

Figure 10.5 Tyler's independent writing. ("Rosie walked over the table.")

Writing-Aloud Intervention

It is essential for teachers to adjust instruction to accommodate changes in students' learning, thus matching the intervention to their needs. This is the basis of accelerated learning. As discussed in Chapter 5, the writing-aloud intervention is designed for children who have good control of foundational knowledge about print but need more assistance in learning about the writing process. In this example, we look at the same students (Billy, Tyler, Karrisa, and Laterica) ten weeks later in their literacy development. At this time, the students have progressed from emergent to transitional reading levels; along the way, their intervention has shifted from interactive writing to writing aloud (see Figure 10.6 for transitions in the writing intervention).

Beginning Lessons (Emergent/Early Writers)	Later Lessons (Late Early/Transitional Writers)
shared reading of ABC chart	no longer used
shared reading of Big Books and poems	shared reading of Big Books and poems
letter and word work; high-frequency words	word study with more complex patterns; spelling charts
personal dictionary	commercial dictionary
interactive writing	writing aloud
writing checklist	editing and revising checklists
journal writing in simple sentences	long, complex texts that may span several days; writing for a variety of purposes

Figure 10.6 Transitions in writing intervention.

Writing Aloud and Independent Writing Over a Three-Day Period

Carla understands that intervention and classroom instruction must be aligned for transfer to occur. In the classroom, the students have been engaged in a unit of study with personal narrative texts. In the writing-aloud intervention, Carla guides the children to write narratives based on their own personal experiences. To model the process, she shares stories from her own life. Her oral rehearsal is a meaningful framework for actively participating in the writing. Furthermore, her expressive use of oral language prepares the children to expect the same expressive elements in the written account. Within the context of this model, the children are guided to apply problem-solving strategies and editing and revising techniques. Carla's instructional goal is achieved when the children can transfer these skills and strategies to their own work.

Day 1

The writing aloud begins as Carla gathers the children around her chair and sets the stage: "Today I have a story to tell you about when I was a little girl. I want you to listen carefully because after I have finished, you can help me write it." The children lean forward with interest.

Karrisa says, "I like your stories."

"Me too," says Tyler.

Carla begins, "When I was a little girl, I lived in this little white house on Crestwood Street and I had a brother." She leans forward slightly and raises her voice. "A pesty brother."

Laterica nods as though she can relate to this type of brother.

Realizing the importance of connecting text to life, Carla says, "You know when we read about that pesty fly who was always making us mad and getting in our way? . . . Well, that is how my brother was. He was a pesty brother!"

Carla watches the children carefully to monitor their understanding. She is prepared to rephrase or repeat information if needed. She knows that the children must understand the story in order to reconstruct it successfully.

Satisfied that the children understand, Carla expands her message with natural, descriptive language:

"He always did things to scare me. He would go out in the yard and get these creepy, crawly bugs and things, and he would throw them on me!"

"Yuk!" Laterica says.

Carla acknowledges Laterica's comment with a slight nod. "I would scream. I would go, 'Aaaa-ahhh!' Do you know what my brother would say? 'Fraidy cat, fraidy cat, fraidy cat!'"

Several voices softly echo, "Fraidy cat, fraidy cat!"

Now Carla changes her voice slightly, signaling that something important is about to happen: "One day it was kind of rainy. It had been raining a lot . . . like it has been here lately. I went into my room and heard the rain pittering and pattering on the roof; it felt so good to get into my bed and snuggle up."

Carla has set the scene extremely well, sprinkling her story with clues about the antics of her pesty brother (he liked to scare her; he would get creepy, crawly things and throw them on her). She hopes the image of a "rainy day" will trigger some expectations of what the brother might do. She continues, "Then my brother came into my room and said, 'Look at this new pair of shoes Mom brought you!' And I thought, Oh, great! I got a new pair of shoes! And I opened up the box and what do you think jumped out!" Her statement is not a question; she goes right on, her voice rising in excitement, the words tumbling out of her mouth. "A frog! It was a bullfrog! And it was going, 'Croak, croak!' It jumped up. . . . It was really big, because bullfrogs are big. It jumped on me and it scared me to death. I was screaming and Mom came running into my room."

By this time, the children are totally involved in the story. Tyler asks, "What did your mom do?"

Carla brings the story to a close: "Well, my brother got sent to his room and he was grounded for a little while. He really didn't think he did anything wrong, because he just kind of had fun doing it."

With her well-told story as background, Carla engages the children in helping her compose a written version of it. "So how am I going to start my story?"

Laterica suggests, "Once upon a time."

Carla accepts Laterica's suggestion and begins to record the phrase. When she comes to the word *upon*, she repeats it two times and says, "Is that one word or two words?"

Billy answers, "I think it's one."

Carla confirms Billy's response as she writes down

the word. She quickly rereads the phrase "Once upon a time" as a language unit and continues writing. As she writes, she thinks out loud, prompting the children to refine their knowledge of spelling patterns, something she has noticed in their journal writing. "I lived in a white house," Carla says. She writes the *h* for *house* and comments, "Now I've got to think about it, because I know two chunks that make that *ou* sound." She writes two spellings (*howse* and *house*) on the practice board and asks the children, "Which one looks right?"

The children answer, "The bottom one."

Carla records the correct spelling and continues writing. When she finishes the sentence, she and the children reread the story as it has been written so far. Some details that were part of the original story have been omitted. Carla prompts the children to recall this information. "I lived in a white house. Where was my white house? Do you think I need to tell you that? Do you think I need to tell you what street I lived on?" As she says this, she rereads the line and inserts a caret. "I lived in a white house on Crestwood Street with my dad, my mom, my sister, and my brother." She hesitates when she comes to the word *brother*. "What did I tell you about my brother that I need to put in my story? What kind of brother was he?"

Laterica and Karrisa exclaim, "Pest!"

"He was a pest brother? Does that sound . . . ?"

"Pesty!" Laterica interjects.

Carla confirms, "Pesty! Okay! That describes my brother, doesn't it!" Next she engages the children in a brief discussion about word patterns. "I've got to come down here to my practice board and try that word out. There's *pest*. What am I going to put on the end of it to make it *pesty*? Think about what we add to the end of *Tyler* to get *Tylery*."

"*Y*," the children respond.

Carla adds the *y* to the end of the word and asks, "Does that look like *pesty*? Yes, because if we took Tyler's name and put a *y* at the end of it, it would be *Tylery*. Let me try that." She writes the two words one on top of the other and invites the children to compare the endings.

"Now where am I going to add this word in the story? Would I say 'my sister and my brother pesty'?"

"No! Put it before *brother*. My pesty brother," says Billy. The writing continues, Carla guiding the children through the process of composing, editing, and revising another sentence. Details are added ("When I was a little girl"), and words are worked on within the context of the story. As the session comes to an end, Carla directs the children's attention to the writing checklist (see Chapter 5). She says, "Okay, that is as far as I am going to get with my story today. Remember, I am right here." She points to Steps 1 and 2 of the checklist. "I'm writing my story. I'm making sure it makes sense, and I'm adding to my story and crossing out what I don't want."

After the children reread the story, Tyler reminds Carla that in the original version she had described the house as a "little white house." Carla asks, "Do you think I should add that?" Then she inserts a caret before *house* and adds the new information.

Day 2

"Raise your hand and tell me where I am in the writing of my story," Carla says.

Tyler looks at the writing checklist and responds, "Writing our story and seeing if it makes sense. And crossing out the things that we don't want."

"Yes," says Carla. "So what do we need to do before we finish writing our story today?"

The children respond in unison, "Go back and reread it."

Carla and the children reread the story together. "Once upon a time, I lived in a little white house on Crestwood Street with my dad, my mom, my sister, and my pesty brother. He always picked up creepy, crawly things and threw them on me."

Now Carla picks up her marker and fluently adds new information: "Then I would scream, 'Stop, Joey!' And he would call me . . ." She pauses to invite the children to contribute.

"Fraidy!" Tyler answers.

Carla rereads the previous phrase and adds "fraidy cat" to the story. She continues thinking out loud as she records the message: "One dark rainy night, I crawled into my warm bed and went to sleep. I was sleeping so good. The rain was going drip, drip, drip on the roof." As she writes the words into the story, she says, "Doesn't that make you sleep good when you hear the rain dripping?" Interestingly, the story is being clarified. For the first time, we learn that Carla was asleep when her pesty brother came into the room.

Carla writes the following sentence: "My pesty brother crawled into my room and flipped on the light." When she hesitates momentarily at the word *light,* Billy comments, "It's like *night.*"

"Wake up, Carla! Look at what Mom brought . . . brought." Again, the hesitation in her voice signals that Carla is thinking about the word. She decides on the correct spelling for the word and records it in her story. She adds the phrase "I popped up," quickly marks through the word *I,* changes it to *My head,* and continues writing. "My head popped up fast and I saw a big shoe box. I opened the box and . . ."

The children say, "Out jumped . . ."

"Out jumped a huge bullfrog," Carla writes as she speaks. "He said, 'Croak, croak.' I screamed, 'Oh, Mom, come here!!'" Carla reflects, "What do you think Mom did?" In response, she adds the new information: "Mom came running. She saw what Joey had done. She said, 'Joey! Go to your room now!'"

"AND DON'T COME OUT!" Tyler says boldly.

Carla repeats Tyler's statement and records it in the story. She continues writing aloud. "The next morning Joey apologized and said, 'I'm sorry, I thought that is what big pesty brothers were supposed to do to little . . .'"

When she hesitates, the children call out, "Sisters!" and the story comes to an end.

"Now what do I need to do?" Carla asks.

"Go back and reread it."

"Cross out what you don't like."

"Add some more things."

Carla and the children reread the story and conclude that it is ready to be edited for punctuation the next day.

Day 3

"Look at our steps in writing. What do I need to do now?" Carla asks the children. "Okay, first I need to go back and reread it. So everybody read it with me."

After the reading, Carla prompts again, "What do I need to do now?"

"Read the story and check the punctuation," says Laterica.

"Right, I need correct punctuation so my story will make sense and sound interesting to other people," Carla says. "So where my voice stops, what am I going to put?"

"Punctuation!" Billy and Karrisa exclaim.

"Some kind of punctuation mark. It could be a period, or talking marks, or an exclamation mark," Carla explains. Tyler adds, "Or it could be a question mark!"

"What am I going to put if my voice just slows down a little?" Carla asks.

"Put a comma," Karrisa answers.

The children still need guidance in this area. They are able to talk about punctuation in an assisted situation, but their writing does not reflect their control of this behavior yet. They need lots of practice listening to how sentences with varied punctuation sound to their ears. Using this rich story as a model, Carla provides the children with opportunities to apply punctuation to enhance meaning. They reread it together with fluency and expression, and they discuss punctuation.

Independent Writing

From an apprenticeship point of view, the purpose of assisted writing is to provide children with clear models and guided practice that will carry over to their independent work. So how are these children doing in their independent writing (see children's writing samples in Figures 10.7–10.10)?

Well, there is evidence that they are applying editing and revising strategies when they compose their texts. Karrisa writes the phrase "Then I went to," rapidly draws a line through it, and revises it to reflect a new beginning ("The next morning"). Tyler edits the unnecessary word *but* from his story and continues to write quickly and fluently. All the children monitor their spellings by circling words and making new attempts.

Not surprisingly, all four children write stories that involve a brother. Karrisa, Tyler, and Laterica write about incidents in which their brother caused a problem for them. Karrisa uses the word *apologized* in her story, probably because she was exposed to it during the writing-aloud experience. Laterica uses the phrase *I'm sorry* and carries the concept further by describing her brother's punishment and his appeal to be forgiven. Tyler includes a frog in his story, also a part of Carla's story. All four children's stories are based on real events in their lives, and they are all reminiscent of Carla's story, even though there was no discussion of journal writing topics.

The children use descriptive language and complex sentence patterns to communicate their messages. Tyler expresses his feelings with his comment, "I was

Figure 10.7 Karrisa's story. ("One day when me and my brother was playing in the living room my brother hit the table. He knocked my mom's favorite glass down. He broke it. He got in trouble but I told mom what happened and then my mom said not to play in the living room again. So then my mom said go to your room. My brother did not watch tv again. Mom apologized to me. I said 'That is ok.' The next morning I woke up. My mom said 'Good morning.' I had to wake up my brother. I did not like to wake up my brother. Then I went to school.")

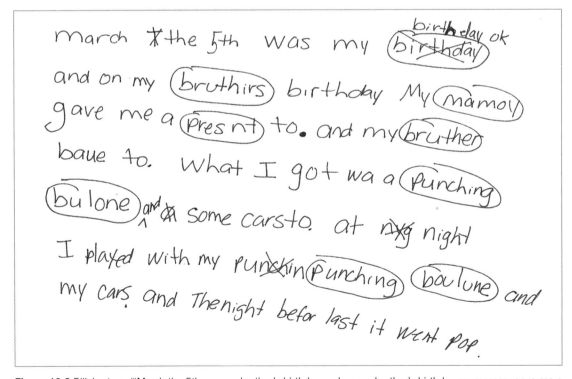

Figure 10.8 Billy's story. ("March the 5th was my brother's birthday and on my brother's birthday my mommy gave me a present too. And my brother gave (me one) too. What I got was a punching balloon and some cars too. At night I played with my punching balloon and my cars, and the night before last it went pop.")

so mad I would jump off 7 steps." The children use transitional words (*then, so, and, but, when*) to connect meaningful units and identify time elements (*one day, March the 5th, when I was a little boy, Friday*). Laterica uses dialogue that requires three types of punctuation to express the appropriate meaning (exclamation point, period, question mark). Although she is unable to apply correct punctuation, Laterica reads the story to the teacher with appropriate phrasing and intonation.

Based on Carla's writing-aloud lesson and the children's journal samples, we can assume that the children applied knowledge gained from the assisted writing activity, including concepts, vocabulary, transitional words, composing strategies, and revising and editing techniques.

At the beginning of the year, the children in Carla's literacy program needed supplemental literacy support. Their instructional program included a high degree of teacher-regulated activities, with special emphasis on modeling, coaching, and scaffolding. Ten weeks later, as they became more competent learners, their literacy lessons reflected an obvious movement toward more child-regulated activities.

A Supplemental-Reading Intervention

An important goal of a reading intervention is volume reading. Teachers must be astute observers of how children read texts with varied support (assisted versus unassisted), plus how they apply problem-solving strategies to different types of texts (familiar or easy versus new texts). In this section, we revisit Tyler, Billy, Laterica, and Karrisa at two points in their reading development (emergent and transitional levels) that correspond with their writing intervention (interactive and writing aloud). On Monday to Thursday, the children participate in the writing intervention; then on Friday, Carla provides a thirty-minute reading intervention to support

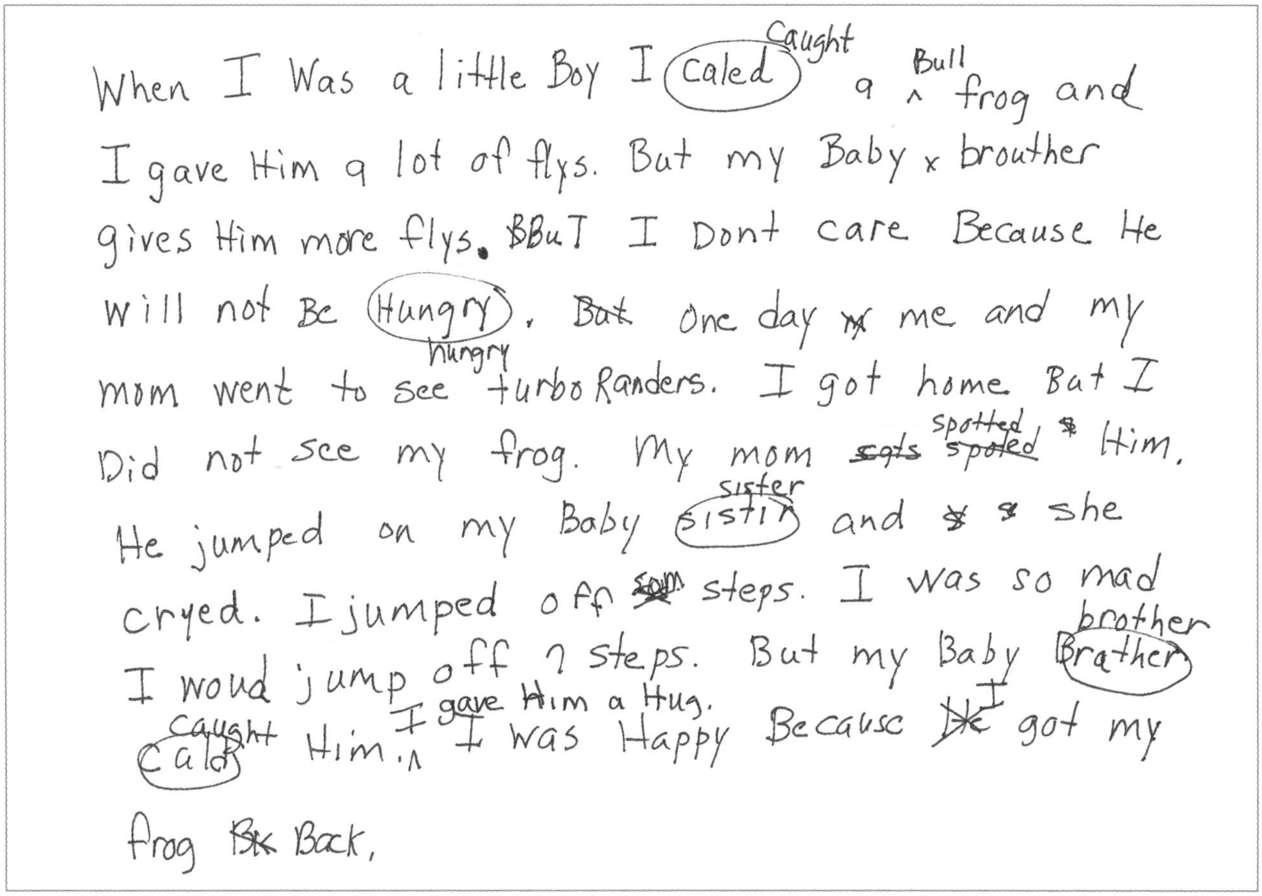
When I Was a little Boy I Caled (caught) a Bull frog and
I gave Him a lot of flys. But my Baby brouther
gives Him more flys. But I Dont care Because He
will not Be Hungry (hungry). One day me and my
mom went to see turbo Randers. I got home But I
Did not see my frog. My mom spoted (spotted) Him.
He jumped on my Baby sistir (sister) and she
cryed. I jumped off steps. I was so mad
I woud jump off 7 steps. But my Baby Brather (brother)
Calo (caught) Him. I gave Him a Hug. I was Happy Because I got my
frog Back.

Figure 10.9 Tyler's story. ("When I was a little boy I caught a bullfrog and I gave him a lot of flies. But my baby brother gave him more flies. But I don't care because he will not be hungry. One day me and my mom went to see Turbo Rangers. I got home but I did not see my frog. My mom spotted him. He jumped on my baby sister and she cried. I jumped off some steps. I was so mad I would jump off 7 steps. My baby brother caught him. I gave him a hug. I was happy because I got my frog back.")

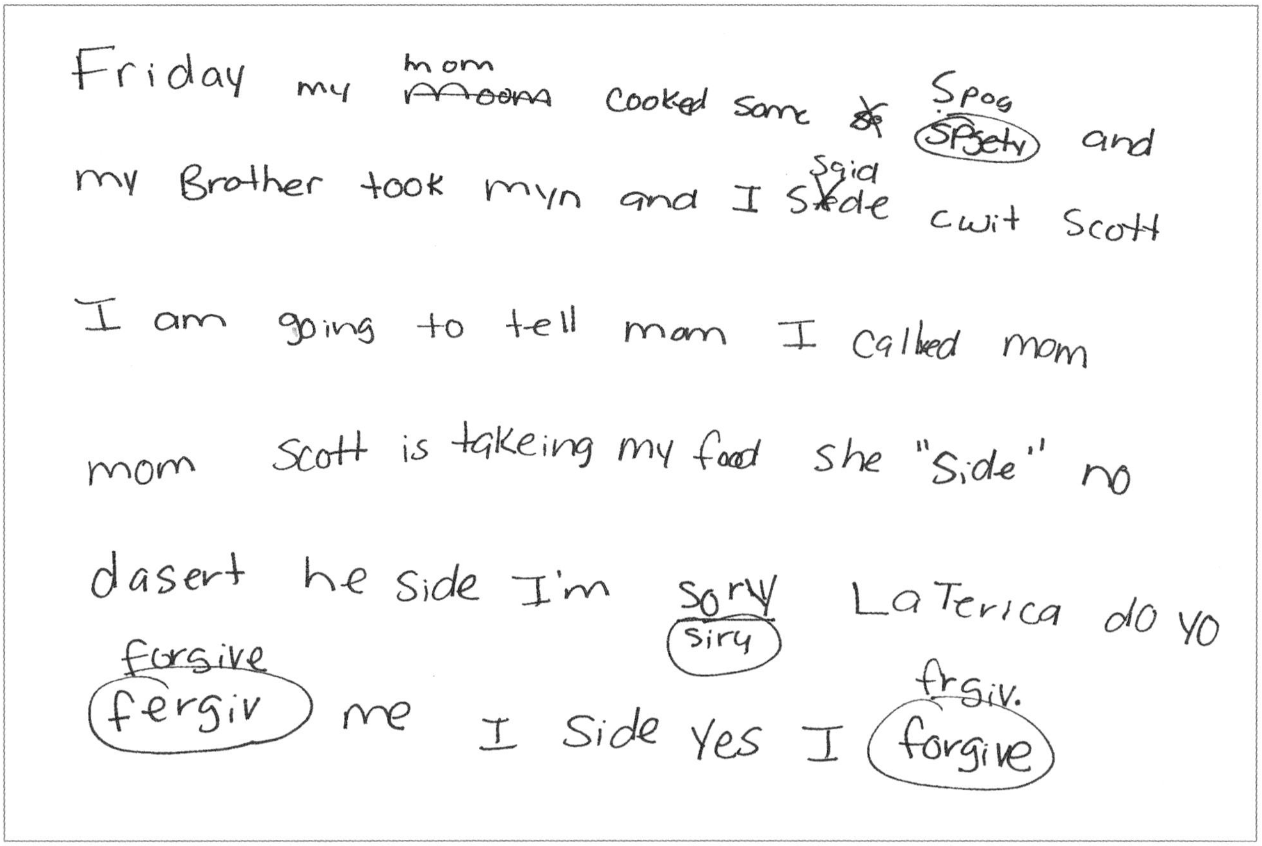

Figure 10.10 Laterica's story. ("Friday my mom cooked some spaghetti and my brother took mine and I said 'Quit Scott.' I am going to tell mom. I called mom. Mom Scott is taking my food. She said 'no dessert.' He said 'I'm sorry Laterica do you forgive me?' I said 'Yes I forgive you.'")

their reading development. The reading intervention consists of two components.

Component 1: 15 minutes (Processing of Easy or Familiar Books)

1. The children read independently several easy or familiar books. This volume reading builds their background knowledge, promotes reading fluency, and allows them to practice effective problem-solving strategies.
2. The teacher takes a running record on two children and provides them with two or three powerful teaching points to boost their processing power.
3. After the running record, the teacher circulates among the students, listening to each child read independently, providing assistance as needed, and taking observation notes.

Component 2: 15 minutes (Processing of a New Book)

1. The teacher introduces a new book and engages the children in an orientation to the text. She focuses on the meaning; then she demonstrates a word-solving strategy that aligns with their reading development. She sets two purposes for reading: (1) to comprehend a particular message and (2) to apply a particular word-solving strategy.
2. The children spread out in the room and read the book, and the teacher circulates among the students, listening to their reading, providing assistance as needed, and taking observation notes.
3. After the reading, the teacher convenes the group to discuss the book, to address any comprehension confusions, and to highlight one or two problem-solving strategies.

A Look at the Emergent Reading Group

When the children enter the room, they are familiar with the routine. Without hesitation, Karrisa, Tyler, Laterica, and Billy go to their book boxes and carry them to a comfortable spot for reading. Billy and Tyler climb the ladder to the reading loft and begin buddy reading, Karrisa curls up on large floor pillows underneath the loft, and Laterica sits in an oversized green-checkered chair. Before the children begin reading, Carla reminds them to use their finger and make their words match what they are saying.

The soft murmur of voices is heard as the children read aloud. Carla observes their reading behavior. She carries a clipboard on which she records significant observations. She is particularly interested in how the children use visual information to monitor language and meaning cues in the text. Each day she takes running records for two children in the group. Today Carla sits beside Karrisa and listens to her as she reads her book.

Like the other children in this group, Karrisa is just beginning to notice the visual cues in the text. Carla notes that Karrisa is using clear, crisp pointing behavior and that she monitors her reading with some known letters. (During shared reading and writing, Karrisa often uses special cues from the ABC chart to help with letter-sound relationships.) During her reading, Karrisa substitutes the word *chair* for *table* and immediately corrects herself. Although Karrisa can control the *t* sound in shared reading and writing, Carla is not sure whether the visual information or the strong picture cue (there is a table in the picture) is responsible for the correction. However, Karrisa's reading behavior gives Carla the chance to help her articulate and reflect on the importance of using her knowledge across changing situations:

Carla: (*Promoting self-reflection*) Karrisa, can you find the part on page four where you did some really good work? (*Karrisa points to the word* table.) (*Promoting articulation*) How did you help yourself?

Karrisa: First, I said *chair,* but then I saw the *t.* So I went back and said *table.*

Carla: That's a good problem-solving strategy. You looked at your picture, and you looked at the first letter to help you with that word.

Based on her observations of the children's strengths, Carla has selected the book *At the Beach* (Parkes 1997) for the guided reading lesson:

- The print is positioned consistently.
- There is enough space between the words so that the children can point and read.
- The words *I* and *a* are used frequently and serve as solid visual anchors for monitoring one-to-one matching.
- There is strong picture support to help the children with unknown words.
- The text consists of simple, complete sentences that are compatible with the children's oral language.
- There is a high correlation between picture and text.
- The text contains more supportive features than challenging features.

Carla begins by handing each child a seashell. The children's excitement is obvious; they ask Carla questions about where she got the shell. Carla tells them a brief story about her trip to the beach and allows the children a few moments to share similar experiences. Then she introduces the new book, which is about a little boy who goes to the beach. Carla encourages the children to think about some things the boy might see at the beach. The children exclaim, "A seashell!" Carla acknowledges their response and invites them to look at the pictures to expand their predictions. When the children turn to the page with the picture of the shell, they cry with excitement, "A seashell!" Although the text contains only the word *shell,* Carla makes no mention of this, for she wants to see if the children will monitor their one-to-one matching on this page. On the final page, Carla directs the children's attention to the visual features of print, asking them to predict the letter at the beginning of the word *picked.* Although this is an unknown word, Carla expects the children to locate the word quickly based on their knowledge of letter and sound associations for *p.* Last, Carla constructs the word *saw,* which occurs frequently throughout the text, with magnetic letters on the overhead projector: "This is an important word in your story. Look on the first page and see if you can find the word *saw.*" The children locate the word and frame it with their fingers. Then Carla instructs them to read the first page so that they can hear the word *saw* in the context of the story pattern.

"Now," Carla says, "turn your book back to the title page and let's read the title and author together." The children begin reading the story in whispers. Carla circulates and observes their behavior. She intervenes only if she believes a child is in danger of losing meaning.

When the children finish reading, Carla engages them in a discussion of the story, followed by a discussion of the importance of first-letter cues for checking on their reading:

Carla: Laterica, on page three you really did some good checking work. First you said *lobster,* but then you changed it to *crab.* Why did you change it?

Laterica: Because it didn't start with *l.*

At the end of the guided reading session, Carla and the children reread the story together fluently. Carla regulates her participation according to the children's control of the task. As the children prepare to leave, they select two or three books from their independent reading boxes to read at home. After the children are gone, Carla quickly records some important observations that she will use to plan her instruction tomorrow.

The Reading Intervention at a Later Time

As the children in the group have become more strategic readers, Carla's focus has shifted to developing an increasing range of comprehension strategies with more time for silent reading. Afterward the children participate in oral and written responses, discuss the texts in terms of story elements, and compare and contrast it with other stories they have read. The discussion-group format presents many opportunities for the children to interact with various types of texts.

Today the children are going to extend their range of experiences by reading and discussing "Little Bear and Owl" (Holmelund 1959). Carla begins by building on the children's background knowledge, talking about make-believe, and asking whether they have ever pretended to be somewhere else when they were playing. The children offer some personal make-believe experiences.

Next Carla gives the children a brief synopsis of the story: "Father Bear is far away at the ocean on a fishing trip, but Mother Bear needs some fish right away. So she sends Little Bear down to the river to catch some fish. As Little Bear and his friend Owl are fishing, Little Bear makes believe he is on a big boat." Carla encourages the children to make predictions about why Little Bear pretends to be on a big boat.

Billy says, "Because he has never been on a boat and he thought it would be fun."

Karrisa responds, "He would be catching lots of fish."

Tyler comments, "So he can be at the ocean like his father."

Carla accepts the children's predictions and then sets the purpose for reading: the children are to read the story to find out what happens in Little Bear's imagination as he pretends to be on a big boat.

Carla tells the children to place a sticky note on the page if they are unable to solve a word. As a brief reminder, she then asks them to articulate some strategic ways to problem-solve at the point where they have difficulty. The children quickly respond with flexible solutions: "Look for something I know about the word." "Look all the way through the word and make sure it makes sense and looks right." Carla praises their understanding of problem-solving actions and then directs them to read the story silently.

After the children finish the story, Carla talks with them about Little Bear's experience: "Why did Little Bear make believe he was fishing on a big boat?"

"Because he wanted to be a real fisherman just like Father Bear," Laterica says.

Tyler adds quickly, "He also wanted to catch something really big, like an octopus."

Karrisa chimes in, "This story is a little bit like the one we read a while back, 'Just Like Daddy.'"

Carla responds enthusiastically, "That's right, Karrisa. How are they alike?" Karrisa explains that both little bears wanted to be like their daddies and both went fishing. Carla draws a Venn diagram on the board summarizing the children's discussion of the similarities and differences between the two stories.

At the end of the guided reading, Carla and the children examine any difficult words they have marked with sticky notes. Carla uses the chalkboard or her magnetic letters to illustrate analysis strategies for solving a few selected words.

Closing Thoughts

In Chapter 1, we discussed the urgency of ensuring that all children become successful readers by the end of third grade. Most children will learn from high-quality classroom instruction, but some will require supplemental instruction to help them learn. For those children, it is critical that classroom teachers and intervention specialists collaborate on aligning instruction across the two contexts. Intervention serves two purposes: (1) to help students acquire essential knowledge about important literacy concepts and (2) to help students acquire strategies for learning how to attain new information. The ultimate goal of a supplemental intervention is for the children to be able to transfer their knowledge, skills, and strategies from the intervention setting to the classroom setting, ensuring that intervention is no longer needed.

Here are three points to consider in designing a supplemental intervention:

1. When learning is new, teachers arouse their students' attention through explicit teaching, clear models, and memorable examples that highlight the concept to be learned.
2. Teachers understand that integration must occur; therefore, they create opportunities for students to consolidate the new learning with the old learning. During the integration phase, teachers use language and nonverbal scaffolds to activate students' problem-solving strategies in connected texts.
3. A literacy intervention must focus on acceleration (in contrast to remediation). Acceleration is fostered when literacy components are linked and students learn how to use their knowledge from one component to assist their learning in another component.

chapter eleven

TEACHERS WORKING TOGETHER FOR CHILDREN

Literacy must be viewed through a wide-angle lens. It takes many dedicated people working together to ensure every child's right to literacy. A single program or a single teacher cannot bring about comprehensive changes within the school. Collaborative approaches to professional learning can promote school change that extends beyond individual classrooms.

The importance of teachers working together as a team of educators whose goal is to support the total child cannot be overstated. Teams of teachers with a common goal can do much more than an individual teacher working alone. Teachers must be knowledgeable about learning theory and research-based literacy practices. Learning teams provide an authentic context for sharing ideas, testing them out in the classroom, and increasing expertise through teacher collaboration. This is a powerful vehicle for refining instruction to best educate all children.

Our work has focused on creating an apprenticeship culture within the school that promotes teacher collaboration. Changing the context of schools to create settings for teachers to construct and share knowledge is essential to produce student learning. The seven principles for apprenticing children into literacy (see Chapter 2) can be applied to teacher learning. The school is a natural learning lab—a place where teachers refine their craft through opportunities to learn together. Schools need structures in place that enable teachers to think like researchers—observing behavior, collecting evidence, collaborating with others, constructing new knowledge, and sharing results.

Literacy teams create a social community for teacher collaboration and shared responsibility for student learning. Teachers identify long- and short-term goals for personal growth. They focus on student learning to guide assessment. They support one another through active demonstrations and follow-up discussions of teaching and learning interactions, and they seek help in specific areas of professional development. They plan together, monitor children's progress, and share the nuts and bolts of what really works in their classrooms. In the process, they build a support system for implementing change in theory and in practice.

A Few Examples of Teacher Collaboration

In Chris's school, the teachers formed a literacy team to actively support one another and the children they each work with. In the beginning, the teachers met and discussed their curriculum and the children they thought were falling through the cracks. They discovered that although they were each using the adopted basal program as their primary method of reading instruction, there were many differences in their two-hour language arts blocks. Some teachers were doing whole-class reading; some used small groups. One grade level used a structured phonics program; one grade level taught phonics within context. When the teachers looked at how they were incorporating writing into the curriculum, they also found many inconsistencies. Many teachers had their students write every day, others only sporadically.

The team set out to revise their teaching practices into a cohesive curriculum across the primary grades. At team meetings, the teachers examined portfolios of children's reading and writing progress and used this information for planning reading and writing groups. The teachers noted that the children who were receiving help from the reading specialists were making significant gains. They thought that all of the children could benefit from a balanced literacy approach in the classroom and began working together toward that goal.

One of the first goals of the team was to examine the materials they had available for teaching reading. All the teachers were somewhat frustrated with the basal program. The levels of difficulty did not appear to be consistent and supportive of the children. One teacher said, "Some of the stories are too easy for the children, and other stories are so hard that the children just fall apart when they try to read them." Several of the first-grade teachers thought that the basal was too difficult for their lowest readers, so they didn't use the book until later in the school year. Lynn, the reading specialist, showed the teachers how to look at features of text and how to determine appropriate levels of difficulty.

At the next team meeting, the teachers brought in their basal readers and began to organize the stories according to emergent, early, and fluent levels. Everyone was shocked and dismayed at the vast range of levels in the basal. After the teachers had identified the stories by level of difficulty, they looked at which ones could be used in a guided reading group and which ones could be used for shared reading or a read-aloud. Recognizing the need for more guided reading materials at the children's instructional reading levels, and with the support of their principal, they purchased guided reading sets for all the teachers to use.

The teachers at Shelby's school recognized the need for more guided reading materials as well. At a team meeting, the teachers initiated a schoolwide "book search" in an effort to locate more books. As teachers began bringing in the books, the principal formed a committee to organize the books according to text difficulty. This committee cleaned out a storage area and created a book room for everyone in the school to use. Another committee devised a checkout system for the book sets. The teachers put each set of little books into a zipper storage bag with the name and level of the book on a library card. When a teacher wanted to check out a set of books, she simply pulled out the library card and placed it into her pocket on the "checkout" wall chart. The teachers were able to keep track of the books they needed for a particular group of children and had access to more appropriate materials for supporting their young readers.

In Donnie's school, the teachers had been using a schoolwide book room for more than ten years, and the shelves were full of leveled texts. The teachers recognized that the book room needed to be expanded to include more trade books. Therefore, they focused their school monies on building an extensive collection of high-quality literary and nonliteracy texts, and they changed the concept of "book room" to "curriculum room." This new focus led to many changes in the curriculum room. For example, they organized the trade books to align with units of study, identified mentor texts for particular units, worked together to create literary planners for specific texts, and designed a computerized checkout system that enabled teachers to easily locate and return materials. In the adjoining room, the teachers created a cozy work area for their team meetings, and the curriculum room became an essential resource for their collaborative planning.

In Michelle's school, the intervention teachers were concerned that too many children were starting first grade at-risk for reading failure. Michelle, the literacy coach, believed that if the children had strong literacy experiences in kindergarten, it would help to ensure their reading success in first grade. Michelle invited Brittany, a kindergarten teacher, to collaborate with her on implementing a literacy-rich writing workshop in Brittany's classroom. Together, they analyzed the children's writing, used data to plan mini-lessons, videotaped Brittany's teaching and discussed her interactions with her children, and presented at conferences on the effect of writing workshop on kindergarten students' literacy development.

In Jennifer's school, the teachers used grade-level literacy teams to support one another as they implemented writing workshop. At each meeting the teachers brought in mentor texts, anchor charts, examples of mini-lessons, and students' writing samples, including the writing portfolios of their hardest-to-teach children. After the meeting, Jennifer, the literacy coach, observed in the classrooms and helped the teachers transfer their knowledge to the writing workshop. Follow-up meetings allowed the teachers to reflect on the successes or difficulties they had encountered and to plan for next steps. These meetings enabled the teachers to make important changes in their theories and practice.

Michael, the school principal, provided ongoing support and assistance with the following:

- regularly scheduled meetings during the school day throughout the year
- professional books for each teacher to use during team meetings and as classroom resources
- a wide variety of mentor texts to be used for read-alouds during mini-lessons and as references during student conferences
- opportunities to observe in other classrooms and to network with other teachers
- professional consultants from the University of Arkansas at Little Rock to provide literacy support in targeted areas of assessment and instruction

Robert, a district administrator, recognized the importance of providing teachers with opportunities to observe one another's teaching and encouraged his intervention teachers to do so. This proved so successful that he expanded the concept to include peer observations with grade-level teachers. He worked with the school's literacy coach to restructure the teachers' instructional day so that grade-level literacy team meetings could take place each Friday. During these team meetings, teachers applied theories of learning to the everyday practices of the classroom, generating new understanding.

At each meeting, team members brought in portfolios of children's progress that included running records and writing samples. The teachers learned how to use materials appropriately for instruction and testing purposes. They identified benchmark books from their guided reading sets and wrote standard book introductions that were used for testing and placement purposes. The team meetings focused on creating a literacy-rich environment for the children. When new topics and approaches were introduced, the teachers implemented them in their classrooms. They brought in videotapes or other documentation of their teaching and learning interactions for discussion and feedback from their colleagues. They planned personal areas of growth, sought out professional guidance, and worked together to address the needs of their children. The literacy teams provided the teachers with a structure for becoming reflective educators.

Why Should Teachers Reflect?

With reflection, teachers become more proactive in directing their teaching: reflection requires teachers to think before acting, which makes them responsible for their behaviors. When teachers are reflective, they become more empowered decision makers; they systematically reflect on their own performance by thinking, writing, and talking about their teaching and by judging the impact of their instruction on their students' learning. Self-reflection frees teachers from impulsive and routine actions and enables them to act in a deliberate and intentional manner (Loughran 2002).

A teacher's identity is determined by his or her belief system, which is shaped by personal and professional experiences. Self-reflection occurs when teachers examine their theories, beliefs, and practices and question how their perceptions are influencing their students' learning. Ferrell (2004) encourages teachers to reflect on the following:

- What am I doing in my classroom? (a description of my practice)
- Why am I doing this? (a look at the theory behind my practice)
- What is the result of my teaching? (a look at the consequences of my practice)
- Will I change anything based on my observations of my students? (a look at my future actions)

When teachers acquire an understanding of reflective practice, they engage in opportunities to heighten awareness and formulate beliefs and theories of teaching. In the process, they refine the craft of teaching through action.

Refining the Craft of Teaching

We believe learning to teach is an ongoing journey, and school is where teachers refine the craft of teaching. Every school should become a learning community where teachers come together frequently to study and work collaboratively as a means for improving their craft. Collaborative approaches to professional learning can promote school change that extends beyond individual classrooms.

Teachers who are more knowledgeable about teaching and learning are more likely to use research-based practices that are associated with increased student achievement. Teachers develop expertise when they observe one another teach and engage in reflective dialogues about teaching and learning. It takes expertise to orchestrate complex academic tasks, and this level of complexity can develop only through reflective and critical thinking.

The Language of Collaboration

Research has shown that a collaborative environment where teachers have structured time to plan instruction, observe each other, and share feedback has a positive effect on the learning climate of the school (Darling-Hammond and McLaughlin 1999). Indeed, collaboration with other teachers on instruction related to teaching strategies, assessing student knowledge, and managing a classroom is essential for increasing teacher expertise. In the previous chapters, we shared how teachers use language to scaffold their students' problem solving on literacy tasks and to create conversational moves during book discussions (see Chapter 9). In a similar way, teachers should attend to the collaborative nature of their language as they interact with colleagues around a common goal (see Figure 11.1 for five principles of collaborative talk).

1. **Keep the focus on the group goal.** Work as a learning team with a common set of goals that benefit all members of the group.
2. **Make the learning meaningful and relevant.** Teachers should see the value in the learning and how it can be applied to their classroom practice.
3. **Set norms for collaborative work.** In the same way that teachers establish routines and conversational norms for their students, they should set similar guidelines for their collaborative work.
4. **Build on one another's ideas.** Build discourse chains where ideas are linked together to form deeper meanings. In the process, the learning moves from the procedural to the conceptual levels.
5. **Use literacy resources.** Ground the work in professional texts and students' work.

Figure 11.1 Five principles of collaborative talk.

When teachers engage in collaborative, problem-solving discussions with one another, they are working in their zones of proximal development, which keeps their learning at the cutting edge. In the final sections of this chapter, we look at multiple examples of how teachers are working together to effect positive changes in their instructional practices. First, we share snapshots of exemplary schools that use teacher collaboration as a tool for school improvement. Then we share examples of how teachers use action research to study the impact of collaboration on their teaching practices. Finally, we look at an example of how teacher observations of student learning are a powerful means for collaboration and self-reflection.

A Look at Council Bluffs Community School District

The Council Bluffs Community School District in Iowa implements a variety of collaborative meetings to meet the instructional needs of teachers. The teachers in each building have ninety minutes of professional development each week courtesy of the district's early-release day. These professional-development sessions provide the teachers with the opportunity to share information related to the Comprehensive Literacy Model (see Dorn and Soffos 2001b, 2011) in a large-group format. In addition to the weekly early-release days, teachers have weekly team meetings, which may consist of grade-level teams, professional-learning communities, and book studies as an extension of weekly professional development. These meeting times are carefully considered through each school's master schedule. The small-group meetings allow principals and literacy coaches to tailor professional development to meet the teachers' needs based on instructional and student data. This allows teams to deepen their understanding of comprehensive literacy.

Four schools in the district share examples of teacher collaboration and its effect on instructional practice and student learning. The examples illustrate the diversity of collaborative activities and how professional development is based on the unique needs of the teacher teams.

Analyzing Student Work in Grade-Level Teams

Team meetings at Carter Lake Elementary School are designed to incorporate the study of student work into effective teaching practices. Teams are made up of grade-level classroom teachers, support/intervention teachers working with that grade level, the principal, Kim Kazmierczak, and the literacy coach, Jane Burgett. Teams meet weekly for forty minutes during their common planning time. Studying student work provides the team with data to monitor student achievement and to think analytically about how best to support each student. For example, one team focused their learning on formative assessments, and the teachers shared the rubrics they had composed with their students about procedural writing and answered questions about the rubrics. The teachers were able to clarify their thinking about how to write a rubric, what expectations they had for their students, where students were in their understanding, and what instruction they needed to provide. Crafting the rubric's language to be student-friendly, clear, and specific was also part of the discussion. The focus was on student achievement, but collaboration helped teachers better understand how to use formative assessments to impact student performance. This conversation showed reflection and self-regulation by all team members.

The team looked at student writing samples from their classrooms. The conversation was centered on effective scoring and additional ways to refine the rubrics. They collectively analyzed how they would score each writing selection. Their insights clarified how students were performing and guided them to where additional instruction needed to take place. The discussion that occurred during the study of procedural writing provided teachers time to make changes in their instruction and to confer with students to scaffold their work and understanding. The process benefited teacher development while creating a formative tool for students. The focus always remained on student achievement and provided a nonthreatening and supportive environment for teachers to problem-solve and refine their instruction.

This type of team meeting provided evidence of the power behind grade-level meetings where teachers were working within a common framework and curriculum. They were able to support and extend the thinking of others around a common goal. Through collaboration and reflective practice, the teachers became self-regulated learners.

Conducting Book Studies to Meet Teacher Needs

As they worked with the comprehensive literacy model for the first time, the teachers and administrators of Franklin Elementary deemed it critical that the teachers develop a deep understanding of the theory and research upon which the model was based. They also needed the opportunity within a professional community to work with the resources and have conversations with others. Choosing a mentor text from which to build a foundation was paramount. The building administrator, Lori Swanson, and the school's literacy coach, Amy Murray, chose to work from the first edition of *Apprenticeship in Literacy* (Dorn, French, and Jones 1998) to build theory and rationale. Teachers had to understand what they were being asked to do and how their instruction affected their students' learning. Teachers read, discussed, and worked through the research to have in-depth conversations about the information from the text and to apply it to their new learning. Building this foundation was critical to the teachers' successful implementation of the literacy model. The text served as a resource that teams of learners could come back to again and again to confirm or adapt the ongoing learning. Much like instruction with students, the teams began to realize that learning takes time and opportunity. When they designated time for collaboration and opportunity, and engaged in reflective dialogue about theory and research, their knowledge deepened. This structure enabled the building team to have a common goal and vision. The value of having a mentor text as a resource was critical to the success of the team meetings.

Any professional text that is chosen to serve as a mentor text for teachers should match the needs of the team and provide opportunities for rich discussion that impact teacher instruction and in turn affect student performance. Mentor texts can be chosen by school leaders or by teams. The following example describes how a team's need led to a book study that included a group-selected text.

At Edison Elementary School, the preschool teachers formed a grade-level team to study writing and the teaching of writing at the early childhood level. The team consisted of Gjoa King, the building literacy coach; four preschool teachers; and Darrin Praska, the principal. The team began by choosing a professional book to read and discuss. It was important to the teachers that the book focus on preschool children's development as well as teaching practices that could be readily implemented. Gjoa presented several book choices, and the team selected one that fit their needs. It was decided that the team would meet for about thirty minutes each week. The team members then set out to learn more about preschool writing development, as well as writing instruction at the preschool level. Each week the teachers set the reading assignment. When the team came together again, passionate and reflective discussions erupted as beliefs and current knowledge were stretched, expanded, and sometimes, challenged. The teachers were very open and honest. These rich discussions led to deeper levels of implementation.

Once the teachers had attended a couple of team meetings and felt comfortable with the process, Gjoa noticed that during the discussions, they often talked about what they had tried in their own classrooms. She suggested that they take the last ten minutes of every meeting to share student work that came out of the lessons they were implementing as a result of the book study. Teachers then had the opportunity to share student writing and the lessons they had taught throughout the week. This sharing time became another opportunity for wonderful discussions as they asked questions about the student work and the lessons that enabled students to work at high levels. Occasionally, a question would arise and team members would take each other back to the text to see what the author had said in relation to their own beliefs, thoughts, and training.

At the end of the book study, the team members discussed the meetings and how they wanted to proceed. They talked about the experience being beneficial to both themselves and their students. They also talked about what was working well for them in writing and the areas in which they were still having problems. Subsequently, they agreed upon a new, more specific focus area within writing and chose to start a new study in that area.

Cluster Conferences

At Roosevelt Elementary, the staff used an apprenticeship framework with cluster conferences for mentoring and coaching teachers. Mark Schuldt, the principal, and Amy Anderson, the literacy coach, believed that teachers learn best when they can observe other teachers. Therefore, model classrooms at each grade level served as learning labs where the teachers observed instructional interactions and engaged in constructive dialogue about their observations. The format of the cluster conference provided a collaborative structure for a small group of teachers to learn together.

To plan for the cluster conference, Mark and Amy engaged the teachers in problem-solving discussions around specific areas of need. The cluster conference was based on two areas: (1) the teachers' instructional goals and (2) the students' reading and writing data. (For example, if students were scoring poorly in writing, a cluster conference would be scheduled to observe writing workshop in a higher-performing classroom.) Before the cluster conference, Amy and the model classroom teacher planned the lesson, including ways to engage the observing teachers in the follow-up discussion.

On the day of the cluster conference, Amy provided the observing teachers with a cluster conference form to complete and norms to follow (see Figure 11.2). The cluster conference followed four steps: (1) Amy and the model teacher engaged in a brief preconference about the teacher's goal for the lesson, and the observing teachers recorded notes on the instructional focus; (2) the teachers observed the lesson and recorded notes of the teaching and learning as it related to the instructional focus; (3) Amy and the model teacher held a postconference, and the teachers recorded notes; and (4) Amy facilitated a follow-up discussion about the lesson, including implications for future instruction. She guided the teachers to the last question on the cluster form: "What have I learned today that can empower my teaching tomorrow?" This question became the catalyst for rich discussions and moved the teachers toward a plan for integrating the learning into their own instruction. The next week during team meetings, Mark and Amy followed up with more reflections around the question, and the teachers shared how their instruction had changed, plus the impact of their actions on their students' learning.

Roosevelt Elementary School

Cluster Conference

Cluster Conference Norms:

- Limit sidebar conversations and refrain from interacting with students.
- Stay focused on our instructional purpose.
- Be on time.

Teacher/Grade Level: _____

Date: _____

Preconference

Instructional Focus:

Notes (Related to the instructional focus)

Postconference

Instructional Focus Reflections:

What have I learned today that can empower my teaching tomorrow?

Figure 11.2 Teachers use the form for planning a cluster visit to observe in a classroom.

At Roosevelt School, the use of peer observations and cluster conferences was a powerful tool for keeping the teachers at the cutting edge of their profession. The staff believed that schools should be places of learning for teachers, as well as for children, and that learning should be suffused with excitement, passion, joy, and challenge (Hargreaves 1995).

Teachers as Action Researchers

Teachers are natural researchers. On a daily basis teachers design and implement instructional actions, observe and analyze behaviors, and modify plans to better meet the needs of their students. This might not sound like research, but it is. In fact, action research may well be the most important kind of research for improving practice. Teacher research is simply good teaching that is planned and written down in a formal way (Mertler 2006). Let's look at how three teachers used action research to study important issues in their schools.

Expanding Teacher Knowledge About Writing

Jennifer, a literacy coach, was interested in how best to support the teachers in her school as they implemented writing workshop. The purpose of her action research (Kimbrell 2009) was to study the impact of her coaching on the teachers' knowledge about writing. Jennifer's theory was based on the work on Meichenbaum and Biemiller (1998), who said that learners develop expertise through skillfully designed opportunities in three unique settings: acquisition, consolidation, and consultation. Jennifer believed that teachers develop knowledge to varying degrees; therefore, a teacher could be an expert in one area while being a novice in another area. She also believed that teachers develop greater expertise by teaching someone else. If her beliefs were accurate, then her role as a literacy coach should focus on scaffolding the teachers to become consultants for one another.

To test her theory, Jennifer collected audio- and videotapes of teaching and coaching interactions, and analyzed these data for changes in the teachers' knowledge as she coached them in the three settings. During the acquisition setting, she provided the teachers with clear demonstrations and explicit models that focused on the procedural aspects of writing workshop, such as organizing the workshop, designing mini-lessons, conducting conferences, and analyzing the students' writing. She also scheduled time for the teachers to observe their peers as they implemented different aspects of the workshop. During the pre- and postconferences, Jennifer asked the teachers to reflect on their lessons and to make plans for improving their practice.

In the consolidation setting, Jennifer looked for evidence of how the teachers were integrating their learning and prompted them to assume more responsibility for their actions. She found that the teachers were developing knowledge at different rates and in different areas; therefore, she adjusted her scaffolding, including her language prompts, to accommodate the uniqueness of each teacher's knowledge.

In the consultation role, Jennifer expected the teachers to provide peer support in at least one of four ways: (1) offer suggestions at team meetings, (2) host a cluster visit, (3) teach a demonstration lesson, or (4) reflect on learning in a log and share this information with others. She discovered that all teachers exhibited strengths and needs in different areas. For example, a teacher might be an expert in organizing the writing workshop while remaining a novice at conducting writing conferences. Jennifer was able to nurture the teachers' knowledge by helping them help others. Through action research, Jennifer had become a better literacy coach, and the teachers had learned more about the writing process.

Collaboration Between Intervention Specialist and Classroom Teacher

Linda, an intervention specialist, provided supplemental instruction to a small group of struggling readers in a first-grade classroom. She wondered if the children would make greater progress if she and the classroom teacher collaborated to implement writing workshop, so she designed an action research study to explore this question (Holman 2010).

During the ten weeks of the study, Linda worked with the classroom teacher to implement all components of writing workshop. She used a writing workshop protocol (see Appendix D-1) to guide her observations and to help the teacher plan effective instruction. Linda and the classroom teacher identified a small group of struggling writers and collaborated on a layered approach for maximizing the writing opportunities for these children. They discussed the importance of congruent instruction in promoting the students' transfer of knowledge across classroom and supplemental contexts. The classroom teacher met with the struggling writers at least three days a week, and Linda provided an additional layer of daily writing intervention to the same group. Throughout the study, Linda and the classroom teacher analyzed the students' writing and reflected on the impact of instruction on the students' progress. At the end of the study, Linda compared the students' writing for growth over time and found that all students had made significant gains according to a writing process rubric (see Dorn and Soffos 2001a). Through action research, Linda became a better intervention coach, the classroom teacher became a better writing teacher, and the students became better writers.

Dianne's Study

Dianne, a literacy coach, was concerned that her literacy team meetings were not as productive as they should be. She had observed frequently that the teachers were disengaged and eager to return to their classrooms. And she felt it was her responsibility to create the conditions for collaborative and reflective practice. She had read about a structured protocol developed by York-Barr, Sommers, Ghere, and Montie (2006) and wondered if this would be a good scaffold for engaging the teachers. The protocol used a four-step process: (1) studying student work, (2) describing the work, (3) identifying next steps for instruction, and (4) reflecting on the experience and identifying next steps for staff development. The eighteen teachers agreed to participate in the action research, and Dianne began collecting data to study the process (Presley 2007).

During the last five minutes of the team meeting, the teachers reflected in their journals on any aspect of the learning experience. During the school day, the teachers used their journals whenever they wanted to ask questions or make comments about their teaching or their students' learning. Dianne believed that if the teachers were engaged in the collaborative process around their students' work, their self-reflections would indicate a deeper level of thinking, as well as more responsibility for their actions. To test this theory, she analyzed the journals for evidence of changes in their reflections over the twelve-week period.

In the early weeks of the literacy team meetings, the teachers' journals contained mostly comments related to problems, yet the responses showed no evidence of reflecting on the causes or solutions to the problems they posed. For example, the teachers frequently expressed frustration with how the children were misbehaving in literacy corners, yet they provided no explanation for the reasons behind the problem. There was no indication that the teachers were reflecting on the relationship between their teaching and the students' behavior. Also, Dianne observed that the reflection logs were full of questions and requests for more outside assistance.

At the end of the study, Dianne discovered that the teachers had indeed shifted in their reflective practice. An overwhelming number of their journal entries focused on the reflective process and its relationship to teaching practice. For example, one teacher wrote, "The learning process fascinates me and I want to know more and understand more as I learn to look at my individual students' needs and understand where they are in the process." The journals revealed that the teachers were using their students' data to plan their instruction. As a result, the students' behavior problems had diminished and they were learning more from instruction.

Dianne found that using the structured protocol created a collaborative environment for the teachers to learn more about the writing process. In the beginning, the teachers' journal reflections focused on simple comments that identified or described a behavior; for example, "He looked at the pictures." Twelve weeks later, their language had moved from simple responses to expanded descriptions and self-initiated questions. During the team meetings, their conversations had shifted from identifying problems to constructive solutions, including ways to use student data to inform instruction. The teachers sought advice from one another and shared specific details for continuous improvement. As a result of her action research, Dianne developed a better understanding of how to help the teachers learn from collaboration. She changed the way she organized her meetings and engaged the teachers in meaningful and reflective discussions around their students' work. In the process, the teachers developed greater expertise for helping their children become successful writers.

Teachers Learning from Children

Marie Clay (1991) wrote that teachers should hold a tentative theory and should always test the theory against their observations of students. If the students are not responding to the teaching, then teachers must be prepared to change their theories. In this final story, the teachers are learning a lot about themselves, and as a result of their collaborations around a child, their theories begin to change.

A Look at LeRoy Elementary School

LeRoy Elementary School in Illinois is transforming into a school based upon an apprenticeship view of literacy. The change in beliefs about teaching and learning began in the fall of 2008 when a literacy consultant, Julie Eckberg, worked with the K–2 faculty (classroom teachers, teacher assistants, and specialists) for four days, training them in the Observation Survey assessment (six reading and writing tasks, one of which is running records) (Clay 2006). As the teachers paired up, administering the assessment to a first-grade student, important conversations evolved, not only about the practical aspects of literacy teaching and learning (for example, guided reading within a reading workshop) but also about the school as a system and where it was headed.

Four Teachers and a Student Named Zeke

One of the most important discussions revolved around a first-grade student, Zeke, identified as developmentally delayed with particular delays in oral lan-

guage development. On the last day of the professional-development experience, the primary special education teacher asked Julie to look at Zeke's Observation Survey results. As the teacher talked with Julie, other teachers who worked with Zeke joined the conversation. The classroom teacher, the teacher assistant, and the speech-language pathologist—along with the special education teacher—were trying to sort through not only the information and ideas discussed within the four days of professional development, but also how that information came together with their previous knowledge and how it could be applied to Zeke's unique learning needs. Sensing their need for support in working through the complexities, Julie offered her help to the teachers; if they were willing to meet once a week with her, perhaps together they could figure out where to go next.

The teachers agreed, and the principal ensured that they were each able to attend the one-hour weekly meeting. This group of teachers represented a unique collaborative team within the building; although teachers had collaborated on behalf of students' learning in the past (even with an outside consultant at times), this team would be the first to do so (a) within an apprenticeship view of literacy based upon the theories of Vygotsky and Clay and (b) with a consultant who was just as focused on teachers' learning and development as she was on students'. In the principal's mind, whatever the teachers needed on behalf of Zeke's learning and their own (within reasonable limits and within the apprenticeship theoretical framework), she was going to get it for them.

The Team's Collaborative Efforts

The weekly meeting followed a simple routine. Julie worked with Zeke while the other teachers observed. Then the teachers talked about what they had observed; during these conversations, Julie linked the teachers' observations to what was discussed during the four-day professional-development experience, thus extending their learning. Finally, the group brainstormed about what the observations and resulting conversation meant for their work with Zeke.

Typically, Julie and Zeke wrote a simple story during their time together. Zeke would draw a picture of something he wanted to write about, and as he drew, the two of them would talk (something that was very important for Zeke's oral language development). Zeke would then tell Julie what to write underneath the picture, contributing to the writing process when appropriate (such as when a word he could write was included in the story). At the end of their time together, Julie and Zeke would read the story, which then became a familiar text. Published Level A books that included any of Zeke's known words (*I, a, Mom, Dad*) were also read with Zeke, enjoyed, and used for instructional purposes.

Under these conditions, Zeke was being apprenticed in the *process* of writing and reading. This apprenticeship was critical for Zeke's learning, because even though he knew many items in isolation (letters, sounds, words), he did not understand how those items came together during writing and reading as part of a meaningful message. In addition, the teachers were being apprenticed in how to provide such learning opportunities and why they were important. The concrete observational experiences stirred rich discussions within the group and resulted in meaningful instructional planning. Within just a few weeks, a simple, doable plan evolved:

- Every teacher working with Zeke needed to focus on talking, writing stories, and reading them. Zeke would simply take his stories with him wherever he went during the day, and the teachers would build on each other's efforts.

- Instructional interactions and observations would focus on Zeke's literacy behaviors. What did he notice during the writing and reading of books? What did he try? What did he talk about? Did he ever pause, stop, or look at the teacher, indicating he knew something wasn't quite right?

- No new words would be taught to Zeke; rather, teachers would take note of the ones he knew and have him use them in the writing of stories (if possible).

- To support Zeke's oral language development (which was the foundation of his reading and writing development), the teacher assistant would read a book aloud to Zeke every day, talking with him about it much like a parent does with a young child. The classroom teacher would also eventually send home a book a couple of evenings a week (as "homework"), which the parents would read to Zeke, enjoy, and discuss; to scaffold the parents, a discussion question would even be included.

- Finally, since Zeke tended to be impulsive (for example, interrupting, grabbing books or pencils during instructional interactions), expectations in the area of social skills would also be consistent across all contexts.

A Team Communication Tool

In order to build on one another's efforts, the teachers needed to communicate during the school day; one communication tool ended up being Zeke's reading log. Since Zeke was proud of his log and wanted to take it with him wherever he went, the teachers began using pages in the back to document observations and send messages to one another.

For instance, every morning, the teacher assistant (who made a point to talk with Zeke as he entered the classroom) documented what she and Zeke discussed; this provided the special education teacher and speech-language pathologist with a starting point for their conversations later in the day. For instance, they'd say, "Mrs. Wohlwend wrote here that you had an interesting evening last night. Tell me about it." For Zeke's oral language development, this link across his day was important; it allowed him to talk more deeply about one topic rather than a little here and a little there about several. These richer conversations led to richer stories, which were then read and reread, further immersing Zeke in the language.

Another kind of message the teachers sent to one another via Zeke's reading log had to do with letters. It was not helpful for Zeke to have four different teachers emphasizing different letters (and their sounds, their formation, and so on) within the same day, expecting him to retain the learning. Rather, it was more meaningful for him if the same letter (or couple of letters) came up in different contexts throughout the day, in different ways. For instance, if one of the teachers brainstormed words with Zeke that started like *mom* (a word in his writing vocabulary), the next teacher could also talk about the letter *m*, perhaps looking through familiar texts for words that began with that letter.

This linking of learning across the day was critical for a student such as Zeke, whose learning needed to accelerate. The linking not only allowed for the important goal of transfer, but created a snowball-like effect as well. The instructional efforts of one teacher were made more powerful when built upon and extended by the next.

A Simple Plan That Led to Significant Results

The above efforts by the teachers—which interestingly cost little money—resulted in significant changes. The team of teachers began noticing that Zeke was interacting with them more, meaningfully communicating and conversing with them throughout the school day. He was also using longer sentence structures, particularly in the morning when chatting with the teacher assistant. This resulted in the assistant documenting one other thing in the back of Zeke's reading log: the longest sentence that she heard Zeke say each morning. This information was important because (a) it documented his progress in the area of oral language development and (b) it provided additional information for teachers working with Zeke later in the day, particularly the speech-language pathologist.

The team also noticed that meaning was driving Zeke's interactions with text, more so than in the past. Before the team's efforts, Zeke approached reading as recognizing a word, saying it, recognizing the next word, saying it, and so on. Under the learning conditions described above, he became aware that print held a message and that, therefore, whatever he read (and wrote) had to make sense. As a consequence of this awareness, self-monitoring behaviors emerged and even self-corrections, signs of a developing "inner control" (Clay 1991). Self-regulatory behavior was also observed as Zeke participated in the writing of stories, talked with teachers (for example, he began to self-correct his language and speech), and interacted with them (for example, he began to self-correct various social behaviors).

In addition to the changes with Zeke, the team of teachers began noticing changes within themselves. The special education teacher and speech-language pathologist were particularly aware of changing, for as they explained, they (and other educators like them) weren't trained in the above-described instructional approach. In fact, reading—let alone its link to writing and oral language—was little discussed in their discipline's coursework. Consequently, the four-day professional-development experience and follow-up collaborative efforts had rocked their minds, so to speak. The two specialists talked about it during the team's sixth meeting. They also talked about how much they appreciated the professional-development experiences, because even though they were mentally and emotionally draining, the experiences were causing them to think differently about literacy and learning.

A striking example can be provided from that meeting. It deals with something the two specialists pursued on their own, without any suggestion from the literacy consultant or the principal: they joined efforts to better understand and better support the literacy learning of a kindergarten student with whom they both worked by administering the Observation Survey to him. At the meeting, the speech-language pathologist and special education teacher shared the results, talking not only about Zeke's responses but also about how they as teachers reacted to them. For example, the special education teacher explained that during the word reading task of the survey, Zeke pointed to *may* and said, "That's *my*." "Before," she commented, "I wouldn't have celebrated that at all."

A bit later, after other aspects of the survey were discussed, the speech-language pathologist shared something similar: "We would have never looked at him in this sort of way before these experiences."

After just four days of professional development, six weeks of a team working and learning collaboratively under the guidance of a knowledgeable other, and countless conversations during that time, things were beginning to change. The teachers on the collaborative team were reflecting upon their own beliefs and practices regarding children's language and literacy learning—*all* children's within the school, typical *and* atypical in development. Additionally, they were reflecting upon the school as a system—how it worked in the past and why, and how it perhaps needed to work in the future and why. Though nothing had been officially decided or implemented within the school, something significant was stirring at its core, not only for this group of teachers but for others as well.

Where the Teachers and School Are Now

Since the story above, much has happened within LeRoy Elementary School. An apprenticeship view of literacy learning—in fact, learning in general—has been officially adopted within the school, influenced by the growing number of teachers who have witnessed what is possible within such a view. As a result, the workshop approach is being used K–6, including a two-and-a-half-hour literacy block for language workshop, reading workshop, and writing workshop. Cross-curricular, standards-based units are being designed at more and more grade levels, creating meaningful links across workshops, and language-literacy rubrics have been created (see Appendices D-2 to D-9), highlighting the major end-of-year goals at each grade level (based upon a synthesis of literacy behaviors discussed in Dorn and Soffos 2001a, 2001b, 2005, and 2011, and Fountas and Pinnell 2001, as well as learning goals outlined in the Common Core State Standards [NGA/CCSSO 2010]). From these big-picture grade-level rubrics, more specific rubrics are then being made (for example, a "Read-Think-n-Write Rubric" for assessing written responses in the reading logs; see Figure 11.3 and Appendix D-9).

The most important feature of all of the rubrics is that they include the same main headings, representing various areas of learning that evolve in complexity over the elementary years. In this way, the alignment across grade levels is clear; the emphasis is not on separate skills or isolated bits of knowledge at each grade level but rather on language and literacy processes that develop in simple but significant ways in kindergarten and then expand in reach and complexity with every year that follows. Essentially, the grade-level language-literacy rubrics represent a continuum of learning across the entire elementary school.

This continuum is particularly helpful to the special education teachers in the building, for the students they support are often in very different learning places. Whereas the "first-grade" language-literacy rubric might be appropriate for a third-grade student with an individualized education plan (IEP), the "second-grade" language-literacy rubric might be more appropriate for another third-grade student with an IEP. The grade level on the rubrics does not matter to these specialists; what matters is the continuum of learning that is represented within the language-literacy rubrics and the place on the continuum where a particular student falls at a particular time in his learning journey.

One other change that has happened in LeRoy Elementary relates, again, to students with IEPs: many are no longer pulled out of the classroom for instruc-

tion. Because of the school's apprenticeship view of literacy and learning (which meets learners where they are along a continuum of learning), because of the workshop approach that is being implemented (which structurally allows for meeting students where they are), and because of the language-literacy rubrics (which scaffold teachers in knowing instructionally how to meet students where they are), the needs of a diverse range of students can be met within grade-level classrooms. In fact, the special education teacher discussed above is pushing into one of the second-grade classrooms in the building with very positive results. Because of the collaborative efforts of the classroom teacher, teacher assistant, speech-language pathologist, and Reading Recovery teacher, students are thriving (as are the teachers). The same is happening in the LeRoy kindergarten, where the special education teacher, speech-language pathologist, and another reading specialist in the school are working closely with the classroom teachers and their assistant to systematically support students who need additional assistance. As these teachers collaborate, they continue to meet with the literacy consultant, who guides their efforts, extends their professional learning, and works to strengthen coherence within the school.

Here lies probably the most important aspect of the whole story: the changes occurring within LeRoy Elementary School have nothing to do with the implementation of a program or even a balanced literacy approach. Instead, the changes have to do with (a) teachers learning about an apprenticeship view of literacy, seeing what is possible, and then continuing to deepen their understandings of *why* what they're seeing is possible through professional collaborations and conversations with one another as well as the literacy consultant, the knowledgeable other in this particular story; and (b) the development of a cohesive system, aligned vertically across grade levels and horizontally across classroom teachers and specialists—not simply through the use of similar instructional practices and assessment techniques but through the development of similar beliefs about language, literacy, and learning. The changes within the school are not being caused by *what* is being done; they are a result of teachers' understanding the *why* behind the what—the developmental theories of Vygotsky and Clay, and the efforts and ideas of others who have built upon those theories.

Read-Think-n-Write Rubric

	Proficiency Levels				
	Below the Standard **1** requires full support	Approaching the Standard **2** requires a lot of support	Meeting the Standard **3** requires some support	Exceeding the Standard **4** requires little to no support	*sub-score*
Focus and Organization of Ideas ✓ states opinion, prediction, question, connection, feeling, etc. ✓ maintains focus on that statement throughout entry	1	2	3	4	x 2 =
Support and Development of Ideas ✓ explains opinion, prediction, question, connection, feeling, etc. ✓ elaborates by referencing specific events, actions, or language in text	1	2	3	4	x 2 =
Language Use and Conventions ✓ spells high-frequency "no-excuse" words correctly ✓ includes spaces between words ✓ uses uppercase letters only in appropriate places ✓ uses end punctuation, followed by a capital letter, most of the time ✓ writes in complete sentences most of the time	1	2	3	4	x 1 =
Entry Format ✓ date ✓ title of text	1	2	3	4	x 1 =
Effort ✓ neatness	1	2	3	4	x 1 =

In this entry, I . . .

offered an opinion.

responded personally to the text.

asked questions.

made predictions/inferences.

shared connections.

responded to the traits and/or actions of the characters.

responded to the theme and/or author's purpose.

responded to the writing style or author's language.

critiqued the text.

Score 28 possible points

Comments

Information and language synthesized from *Teaching for Deep Comprehension*, Dorn and Soffos 2005.
Julie Eckberg 2011, in collaboration with LeRoy CUSD 2, IL.

Figure 11.3 The Read-Think-n-Write Rubric is used to assess students' writing responses in their reading logs.

Closing Thoughts

The stories in this chapter are only a small glimpse into the powerful interactions of teacher collaboration. During the past two decades, we have worked closely with teachers and had the opportunity to observe their changes in practices and theories. Our goal from the beginning has been to guide teachers to become self-regulated learners who design their own questions and seek their own answers through problem-solving discussions with other professionals. As teachers observe and analyze children's reading behavior, they acquire an important tool for testing and refining their theories of how children learn. When teachers apply theory to practice, they understand the significance of important concepts associated with apprenticeship learning: they learn the relevance of scaffolded instruction aimed at children's potential levels of development; the importance of modeling and coaching as instructional tools that enable children to accomplish new learning tasks; and the value of establishing routines, assisted versus independent activities, explicit feedback, and problem-solving solutions to common issues.

Literacy learning is complex—not only for our children, but for us as well. As teachers, we are constantly learning and experiencing transitions that reflect our new understanding. The children in our classrooms need us to work together as a team to support them on their pathway to literacy. Systemic change lies in our understanding how our children learn and in our ability to problem-solve with colleagues who work with our children, share our common experiences, and speak our language of literacy.

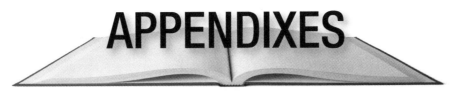

APPENDIXES

All of the forms in Appendixes A–E are also available online at www.stenhouse.com/apprenticeship.

Appendix A-1

Gradual Release of Responsibility Teaching Prompts

Whether teaching strategies for self-monitoring, phonological awareness, phonics, vocabulary, comprehension, or fluency, teaching prompts must match your instructional focus and the students' needs. Here are some examples of prompts that align with levels of support.

Prompting Type	Purpose	Stems
Awareness Level	Use these prompts for the reader who is not using the targeted strategy or skill at all. The prompts offer a model or benchmark of how the strategy or skill is used in reading.	• Listen to how I ___. • Read it like this. • Watch how I ___ . • ____ is not _____ . • When I _____, I _____. • Notice what I do when I _____. • Describe or define _____. Point out an example. _____ • I'm going to _____. • Listen to how I read this.
Control Level	Use these prompts for students who are beginning to use the strategy or skill but still need direct teaching or coaching on how to use it properly.	• Now read _____. • Can you _____? • Do this _____. • Change this: _____. • Try that again and _____. • Try doing this and _____. • Repeat after me: _____. • Read it like this: _____.
Self-Control/Reflective	Use these prompts for students who have previously exhibited use of the strategy or skill in reading but are not consistent. These prompts remind students to be more reflective and to think about the importance of using the strategy or skill at the right time.	• How did you _____? • How did you know ____? • What did you notice about _____? • Did you have any trouble _____? • Were you reading ____ or _____? • When did you know to _____? • What made you _____? • Where did you _____?
Validating/Confirming	Use these prompts at any time to validate or confirm a student's strategies and skills.	• I like the way you _____. • Good job at _____. • You _____. • I noticed _____. • You took ____. • You made _____. • You are _____.

Appendix A-2

Target Reading Strategy Prompts

Concepts About Print	
Front of book	Where can we find the front of the book?
Difference between a picture and a page of print	Does this page have pictures or words on it?
One-to-one matching, left-to-right directionality, and return sweep	Who can help me follow along with a pointer? Where do I start? Which way do I go?
Beginning and end	Where do we begin reading? Where do we finish?
Bottom of picture	Nonfiction: What do we call these words below the picture? (caption) Fiction: Sometimes books will continue with words below pictures. We follow the text down the page even when it is below pictures.
Inverted page of print	Sometimes authors put the print in different places. Who can tell me what is different about this page of print?
Left page beginning a text	Where do we begin reading? Sometimes an author puts words on the left page instead of beginning on the right side. It is important to always look for the title page and where the story begins.
Word order	Notice how the author used words in the sentence. Does the sentence start with a person, place, or thing? If it does, the author will then tell us what the person, place, or thing is doing.
Letter order	How would you start that word if you were writing it?

Making Connections	
Text-to-self	How does the text remind you of your own experiences?
Text-to-text	How does the text connect to something else you have read?
Text-to-world	How does the text connect to the world around you?

Questioning	
Constructing meaning	What do you think the story means?
Enhancing understanding	What other stories have you read that remind you of this one?
Finding answers	Where can we find the answer to this?
Finding specific information	Let's go back and look for . . .
Clarifying confusion	This seems a little confusing. What facts from the story can we use to clarify what the author means?
Identifying research topics	We read about many things. What might we want to find out more about?

Visualizing	
Creating mental images from text	Close your eyes. What do you see when you think about the story?
Placing yourself in text	If you were in the story, what would you do?
Stimulating imaginative thinking	Everyone close your eyes. Imagine you are in the story. What would you do next?

Appendix A-2 continued

Determining Text Importance	
Remembering important information	This is very important. Let's mark this with a sticky note so we will remember it later.
Distinguishing what is important from what is interesting	What things are important in this story? What things are interesting?
Discerning a theme, opinion, or perspective	What is the moral of this story?
Determining if the author's perspective is to inform, persuade, or entertain.	Why do you think the author wrote this story?

Making Inferences	
Drawing conclusions	We finished reading _____. Can you come up with three words to describe ____? What in the story led you to use those three words?
Making predictions	What do you think will happen next in the story?
Using implicit information to make meaning	Page ____ says _____. What does that mean in this story?

Synthesizing Information	
Stopping to collect your thoughts	Let's stop here and think about what we have read.
Summarizing information	How would you summarize this story?
Combining main points and big ideas	Let's combine all the main points into one big idea
Making generalizations	Think about what we read. How would you describe it?
Making judgments	What is your opinion of this passage?
Assimilating information	How would you put all thin information together? What does it mean to you?

Apprenticeship in Literacy, Second Edition: Transitions Across Reading and Writing, K–4
by Linda J. Dorn and Tammy Jones. © 2012. Stenhouse Publishers.

Appendix A-3

Examples of Language Starters for Literature Discussion Groups

- I already know that _____.

- We are reading this piece because _____.

- When I think about this piece, I am reminded of_____.

- When I hear this piece, I wonder about _____.

- I am confused about _____.

- I need to know more about _____ because _____.

- I don't understand the word _____.

- I don't understand why the character did _____.

- I noticed this piece is organized like _____.

- This picture is what I think the author meant when he wrote about _____.

- The point of this piece is _____.

- The author obviously thinks _____ is important because _____.

- The author's words show me that _____.

- I can help myself understand this book by _____.

Appendix A-4

Before, During, and After Reading Strategies

Before Reading	During Reading	After Reading
• Brainstorm/categorize • Preview and survey text • Pose questions • Predict/hypothesize • Use background knowledge	• Make personal connections • Reread to clarify • Use background knowledge • Adjust predictions • Identify confusing parts • Visualize • Ask questions • Summarize • Analyze • Infer • Take notes • Monitor comprehension • Self-correct when meaning breaks down	• Reread to clarify or extend comprehension • Ask questions • Write about reading • Compare/contrast information • Retell • Summarize • Critique

Appendix A-5

Problem-Solving Prompts

Prompts for Checking on Meaning Information

- You said, _____. Does that make sense?
- What would make sense there?
- Look at the picture. What is happening?
- Reread that part and think about what would make sense.

Prompts for Checking on Structure Information

- You said, _____. Does that sound right?
- Reread that part and think about what would sound right.

Prompts for Checking on Visual Information

- Does _____ look right?
- Look at the first letter.
- Search into the word.
- It could be _____, but look at _____ . Check to make sure that looks right.
- Is there something about that word that you know?

Prompts for Self-Monitoring

- Were you right?
- Why did you stop?
- What did you notice?
- What's wrong?
- Try that again.
- You almost got that right. Can you fix it?

Appendix B-1

Assisted Writing Observation Record

Student Name_____

Chart Coding Legend: √ spelling behavior identified from writing sample

Writing Behaviors

Behavior	Date	Date	Date	Date	Date	Date	Date	Comments
Consistent use of directional principles.								
Writing is represented by scribbles.								
Writing is represented by a few letter forms.								
Strings letters together with a few spaces.								
Forms most letters correctly.								
Consistent use of spacing.								
Attempts sound/symbol correspondence with one or two letters.								
Articulates words slowly.								
Analyzes sounds in words.								
Hears and records beginning, middle, and ending sounds in words.								
Hears and records sounds in sequence.								
Writes high-frequency words fluently.								
Uses meaningful chunks (-s, -ed, -ing).								
Uses simple analogies to write unknown words.								
Composes one-sentence messages.								
Composes two- to three-sentence message.								
Composes longer messages.								
Rereads to confirm and extend message.								
Uses visual patterns to write new words.								
Monitors writing by crossing out words that do not look right.								
Uses punctuation.								
Uses known words to write unfamiliar words.								

Apprenticeship in Literacy, Second Edition: Transitions Across Reading and Writing, K–4
by Linda J. Dorn and Tammy Jones. © 2012. Stenhouse Publishers.

Appendix B-2

High-Frequency Word Lists

Word List A #1–25

the	of	and	a	to
in	is	you	that	it
he	was	for	on	are
as	with	his	they	I
at	be	this	have	from

Word List B #26–65

or	one	had	by	word
but	not	what	all	were
we	when	your	can	said
there	use	an	each	which
she	do	how	there	if
will	up	other	about	out
many	then	them	these	so
some	her	would	make	like

Word List C #66–100

him	into	time	has	look
two	more	write	go	see
number	no	way	could	people
my	tan	first	water	been
call	who	oil	now	find
long	down	day	did	get
come	made	may	part	over

Word List D #101–150

new	sound	take	only	little
work	no	place	year	live
me	give	back	most	very
after	our	thing	just	name
good	sentence	man	think	say
great	where	help	through	much
before	line	right	too	mean
old	any	same	tell	boy
follow	came	want	show	also
around	form	three	small	set

Appendix B-2 continued

Word List E #151–200				
put	end	does	another	well
large	must	big	even	such
because	turn	here	why	ask
went	men	read	need	land
different	home	us	move	try
kind	hand	picture	again	change
off	play	spell	air	away
animal	house	point	page	letter
mother	answer	found	study	still
learn	should	America	world	high

Word List F #201–250				
every	near	add	food	between
own	below	country	plant	last
school	father	keep	tree	never
start	city	earth	eye	light
thought	head	under	story	saw
left	don't	few	while	along
might	close	something	seem	next
hard	open	example	begin	life
always	those	both	paper	together
got	group	often	run	important

Word List G #251–300				
until	children	side	feet	car
mile	night	walk	white	sea
began	grow	took	river	four
carry	state	once	book	hear
stop	without	second	late	miss
idea	enough	eat	face	watch
far	wouldn't	real	almost	let
above	girl	sometimes	boy	should
young	talk	list	soon	song
being	leave	family	it's	afternoon

Appendix B-3

High-Frequency Word List Summary

StudentName_____Date:_____

Date	Word List	Beginning of Year	Middle of Year	End of Year
		Part One: Reading Total Number of Words Attempted:_____ Total Number of Words Read Accurately:_____ **Part Two: Spelling** Total Number of Words Attempted:_____ Total Number of Words Spelled Correctly:_____ **Next Five Words to Learn:**	**Part One: Reading** Total Number of Words Attempted:_____ Total Number of Words Read Accurately:_____ **Part Two: Spelling** Total Number of Words Attempted:_____ Total Number of Words Spelled Correctly:_____ **Next Five Words to Learn:**	**Part One: Reading** Total Number of Words Attempted:_____ Total Number of Words Read Accurately:_____ **Part Two: Spelling** Total Number of Words Attempted:_____ Total Number of Words Spelled Correctly:_____ **Next Five Words to Learn:**
		Part One: Reading Total Number of Words Attempted:_____ Total Number of Words Read Accurately:_____ **Part Two: Spelling** Total Number of Words Attempted:_____ Total Number of Words Spelled Correctly:_____ **Next Five Words to Learn:**	**Part One: Reading** Total Number of Words Attempted:_____ Total Number of Words Read Accurately:_____ **Part Two: Spelling** Total Number of Words Attempted:_____ Total Number of Words Spelled Correctly:_____ **Next Five Words to Learn:**	**Part One: Reading** Total Number of Words Attempted:_____ Total Number of Words Read Accurately:_____ **Part Two: Spelling** Total Number of Words Attempted:_____ Total Number of Words Spelled Correctly:_____ **Next Five Words to Learn:**

Appendix B-3 continued

<table>
<tr>
<td></td>
<td></td>
<td>

Part One: Reading
Total Number of Words
Attempted:_____
Total Number of Words Read
Accurately:_____

Part Two: Spelling
Total Number of Words
Attempted:_____
Total Number of Words Spelled
Correctly:_____

Next Five Words to Learn:

</td>
<td>

Part One: Reading
Total Number of Words
Attempted:_____
Total Number of Words Read
Accurately:_____

Part Two: Spelling
Total Number of Words
Attempted:_____
Total Number of Words Spelled
Correctly:_____

Next Five Words to Learn:

</td>
<td>

Part One: Reading
Total Number of Words
Attempted:_____
Total Number of Words Read
Accurately:_____

Part Two: Spelling
Total Number of Words
Attempted:_____
Total Number of Words Spelled
Correctly:_____

Next Five Words to Learn:

</td>
</tr>
<tr>
<td></td>
<td></td>
<td>

Part One: Reading
Total Number of Words
Attempted:_____
Total Number of Words Read
Accurately:_____

Part Two: Spelling
Total Number of Words
Attempted:_____
Total Number of Words Spelled
Correctly:_____

Next Five Words to Learn:

</td>
<td>

Part One: Reading
Total Number of Words
Attempted:_____
Total Number of Words Read
Accurately:_____

Part Two: Spelling
Total Number of Words
Attempted:_____
Total Number of Words Spelled
Correctly:_____

Next Five Words to Learn:

</td>
<td>

Part One: Reading
Total Number of Words
Attempted:_____
Total Number of Words Read
Accurately:_____

Part Two: Spelling
Total Number of Words
Attempted:_____
Total Number of Words Spelled
Correctly:_____

Next Five Words to Learn:

</td>
</tr>
</table>

Appendix B-4

Individual Developmental Spelling Checklist

Student Name_____

Chart Coding Legend: √ spelling behavior identified from writing sample

Spelling Stage	Date	Date	Date	Date	Date	Date	Date	Comments
Precommunicative								
Strings together symbols, numbers, and letter forms without sound symbol relationships								
Semiphonetic								
Recognizes that letters have sounds								
Hears and records some beginning and ending consonant sounds								
Letter names are used to record sounds and syllables								
Phonetic								
Spells one-syllable regular cvc words, including vowels								
Spells two-/three-syllable words, including vowels								
Records letters for every sound in the word, including some vowels								
Transitional								
Flexible control of known words								
Spells words according to how they should look in print								
Uses alternative spellings for the same sound								
Spells using inflectional endings								
Includes vowels in every syllable of the word								
Correct								
Spells words using a variety of word structures (prefixes, suffixes, and compound words)								
Initiates a problem-solving action when a word does not look right								
Controls a wide variety of visual patterns for spelling words								

Appendix C-1

Integrated Workshop Planner

Word Study – Spelling – Vocabulary 30 min.				

Language Studies 30 min.				

Reading Workshop 1 hour, 25 min.				
15-min. mini-lesson				
20-min. groups				
10-min. debriefing				

Writing Workshop 40 min.				
15-min. mini-lesson				
15 min. of conferences w/ individuals and/or groups				
10-min. debriefing				

Content Workshop 45 min.				
35-min. lesson				
10-min. debriefing				

Apprenticeship in Literacy, Second Edition: Transitions Across Reading and Writing, K–4
by Linda J. Dorn and Tammy Jones. © 2012. Stenhouse Publishers.

Appendix C-2

Guided Reading Lesson Planner

Book Selection	Focus of Lesson
Title:	• What strategies are the students in this group using? (e.g., rereading, searching pictures, using first-letter cues, noticing chunks in words) • What strategies are they neglecting?
Level:	• Do I need to focus on deepening their understanding of the text?

Book Orientation

Plan for Activating Background Knowledge

Plan for Supporting Students' Construction of Meaning and Problem Solving

Multiple sources of information (meaning, structure, visual cues) should be addressed within an introduction, to support the integration of them during the first read:

- M—When I show the students the book, what could I say in one or two sentences to provide a brief overview? "This book is about . . ."

- S—Are there recurring phrases in the book that I could use as I naturally talk with the students? Any unusual language that I should point out (e.g., "Away we go")? Any specialized vocabulary (e.g., apartment building)?

- VC—Is there a word in the book the students will frequently encounter that I could have them locate? Or a potentially tricky word for which I could ask, "What letter(s) would you expect to see at the beginning [or in the middle, or at the end] of _____?"

Plan for Setting a Purpose for Reading

Two purposes should be set for reading, both of which relate to the orientation (and probably relate to the focus of the lesson):

- Read for meaning—"When you're reading, think about . . . "

- Word-solving strategy—"Also, if you come to a tricky part, remember what we just discussed . . . "

Oral Reading and Teacher Conference

Plan for Prompting

Based upon previous lessons, what prompts do I anticipate using with these students? (Document observations and prompts used on back.)

Guided Discussion After First Read

This component involves

- a brief discussion of the story, with a focus on the purpose that was set for reading; and
- one or two teaching points, based upon observations of the children's problem-solving efforts during the first read. (Document below.)

Appendix C-2 continued

Observations and Prompts Used	Sample Prompts
• The first teaching point should validate a strategic behavior that was observed. • The second teaching point should activate a strategic behavior that the student needs to use.	Use your pointing finger to help you read. Read it with your eyes. I like how . . . What did you notice? Why did you stop? It could be . . . , but look at . . . Check it. Does it look right and sound right to you? You said . . . Does that make sense? You said . . . Can we say it that way? You said . . . Does it look right? Try that again and think what would make sense. Reread and see if that helps. Do you know a part of that word? What could you try? You made a mistake on that page. Can you find it? Something doesn't seem quite right. How did you know . . . ? How would the character say that? Can you read all of this together? Let me show you. . . . Now you try.

Apprenticeship in Literacy, Second Edition: Transitions Across Reading and Writing, K–4
by Linda J. Dorn and Tammy Jones. © 2012. Stenhouse Publishers.

Appendix C-3

Language Arts Planner

Independent Reading – Running Records 15 min.				

Shared Reading – Read Aloud – Word Study 45 min.				

Guided Reading – Literacy Centers 1 hour				
20-min. groups				

Writing Workshop 30 min.				
10-min. mini-lesson				
15 min.of conferences w/ individuals and/or groups				
5-min. debriefing				

Appendix C-4

Word Study Mini-Lesson Planner

Developing Letter Categories	Chant the alphabet chart by pointing to and saying the name of each letter and naming the object.
Letter Discrimination	Sort the letter cards or magnetic letters by attribute: • Letters with sticks • Letters with straight sticks, slanted sticks, or straight and slanted sticks • Letters with circles • Letters with open circles or closed circles • Letters with sticks and circles • Letters with sticks, circles, or sticks and circles • Tall or small letters • Letters that look alike • Letters that look different • Uppercase letters or lowercase letters • Trace the letter with your finger as you say the movement (down, up, and over).
Letter Name Identification	• Sort the letters by letter name. (Example: Find all the *t*s.) • Quickly pull down each letter card and say its name. • Quickly pull down each letter card and say a word that begins with that letter. • Write the letter quickly several times on your paper as you say the movement. • Locate the letter in your guided reading book.
Sound/Symbol Relationships	• Initial consonants: b, c, d, f, g, h, j, k, l, m, n, p, q, r, s, t, v, w, x, y, z • Short vowels • Long vowels • Initial digraphs: ch, sh, th, wh • *R*-family blends: br, cr, dr, fr, gr, pr, tr, wr • *L*-family blends: bl, cl, fl, gl, pl, sl • *S*-family blends: sc, sk, sm, sn, sp, st, sw • Silent letters: tw, qu, kn, gn • Variant Vowels: ai, ea, ee, ei ,oa, oe, oi, ou, ue, etc. • Vowel and r combinations: ar, er, ir, or, ur • Vowel with silent e • Words that have endings: –s, -ed, -ing, -er, -ly, -ful • Words that begin with a vowel • Contractions • Compound words • Prefixes • Suffixes • Singular and plural words • Words that sound the same but are spelled differently • Double medial consonants: dd, ff, gg, ll, mm, nn, rr, ss, tt • Final consonant sounds: d, f, k, l, m, n, p, r, s, t, w • Final consonant digraphs: ck, nk, sh ,tch • Final consonant clusters: -mp,-nk, -st • Words that have two, three, or more syllables

Apprenticeship in Literacy, Second Edition: Transitions Across Reading and Writing, K–4
by Linda J. Dorn and Tammy Jones. © 2012. Stenhouse Publishers.

Appendix D-1

Writing Workshop Observation Protocol

Classroom: _____   Date: _____

Instructional Setting: Writing Workshop	Teacher and Student Interactions
Analyzing Data: Planning for Mini-Lesson Using assessment to inform instruction Goal: Teachers to use summative and formative assessments to inform their instruction	Teacher uses observation notes, conference notes, and analyses of students' writing to determine the following: • What do students already know about the writing process? • What do they need to know at this time? Teacher uses these data sources to develop an appropriate mini-lesson that meets the needs of the majority of writers in the classroom.
Explicit Teaching: Mini-Lesson/Guided Practice Goal: Students become skilled with the writing process, i.e.: • Process and Habits • Audience and Purposes/Author's Craft • Language Use and Conventions	Teacher explicitly teaches a "how-to" (strategy) lesson that focuses on a specific goal using one of the following tools to make the strategy or thinking visible: 1. Teacher and students draft a text together—i.e., they engage in shared writing. The teacher is the scribe, and together they compose, revise, or edit the message, depending on the goal. <div align="center">**or**</div>2. Teacher models a "how-to" (strategy) by writing aloud—i.e., thinking aloud about his or her thinking processes while composing, revising, or editing. <div align="center">**or**</div>3. Teacher uses mentor text/s (literature) to identify and discuss the power of the author's thinking—i.e., organization, crafting, revising, or editing processes. <div align="center">**or**</div>4. Teacher uses a student's partially completed or completed writing piece to highlight an identified skill or strategy. Teacher conducts a brief mini-lesson—i.e., 8–10 minutes in length. **Guided Practice:** Teacher provides the students with and supports an opportunity to apply the "how-to" (strategy) to their own writing if needed.
Independent Writing Goal: Students to develop a habit of writing and view themselves as writers by writing daily inside and outside school.	Teacher provides students with an opportunity to choose their own topics for writing (can be a choice within a specific mode). Teacher provides students with an opportunity to apply writing strategies to their own work with support (a writing assessment). Students are engaged and on task during independent writing time—i.e., they understand what to do and how to use resources to help themselves (peers, thesaurus, dictionary).
Writing Conferences; The Heartbeat of Writing Workshop Goal: Students' knowledge base of the writing process will be strengthened, thus writing daily for multiple purposes.	Teacher holds one-on-one conferences with 3–5 individual students per day lasting approximately 3–5 minutes each and/or confers with small groups of writers around a common writing goal. Teacher begins conference by asking the student where he or she is in the writing process and gets the student talking. Teacher responds to the student's writing with a reaction to the meaning and then lifts the writer by focusing on 1–2 "how-to" strategies the writer might want to try. Teacher confers with the writer by focusing on the writer, not the writing—i.e., talk is around developing writing strategies, not a set of items. Teacher makes notes and keeps documentation of the student's writing skills (underground strategies) and strategies (thinking processes) that need more attention. Teacher allows students to confer with other writers if they choose to do so, thus receiving feedback and learning from other writers. Teacher provides the students with portfolios to house their completed pieces of work. These pieces can be revisited later if the writer chooses to do so.
Share Time Goal: Students see themselves as writers and value other writers' feedback.	• Teacher provides an opportunity for all students to come together as a community of learners to reflect on their engagement within the workshop if needed. • Teacher provides an opportunity for 3–5 writers to share their writing and receive feedback and learn from other writers.

Appendix D-2

Language-Literacy Rubric

KINDERGARTEN

The behaviors listed below represent end-of-year goals for students in kindergarten.

		Proficiency Levels			
		Below the Standard **1** requires full support	Approaching the Standard **2** requires much support	Meeting the Standard **3** requires some support	Exceeding the Standard **4** requires little support
Reading	**Foundational Language Skills** √ recognizes and produces rhyming words √ generates words that begin with the same sound √ recognizes and names all upper- and lowercase letters √ knows the five major vowels and that they have two primary sounds	1	2	3	4
	Strategic Reading of Text √ can read 2–3 lines of patterned text with strong picture support, pointing to words with one-to-one correspondence √ self-monitors reading, noticing errors and searching for information to self-correct	1	2	3	4
	Comprehending of Text √ talks about text, sharing opinions, making personal connections, comparing and contrasting across texts (the latter with support) √ retells familiar stories, referencing key details (with support); identifies main topic in informational text, sharing key details (with support)	1	2	3	4
	Amount of Text Read √ rereads easy, familiar books at home	1	2	3	4
Writing	**Focus and Organization of Text** √ states an opinion or introduces a topic through drawing, dictating, or writing √ writes about a specific real event, telling what happened in the correct order, and ending with a reaction	1	2	3	4
	Support and Development of Ideas Within Text √ shares facts about a topic through drawing, dictating, or writing	1	2	3	4
	Strategic Writing of Text √ problem-solves tricky words by saying them slowly or clapping them to hear their parts √ rereads what has been written in order to determine what should be written next; crosses out unwanted letters/words	1	2	3	4
	Language Use and Conventions in Text √ records most beginning and ending consonant sounds √ capitalizes the word *I* √ includes spaces between words √ writes most letters with correct formation	1	2	3	4
	Engagement in Workshop Experiences whole-group and small-group discussions, independent reading and writing √ actively listens when texts are read aloud √ participates in discussions, sharing ideas and listening respectfully to others √ quietly reads, writes, and/or completes tasks during independent work time	1	2	3	4

Julie Eckberg, in collaboration with LeRoy CUSD 2, IL. Information/language based upon *Shaping Literate Minds* (Dorn and Soffos 2001b), *Interventions That Work* (Dorn and Soffos 2011a), Common Core State Standards (NGA/CCSSO 2010), and *Teaching for Deep Comprehension* (Dorn and Soffos 2005).

Appendix D-3

Language-Literacy Rubric

FIRST GRADE

The behaviors listed below represent end-of-year goals for students in first grade.

		Proficiency Levels			
		Below the Standard **1** requires full support	Approaching the Standard **2** requires much support	Meeting the Standard **3** requires some support	Exceeding the Standard **4** requires little support
Reading	**Foundational Language Skills** √ distinguishes short- and long-vowel sounds in spoken one-syllable words √ decodes regularly spelled, one-syllable, short- and long-vowel words √ knows common consonant digraphs: sh, ch, th, wh, ck, ph	1	2	3	4
	Strategic Reading of Text √ self-monitors reading, noticing when something isn't quite right √ initiates action at tricky spots: rereads; makes additional attempts at unknown word, breaking it apart in a left-to-right process √ self-monitors how reading sounds, working to read groups of words together so the reading sounds similar to how we naturally talk	1	2	3	4
	Comprehending of Text √ talks about text, sharing opinions, making personal connections, comparing and contrasting across texts √ retells familiar stories, demonstrating understanding of lesson/message; identifies main topic of informational text and shares key details	1	2	3	4
	Amount of Text Read √ easy, successful, independent reading; based on student's reading log	1	2	3	4
Writing	**Focus and Organization of Text** √ states an opinion when writing an opinion piece; introduces a topic when writing an informative piece √ focuses on 2–3 specific, real events when writing a story, using transitional words (*first, next, then, finally*), and ending with a closing	1	2	3	4
	Support and Development of Ideas Within Text √ gives reason for opinion in opinion piece; shares facts in an informative piece; provides details in a story	1	2	3	4
	Strategic Writing of Text √ problem-solves tricky words by saying them slowly or clapping them to hear their parts √ rereads writing to reflect on meaning; crosses out unwanted letters/words; adds new words/ideas with caret; circles words that do not look right and corrects them	1	2	3	4
	Language Use and Conventions in Text √ spells high-frequency "no-excuse" words correctly √ includes spaces between words consistently √ writes all letters using correct formation √ capitalizes the pronoun *I* and names of people √ begins to use end punctuation, followed by a capital letter	1	2	3	4
	Engagement in Workshop Experiences whole-group and small-group discussions, independent reading and writing √ actively listens when texts are read aloud √ participates in discussions, sharing ideas and listening respectfully to others √ quietly reads, writes, and/or completes tasks during independent work time	1	2	3	4

Julie Eckberg, in collaboration with LeRoy CUSD 2, IL. Information/language based upon *Shaping Literate Minds* (Dorn and Soffos 2001b), *Interventions That Work* (Dorn and Soffos 2011a), Common Core State Standards (NGA/CCSSO 2010), *Guiding Readers and Writers* (Grades 3–6) (Fountas and Pinnell 2001), and *Teaching for Deep Comprehension* (Dorn and Soffos 2005).

Appendix D-4

Language-Literacy Rubric

SECOND GRADE

The behaviors listed below represent end-of-year goals for students in second grade.

		Proficiency Levels			
		Below the Standard **1** requires full support	Approaching the Standard **2** requires much support	Meeting the Standard **3** requires some support	Exceeding the Standard **4** requires little support
	Foundational Language Skills √ solidifies knowledge of common word parts and how words work √ knows common prefixes and suffixes and uses them to understand word meanings: dis-, re-, un-, -y, -ly, -est, -less, -ful	1	2	3	4
Reading	**Strategic Reading of Text** √ self-monitors, noticing when meaning is lost and rereading is necessary √ initiates action at tricky spots: rereads; makes additional attempts at unknown word, breaking it apart left-to-right at larger word parts √ pauses at appropriate places (3- to 4-word phrase groups or longer) and alters expression, guided by meaning of story and punctuation	1	2	3	4
Reading	**Comprehending of Text** √ talks/writes about text, explaining opinions, making personal connections, comparing and contrasting across texts, and citing evidence √ retells stories and determines lesson/message/moral; identifies main topic of multiparagraph informational text and focus of specific paragraphs	1	2	3	4
Reading	**Amount of Text Read** √ easy, successful, independent reading; based on student's reading log	1	2	3	4
Writing	**Focus and Organization of Text** √ states an opinion when writing an opinion piece and introduces a topic when writing an informative piece; groups related information together; ends with a concluding statement or section √ focuses on several real events when writing a story, using transitional words/phrases (*next, then, after that, later on*), and ending with a closing	1	2	3	4
Writing	**Support and Development of Ideas Within Text** √ gives reasons for opinion in opinion piece; shares facts and definitions in an informative piece; describes actions, thoughts, and feelings in a story	1	2	3	4
Writing	**Strategic Writing of Text** √ problem-solves words by saying them slowly or clapping them to hear their parts √ rereads writing to reflect on meaning and word choice; crosses out unwanted letters/words; adds new words/ideas with caret; circles words that do not look right and corrects them; uses circles/arrows to rearrange parts of text	1	2	3	4
Writing	**Language Use and Conventions in Text** √ correctly spells high-frequency "no-excuse" words √ uses uppercase letters only in appropriate places (e.g., proper nouns) √ uses commas in a series and in parts of a letter; uses apostrophes in contractions and common possessives √ uses end punctuation, followed by a capital letter, most of the time √ writes in complete sentences most of the time	1	2	3	4
	Engagement in Workshop Experiences whole-group and small-group discussions, independent reading and writing √ actively listens when texts are read aloud √ participates in discussions, sharing ideas and listening respectfully to others √ quietly reads, writes, and/or completes tasks during independent work time	1	2	3	4

Julie Eckberg, in collaboration with LeRoy CUSD 2, IL. Information/language based upon *Shaping Literate Minds* (Dorn and Soffos 2001b), *Interventions That Work* (Dorn and Soffos 2011a), Common Core State Standards (NGA/CCSSO 2010), *Guiding Readers and Writers* (Grades 3–6) (Fountas and Pinnell 2001), and *Teaching for Deep Comprehension* (Dorn and Soffos 2005).

Apprenticeship in Literacy, Second Edition: Transitions Across Reading and Writing, K–4
by Linda J. Dorn and Tammy Jones. © 2012. Stenhouse Publishers.

Appendix D-5

Language-Literacy Rubric

THIRD GRADE

The behaviors listed below represent end-of-year goals for students in third grade.

		Proficiency Levels			
		Below the Standard **1** requires full support	Approaching the Standard **2** requires much support	Meeting the Standard **3** requires some support	Exceeding the Standard **4** requires little support
Reading	**Foundational Language Skills** √ can explain the function of nouns, pronouns, verbs, adjectives, adverbs √ can recognize and produce simple, compound, and complex sentences	1	2	3	4
	Strategic Reading of Text √ self-monitors, noticing when meaning is lost and rereading is necessary √ initiates action at tricky spots: rereads; makes additional attempts at unknown word, breaking it apart left-to-right at larger word parts √ pauses at appropriate places (3- to 4-word phrase groups or longer) and alters expression, guided by meaning of story and punctuation √ uses sentence-level context clues to clarify meaning of words/phrases	1	2	3	4
	Comprehending of Text √ talks/writes about text, explaining opinions, making personal connections,comparing/contrasting across texts, analyzing characters, citing evidence √ retells stories and determines lesson/message/moral, discussing key details the author used to convey it; determines central idea of informational text, explaining how it is supported by key details	1	2	3	4
	Amount of Text Read √ easy, successful, independent reading; based on student's reading log	1	2	3	4
Writing	**Focus and Organization of Text** √ states an opinion when writing an opinion piece and introduces a topic when writing an informative piece; groups related information together, using paragraphs; uses words/phrases to link ideas within paragraphs (*therefore, since, for example*); ends with a concluding statement/section √ focuses on several events when writing a real or imagined story; uses transitional words/phrases (*next, after that, later on*); ends with closing	1	2	3	4
	Support and Development of Ideas Within Text √ gives reasons for opinion in opinion piece; shares facts, definitions, details in an informative piece; describes actions, thoughts, feelings in a story	1	2	3	4
	Strategic Writing of Text √ problem-solves words by listening for known parts and using analogy √ rereads writing to reflect on meaning and word choice; crosses out unwanted letters/words; adds new words/ideas with caret; circles words that do not look right and corrects them; uses circles/arrows to rearrange parts of text	1	2	3	4
	Language Use and Conventions in Text √ spells high-frequency "no-excuse" words correctly √ capitalizes all pronouns; uses commas in a series and in a letter; uses apostrophes in contractions and common possessives; punctuates dialogue √ uses end punctuation, followed by a capital letter, consistently √ writes in complete sentences consistently	1	2	3	4
	Engagement in Workshop Experiences whole-group and small-group discussions, independent reading and writing √ actively listens when texts are read aloud √ participates in discussions, sharing ideas and listening respectfully to others √ quietly reads, writes, and/or completes tasks during independent work time	1	2	3	4

Julie Eckberg, in collaboration with LeRoy CUSD 2, IL. Information/language based upon *Shaping Literate Minds* (Dorn and Soffos 2001b), *Interventions That Work* (Dorn and Soffos 2011a), Common Core State Standards (NGA/CCSSO 2010), *Guiding Readers and Writers* (Grades 3–6) (Fountas and Pinnell 2001), and *Teaching for Deep Comprehension* (Dorn and Soffos 2005).

Appendix D-6

Language-Literacy Rubric

FOURTH GRADE

The behaviors listed below represent end-of-year goals for students in fourth grade.

		Proficiency Levels			
		Below the Standard **1** requires full support	Approaching the Standard **2** requires much support	Meeting the Standard **3** requires some support	Exceeding the Standard **4** requires little support
Reading	**Foundational Language Skills** √ can form and use prepositional phrases √ can recognize and interpret figures of speech such as similes and metaphors √ continues to develop knowledge of meaningful word parts (Greek and Latin affixes and roots) for use in problem-solving words in reading and writing	1	2	3	4
	Strategic Reading of Text √ self-monitors, noticing when meaning is lost and rereading is necessary √ breaks unknown words apart at larger, meaningful word parts √ pauses at appropriate places (3- to 4-word phrase groups or longer) and alters expression, guided by meaning of story and punctuation; works to read longer stretches of text together (e.g., introductory clauses) √ uses context of sentence, paragraph, and section to determine/clarify meaning of words/phrases; also uses dictionary, glossary, thesaurus	1	2	3	4
	Comprehending of Text √ talks/writes about text, explaining opinions, making personal connections, comparing/contrasting across texts, analyzing characters, citing evidence √ summarizes story, drama, poem, determining theme and key details used to convey it; summarizes informational text, determining central idea and explaining how it is supported by key details	1	2	3	4
Writing	**Focus and Organization of Text** √ states opinion/introduces topic when writing opinion/informative pieces; uses words/phrases to link ideas within paragraphs (e.g., *for instance, in addition, consequently, specifically*); ends with a concluding statement/section, related to the opinion or information presented √ begins stories in a way that helps to orient the reader; ends with a closing that follows from the experiences or events described	1	2	3	4
	Support and Development of Ideas Within Text √ gives reasons in an opinion piece, supporting them with facts/details √ shares facts, definitions, details in an informative piece, elaborating with examples; integrates information from two texts on the same topic √ describes actions, thoughts, feelings in a story, using dialogue	1	2	3	4
	Strategic Writing of Text √ problem-solves words by listening for known parts in word and using analogy √ rereads writing to reflect on meaning, development of ideas, word choice; works to grab the reader's attention more effectively in the opening	1	2	3	4
	Language Use and Conventions in Text √ capitalizes words appropriately, uses end punctuation, and correctly spells high-frequency "no-excuse" words in all written work √ correctly spells frequently confused words: *to, two, too; there, their; its, it's* √ recognizes fragments and run-ons in sentences and corrects them √ uses comma after when/if introductory clause; uses comma before coordinating conjunction in compound sentence	1	2	3	4
	Engagement in Workshop Experiences whole-group and small-group discussions, independent reading and writing √ actively listens when texts are read aloud; participates in discussions, sharing ideas and listening respectfully to others; quietly reads, writes, and/or completes tasks during independent work time	1	2	3	4

Julie Eckberg, in collaboration with LeRoy CUSD 2, IL. Information/language based upon *Shaping Literate Minds* (Dorn and Soffos 2001b), *Interventions That Work* (Dorn and Soffos 2011a), Common Core State Standards (NGA/CCSSO 2010), *Guiding Readers and Writers* (Grades 3–6) (Fountas and Pinnell 2001), and *Teaching for Deep Comprehension* (Dorn and Soffos 2005).

Appendix D-7

**KINDER
GARTEN**

Dictated

Text

Text
ReadAloud

A
1

B
2

C
3–4

Emergent Processing Level
become aware

Strategic Behaviors and Foundational Skills

Emergent Level

"The goal of instruction at the emergent level is to create a textual context where children can learn how to attend to print. . . . At the emergent level, the teacher carefully selects easy texts with repetitive patterns that contain some letters and words that the child is beginning to notice" (Dorn and Soffos 2001, 34).

Using the Checklist

The below checklist should guide a teacher's daily planning and decision making, in that the below behaviors are the learning goal. Book choice (including its level), book introduction, and instructional moves will affect whether or not the below behaviors will be observed in any given teaching-learning situation. For the systematic monitoring of progress, complete the checklist based upon running records derived from the Keystone book assessment (see Dorn and Soffos 2011a for a description of Keystone assessments).

Very early on, does the student . . .

- tell the story that could be in print
- have some concepts about print under control
  (e.g., front/back of book, some understanding of moving left to right and down the page)
- know some letters; recognize two or more words with lapses

A bit later, does the student . . .

- try to use the language of the book
- attend to shape, size, position, and pattern in print
- orient to print, knowing where to start and where to move
- attempt to point to words as he or she reads

Later on, does the student *self-monitor* his or her reading . . .

- noticing when something isn't quite right—stopping, pausing, commenting, or appealing for help
  (e.g., child "runs out of words" when pointing and reading and then looks at the teacher)

Does the student use various *sources of information* to predict what the print might say?

- knowledge of the story—meaning
  (i.e., whether something makes sense, based upon the story and the illustrations)
- knowledge of language—structure
  (i.e., whether something sounds right, based upon English grammar)
- knowledge of letters and/or words—visual information
  (i.e., whether something looks right, based upon the child's known words and the first letter in unknown words)

Does the student *cross-check* these sources of information, resulting in self-correction?

- Example: For the text, *Mom is resting*, a child reads, "Mom is sleeping." The child used knowledge of the story (meaning) and knowledge of language (structure) to predict "sleeping." The child then checks that information *against* the first letter of *resting* (visual information that the child hasn't used yet) and self-corrects.

At unknown words, does the student *initiate action* and *search for information* . . .

- looking at pictures
- rereading
- articulating first letter
  using resources—ABC chart, name chart, knowledge of known words—to support letter-sound links

Does the child . . .

- read 2–3 lines of patterned text with picture support, using one-to-one correspondence
- begin to transition in book Level C to "pointing with eyes" instead of the finger

On *print concepts, phonological awareness, phonics*, and *word recognition*, does the child . . .

- recognize and produce rhyming words
- generate words that begin with the same sound
- recognize and name all upper- and lowercase letters
- know the five major vowels and that they have two primary sounds (long and short)
- read common high-frequency words by sight

Appendix D-7 continued

FIRST GRADE beg to mid-year	Early Processing Level *gaining control*	**Early, Transitional, and Fluent Levels**

Early, Transitional, and Fluent Levels

Readers at the early, transitional, and fluent levels of processing are similar in the strategic reading behaviors they use. The difference is in the types of texts they read. As students move through these levels, they read increasingly longer text with richer content and vocabulary and more complex sentence structures. In this way, teaching revolves around supporting students as they use a set of strategic behaviors within a broader range of reading circumstances.

One other difference between the processing levels is the speed at which the strategic processing system works. For instance, although searching for information is a strategic behavior of both first-grade students in the early level and third-grade students at the fluent level, the process for the latter will be quicker and more efficient.

On comprehension, the behaviors below provide evidence of comprehending during the process of reading, as part of the active thinking process.

Does the student *self-monitor* his or her reading . . .

- noticing when something isn't quite right—stopping, pausing, commenting, or appealing for help

Does the student shift from cross-checking information after an error has been made to *integrating* information at error?

- Running record analysis moves from ⓂⓈ V   M SⓋ
  to . . . ⓂⓈⓋ   M S V

At point of difficulty, does the student *initiate action* and *search for information* . . .

- rereading
- making additional attempts at tricky words
- searching through words in a left-to-right process, taking them apart at larger units of analysis
  s-un, *wh-ite*, *look-ing* at the early level
  far-mer, *un-der-st-and* at the transitional level
  con-tain-er, *ex-plan-a-tory* at the fluent level
- using word parts—such as prefixes, suffixes, roots, compound parts—to help with word meanings
  emphasized within transitional and fluent levels

Does the student *reread for various purposes*?

- to confirm meaning
- to pick up new information for solving problems (searching)
- to put stretches of language "together" to make better sense of the text and improve how the reading sounds

Does the student *orchestrate* . . .

- the above problem-solving behaviors efficiently (i.e., smoothly, "on the run")?

On *fluency*, does the student's reading . . .

- flow at an appropriate rate
- include pauses at appropriate places, guided by the author's meaning and use of punctuation, resulting in 3- to 4-word meaningful phrase groups or longer
- include appropriate changes in pitch (i.e., intonation) and stress (i.e., emphasis), guided by the author's meaning and use of punctuation and text features

On *phonological awareness*, *phonics*, and *word recognition* does the child . . .

- distinguish long from short-vowel sounds in spoken single-syllable words (grade 1)
- know the spelling-sound correspondences for common consonant digraphs: sh, ch, th, wh, ck, ph (grade 1)
- decode regularly spelled one-syllable words, including those with consonant blends; read words with inflectional endings (grade 1)
- know final -*e*, common vowel teams (grade 1), and other vowel teams (grade 2) for representing long sounds
- decode two-syllable words (grade 1, depending on the word, and grade 2)
- decode words with common prefixes and suffixes (grade 2)
- identify and know the meaning of common prefixes and derivational suffixes (grade 3)
  -*ment*, -*ity*, -*tion* turn words into nouns; -*ful*, -*ous*, -*al* turn words into adjectives; -*ly* turns words into adverbs
- decode multisyllable words (grade 3)

Left column grade/level labels:

FIRST GRADE beg to mid-year — **Early Processing Level** *gaining control*
D 5–6
E 7–8
F 9–10
G 11–12

end of **FIRST GRADE** to end of **SECOND GRADE** — **Transitional Processing Level** *extending control*
H 14
I 16
J 18
K
L
M

THIRD GRADE — **Fluent Processing Level** *enlarging the system*
N
O
P

Information and language drawn from *Shaping Literate Minds* (Dorn and Soffos 2001b) and *Change Over Time in Children's Literacy Development* (Clay 2001). Synthesis of information and formatting, Julie Eckberg in collaboration with LeRoy CUSD 2, IL.

Apprenticeship in Literacy, Second Edition: Transitions Across Reading and Writing, K–4
by Linda J. Dorn and Tammy Jones. © 2012. Stenhouse Publishers.

Appendix D-8

Read-Think-n-Write Rubric

GRADE 2

A one-paragraph written response to text

	Proficiency Levels				
	Below the Standard **1** requires full support	Approaching the Standard **2** requires much support	Meeting the Standard **3** requires some support	Exceeding the Standard **4** requires little support	sub-score
Focus and Organization of Ideas √ states opinion, prediction, question, connection, feeling, etc. √ maintains focus on that statement/topic throughout paragraph	1	2	3	4	x 2 =
Support and Development of Ideas √ explains opinion, prediction, question, connection, feeling, etc. √ elaborates by referencing specific events, actions, or language in text	1	2	3	4	x 2 =
Language Use and Conventions √ correctly spells high-frequency "no-excuse" words √ uses uppercase letters only in appropriate places (e.g., proper nouns) √ uses commas in a series; uses apostrophes in contractions and common possessives √ uses end punctuation, followed by a capital letter, most of the time √ writes in complete sentences most of the time	1	2	3	4	x 2 =
Effort √ neatness √ timeliness	1	2	3	4	x 1 =
Comments			**Entry Format** add one point if date and title of text are included		
			Total Score 29 possible points		

Julie Eckberg, in collaboration with LeRoy CUSD 2, IL. Grade 2 Read-Think-n-Write Rubric aligns with Grade 2 Language-Literacy Rubric (Eckberg). The latter includes synthesized information/language drawn from *Shaping Literate Minds* (Dorn and Soffos 2001b), *Interventions That Work* (Dorn and Soffos 2011a), Common Core State Standards (NGA/CCSSO 2010), *Guiding Readers and Writers* (Grades 3–6) (Fountas and Pinnell 2001), and *Teaching for Deep Comprehension* (Dorn and Soffos 2005).

Appendix D-9

Read-Think-n-Write Rubric

GRADE 4

A two-paragraph written response to text

	Proficiency Levels				
	Below the Standard **1** requires full support	Approaching the Standard **2** requires much support	Meeting the Standard **3** requires some support	Exceeding the Standard **4** requires little support	sub-score
Summary of Text (paragraph one) √ briefly summarizes text, including relevant information about characters, setting, and plot	1	2	3	4	x 2 =
Focus and Organization of Ideas (paragraph two) √ states opinion, prediction, question, connection, feeling, etc. in topic sentence of paragraph √ maintains focus on that statement/topic throughout paragraph	1	2	3	4	x 2 =
Support and Development of Ideas (paragraph two) √ explains opinion, prediction, question, connection, feeling, etc. √ elaborates by referencing specific events, actions, or language in text	1	2	3	4	x 2 =
Language Use and Conventions √ capitalizes words appropriately, uses end punctuation, and correctly spells high-frequency "no-excuse" words √ correctly spells frequently confused words: *to, two, too; there, their, its, it's* √ recognizes fragments and run-ons in sentences and corrects them √ uses comma after when/if introductory clause; uses comma before coordinating conjunction in compound sentence	1	2	3	4	x 2 =
Effort √ neatness √ timeliness	1	2	3	4	x 1 =
Comments			**Entry Format** add one point if date and title of text are included		
			Total Score 37 possible points		

Julie Eckberg, in collaboration with LeRoy CUSD 2, IL. Grade 4 Read-Think-n-Write Rubric aligns with Grade 4 Language-Literacy Rubric (Eckberg). The latter includes synthesized information drawn from *Shaping Literate Minds* (Dorn and Soffos 2001b), *Interventions That Work* (Dorn and Soffos 2011a), Common Core State Standards (NGA/CCSSO 2010), *Guiding Readers and Writers* (Grades 3–6) (Fountas and Pinnell 2001), and *Teaching for Deep Comprehension* (Dorn and Soffos 2005).

Appendix D-10

Writing Continuum of Emergent to Fluent Writing Behaviors: Text Types and Purposes

Emergent	Beginning Early	Late Early	Transitional	Fluent
Write opinion pieces about a book they are reading (e.g., My favorite part is); use drawings that match and elaborate on the message. Write informative/ explanatory texts that name what they are writing about, include some information about the topic, use drawings that match and elaborate on the message. Write a narrative piece that tells about the events in the order in which they occurred; use drawings that match and elaborate on the message.	Write opinion pieces that introduce the topic, state an opinion, supply a reason for the opinion, and provide some sense of closure. Write informational/ explanatory texts on a known topic, name the topic, supply some facts about the topic, and provide some sense of closure. Write narratives that recount two or more appropriately sequenced events, provide some details regarding what happened, and use temporal words to signal events order and provide some sense of closure.	Write opinion pieces that introduce the book, state an opinion, supply reasons that support the opinion, use linking words (e.g., *because*, and, *also*) to connect opinion and reasons, and provide a concluding statement or section. Write informative/ explanatory texts that introduce a topic, use facts and definitions to develop points, and provide a concluding statement or section. Write narratives that recount a well-elaborated event or short sequence of events, including details to describe actions, thoughts, and feelings; use temporal words to signal event order, and provide a sense of closure.	Write opinion pieces on topics or texts that support a point of view with reasons. Pieces include organizational structures that list reasons, use linking words or phrases, and provide a concluding statement. Write informative/ explanatory texts that examine a topic and convey ideas and information clearly. Pieces include organizational structures that link related information, develop topics with facts, definitions, and details, use ideas within categories of information, use words and phrases to connect ideas, and provide a concluding statement. Write narratives to develop real or imagined events using crafting techniques, descriptive details, and clear event sequences. Pieces establish relationships between characters and situation, use dialogue appropriately, use temporal words and phrases to signal event order, and provide a sense of closure.	Write opinion pieces on topics or texts that support a point of view with reasons. Pieces include organizational structures that group related ideas to support the writer's purpose, provide reasons that are supported by facts and details, link opinion and reason by using words and phrases, and provide a concluding statement. Write informative/ explanatory texts to examine a topic and convey ideas and information clearly. Pieces include organizational structures (paragraphs, headings, illustrations, etc.); use precise language and domain-specific vocabulary; develop topic with facts, definitions, concrete details, quotations, etc.; link ideas by using words and phrases; and provide a sense of closure. Write narratives to develop real or imagined events using crafting techniques, descriptive details, and clear event orders. Pieces establish relationships between characters and situations, use dialogue effectively, use concrete words and phrases, use figurative language and sensory details to convey events precisely, and provide a conclusion that follows from the narrated events.

Based on Common Core State Standards (NGA/CCSSO 2010).

Appendix E

Selected Lessons from a Ten-Week Program of Independent and Assisted-Writing Activities

Lesson 1

Journal Analysis (semiphonetic stage of spelling)
- Writes name.
- Hears *l* in beginning and ending positions.
- Adds letters to a word to make a word look longer (*oatmeal*).
- Returns to second line and makes new attempt for *likes*.
- Experiments with periods.
- Shows directional movement.
- Does not use spacing between words.

Focus of Group-Assisted Writing (interactive writing at the emergent level)
- Focus on spacing and hearing sounds in words.
- Demonstrate early strategies (rereading, letter formation, linking to ABC chart, etc.).

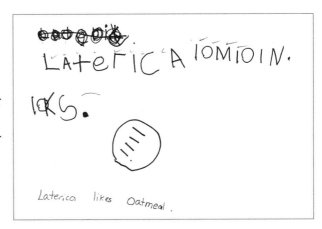

Figure E-1

Lesson 3

Journal Analysis (semiphonetic stage of spelling)
- Shows risk-taking behavior through early editing attempts.
- Hears consonant sounds (c, k, l, t) in beginning and ending positions.
- Writes familiar word from shared reading (*pig*).
- Uses exclamation point.
- Does not use spacing.

Focus of Group-Assisted Writing (interactive writing at the emergent level)
- Focus on spacing, hearing sounds in words, and rereading.
- Introduce dictionary for recording known and partially known words.

Figure E-2

Lesson 8

Journal Analysis (phonetic stage of spelling)
- Shows good control of spacing.
- Writes known words.
- Hears consonant sounds in beginning, middle, and ending positions.
- Shows awareness of visual features in common words.
- Writes more complex sentence.
- Ignores ending punctuation.

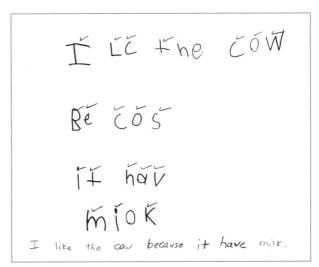

Figure E-3

Focus of Group-Assisted Writing (interactive writing at the emergent level for one or two more lessons)

- Focus on hearing sounds in sequence.
- Attend to visual features of frequently encountered words.
- Introduce role of punctuation (quotation marks) in expressive reading.

Lesson 11

Journal Analysis (phonetic stage of spelling)

- Good control of spacing.
- Uses known word (*the*).
- Uses punctuation (exclamation point) for emphasis (also underlines text to show excitement).
- Experiments with dialogue in text and bubble.
- Hears beginning and ending consonant sounds.
- Shows awareness that words contain vowels, and experiments with these as visual markers (with no letter/sound correspondence).
- Edits attempt for *now* (crosses out *a* and revises with *o*).

Focus of Assisted Writing (interactive writing at early level with two or three sentences)

- Introduce how to use key words (*where, when, why, how*) to build on meaning.
- Continue to use varied punctuation (exclamation points, quotation marks, periods) to support meaning.
- Continue to work on hearing sounds in sequence and attending to visual information in frequently encountered words.

Figure E-4

Lesson 15

Journal Analysis (phonetic stage of spelling)

- Hears consonant sounds in beginning, middle, and ending positions.
- Hears some vowels.
- Uses known words.
- Uses two sentences to communicate message.
- Uses lead sentence to include "when" element.
- Experiments with commas.
- Uses quotation marks and exclamation point to express meaning.

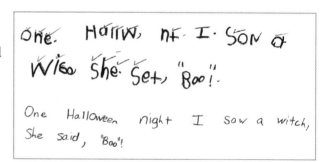

Figure E-5

Focus of Assisted Writing (early revisions with overhead transparency)

- Display on whiteboard children's writing samples to illustrate how to add details for writing longer stories.
- Display page from guided reading book to illustrate writer's techniques (descriptive language, lead sentences, etc.).
- Invite peer prompting using key words (*where, when, why, how*, etc.).

- Begin writing-aloud demonstrations.
- Introduce editing and revising techniques (carets, insertions, crossing out, etc.).
- Emphasize use of punctuation for expressive reading.
- Demonstrate simple analogies with visual patterns from known words.

Lesson 20

Journal Analysis (transitional stage of spelling)

- Uses lead-in sentence (when).
- Expands message to three sentences.
- Edits on the spot to include descriptive information (starts to write *day* and changes it to *Thanksgiving day*).
- Uses varied punctuation (period, comma, quotation marks, and exclamation point).
- Uses known words.

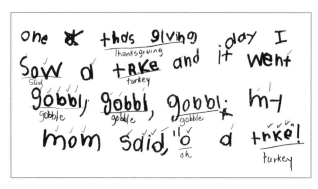

Figure E-6 ("One Thanksgiving day I saw a turkey and it went gobble, gobble, gobble. My mom said, 'Oh, a turkey!'")

Focus of Assisted Writing (writing aloud with revising and editing)

- Continue to emphasize editing and revising techniques while writing aloud.
- Illustrate importance of writing for different purposes and audiences.
- Demonstrate problem-solving analogies visually.
- Use personal resources, such as the dictionary and word wall.

Lesson 30

Journal Analysis (transitional stage of spelling)

- Uses a balance of problem-solving techniques for editing spelling (corrects the spelling at the time of error, circles the spelling after the story is completed, and uses other resources to confirm spelling).
- Understands how to write a letter.
- Uses commas and periods to communicate meanings.
- Attends to visual patterns in words.

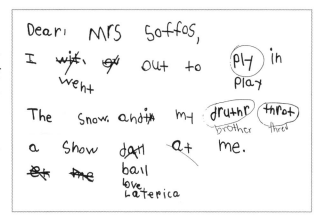

Figure E-7 ("Dear Mrs. Soffos, I went out to play in the snow and my brother threw a snowball at me. Love Laterica.")

Focus of Assisted Writing (writing aloud with revising and editing)

- Continue to demonstrate flexible ways to problem-solve on the spot.
- Continue to demonstrate editing and revising techniques.
- Continue to demonstrate composing process with various topics.

Lesson 48

Journal Analysis (transitional stage of spelling)

- Composes well-organized and coherent texts.
- Uses punctuation to support meaning.
- Uses editing and revising techniques.
- Applies problem-solving strategies on the spot.

Focus of Assisted Writing (writing aloud with revising and editing)

- Continue to focus on composing various texts for different purposes.
- Continue to emphasize editing and revising techniques.

Lesson 50

Journal Analysis (transitional and conventional stages of spelling)

- Retells a detailed and chronologically organized version of a story.
- Includes various punctuation to express meaning.
- Identifies first draft as "sloppy copy."
- Uses editing and revising techniques (lines drawn through phrases, crossing out, carets and insertions, circling).

Focus of Assisted Writing (writing aloud with revising and editing)

- Phase out the assisted writing activities.
- Devote extended periods to independent writing.
- Be ready to model the writing process and provide assisted-writing activities as needed.

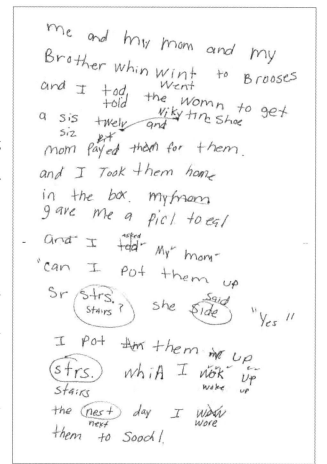

Figure E-8 ("Me and my mom and my brother went to Bruces and I told the woman to get a size twelve Nike tennis shoe and my mom paid for them and I took them home in the box. My mom gave me a pickle to eat and I told my mom 'Can I put them upstairs?' She said 'Yes.' I put them upstairs. When I woke up the next day I wore them to school.")

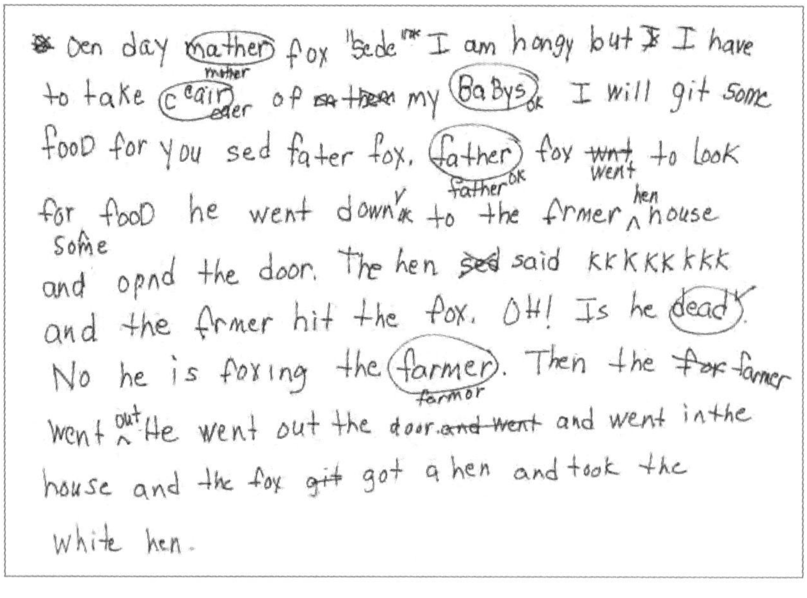

Figure E-9 ("One day mother fox 'said' I am hungry but I have to take care of my babies. I will get some food for you said father fox. Father fox went to look for some food. He went down to the farmer's hen house and opened the door. The hen said kkkkkkk and the farmer hit the fox. Oh! Is he dead? No. Hen is foxing the farmer. Then the farmer went out. He went out the door and went in the house and the fox got a hen and took the white hen.")

REFERENCES

Adams, M. 1996. *Beginning to Read: Thinking and Learning About Print*. 9th ed. Cambridge, MA: MIT Press.

Adler, D. 2009. *The Mystery of the Stolen Diamonds*. St. Louis, MO: Turtleback Books.

Allington, R. L. 2002a. "What I've Learned About Effective Reading Instruction: From a Decade of Studying Exemplary Elementary Classroom Teachers." *Phi Delta Kappan* 83 (10): 740–747.

———. 2002b. "Research on Reading/Learning Disability Interventions." In *What Research Has to Say About Reading Instruction*. 3rd ed., ed. A. E. Farstrup and S. Samuels. Newark, DE: International Reading Association.

Anderson, C. 2000. *How's It Going? A Practical Guide to Conferring with Student Writers*. Portsmouth, NH: Heinemann.

Anderson, R., E. H. Hiebert, J. A. Scott, and I. Wilkinson. 1985. *Becoming a Nation of Readers: The Report on the Commission on Reading*. Washington, DC: The National Institute of Education, U.S. Department of Education.

Annie E. Casey Foundation. 2010. *EARLY WARNING! Why Reading by the End of Third Grade Matters*. A KIDS COUNT Special Report from the Annie E. Casey Foundation. Baltimore: Annie E. Casey Foundation.

Bruner, J. 1967. *Studies in Cognitive Growth: A Collaboration at the Center for Cognitive Growth*. New York: Wiley.

———. 1986. *Actual Minds, Possible Worlds*. Cambridge: Harvard University Press.

Bryson, T. 2010. *Balloon Ride*. Pelham, NY: Benchmark Education.

Burton, M., C. French, and T. Jones. 2010. *Families*. Pelham, NY: Benchmark Education.

Button, K., M. Johnson, and P. Furgerson. 1996. "Interactive Writing in a Primary Classroom." *The Reading Teacher* 49 (6): 446–454.

Calkins, L. 1994. *The Art of Teaching Writing*. Portsmouth, NH: Heinemann.

Campione, J., A. Shapiro, and A. Brown. 1995. "Forms of Transfer in a Community of Learners: Flexible Learning and Understanding." In *Teaching for Transfer: Fostering Generalization in Learning*, ed. A. McKeough, J. Lupart, and A. Marini. Hillsdale, NJ: Lawrence Erlbaum.

Carle, E. 1990. *The Very Quiet Cricket*. New York: Philomel.

Castor, Debra. 2009. *Habitats Around the World*. Pelham, NY: Benchmark Education.

Center for Labor Market Studies. 2009. *Left Behind: The Nation's Dropout Crisis*. Boston: Department of Economics of Northeastern University. http://www.northeastern.edu/clms/wp-content/uploads/CLMS_2009_Dropout_Report.pdf.

Clay, Marie. 1975. *What Did I Write?* Portsmouth, NH: Heinemann.

———. 1991. *Becoming Literate: The Construction of Inner Control*. Portsmouth, NH: Heinemann.

———. 2000. *Running Records for Classroom Teachers*. Portsmouth, NH: Heinemann.

———. 2001. *Change Over Time in Children's Literacy Development*. Portsmouth, NH: Heinemann.

———. 2006. *An Observation Survey of Early Literacy Achievement*. 2nd ed. Portsmouth, NH: Heinemann.

Clay, M., and C. Cazden. 1990. "A Vygotskian Interpretation of Reading Recovery." In *Vygotsky and Education: Instructional Implications and Applications of Sociohistorical Psychology*, ed. L. Moll. Cambridge, UK: Cambridge University Press.

Collins, A., J. Brown, and S. Newman. 1989. "Cognitive Apprenticeship: Teaching the Crafts of Reading, Writing, and Mathematics." In *Knowing, Learning, and Instruction: Essays in Honor of Robert Glaser*, ed. L. Resnick. Hillsdale, NJ: Lawrence Erlbaum.

Cowley, J. 1990. *Nighttime*. Bothell, WA: Wright Group.

———. 1996. *The Seed*. Bothell, WA: Wright Group.

Cunningham, P. 1996. *Phonics They Use*. New York: HarperCollins.

Cutting, J. 1988. *I Like . . . .* Bothell, WA: Wright Group.

Darling-Hammond, L. and M. W. McLaughlin. 1999. "Investing in Teaching as a Learning Profession: Policy Problems and Prospects." In *Teaching as the Learning Profession: Handbook of Policy and Practice*, ed. L. Darling-Hammond and G. Sykes. San Francisco: Jossey-Bass.

Dewey, J. 1935. *Liberalism and Social Action*. New York: Putnam.

———. 2010. *How We Think*. Boston: D. C. Heath.

Diaz, R., C. Neal, and M. Amaya-Williams. 1990. "The Social Origins of Self-Regulation." In *Vygotsky and Education: Instructional Implications and Applications of Sociohistorical Psychology*, ed. L. Moll. Cambridge, UK: Cambridge University Press.

Donaldson, M. 1978. *Children's Minds*. New York: W. W. Norton.

Dorn, L. 1996. "A Vygotskian Perspective on Literacy Acquisition: Talk and Action in the Child's Construction of Literate Awareness." *Literacy, Teaching, and Learning: An International Journal of Early Literacy* 2 (2): 15–40.

Dorn, L. J., C. French, and T. Jones. 1998. *Apprenticeship in Literacy: Transitions Across Reading and Writing*. 1st ed. Portland, ME: Stenhouse.

Dorn, L. J., and S. C. Henderson. 2010. "A Comprehensive Intervention Model: A Systems Approach to Response to Intervention." In *Successful Approaches to RTI: Collaborative Practices for Improving K–12 Literacy*, ed. M. J. Lipson and K. K. Wixson. Newark, DE: International Reading Association.

Dorn, L. J., and B. Schubert. 2008. "A Comprehensive Intervention for Preventing Reading Failure: A Response to Intervention Process." *The Journal of Reading Recovery* 7 (2): 29–41.

Dorn, L., and C. Soffos. 2001a. *Scaffolding Young Writers: A Writers' Workshop Approach*. Portland, ME: Stenhouse.

———. 2001b. *Shaping Literate Minds: Developing Self-Regulated Learners*. Portland, ME: Stenhouse.

———. 2005. *Teaching for Deep Comprehension: A Reading Workshop Approach*. York, ME: Stenhouse.

———. 2011a. *Interventions That Work: A Comprehensive Intervention Model for Preventing Reading Failure in Grades K–3*. Boston: Allyn and Bacon.

———. 2011b. *Interventions That Work: Assisted Writing Group.* DVD. Boston: Allyn and Bacon.

Dweck, C. 2000. *Self-theories: Their Role in Motivation, Personality, and Development.* Philadelphia: Psychology Press.

———. 2006. *Mindset.* New York: Random House.

Eisner, E. 2002. *The Kind of Schools We Need.* Portsmouth, NH: Heinemann.

Ferrell, T. S. 2004. *Reflective Practice in Action.* Thousand Oaks, CA: Corwin.

Fountas, I., and G. S. Pinnell. 1996. *Guided Reading: Good First Teaching for All Children.* Portsmouth, NH: Heinemann.

———. 2001. *Guiding Readers and Writers (Grades 3–6): Teaching Comprehension, Genre, and Content Literacy.* Portsmouth, NH: Heinemann.

Gentry, R., and J. W. Gillet. 1993. *Teaching Kids to Spell.* Portsmouth, NH: Heinemann.

Gersten, R., Fuchs, L. S., Williams, J. P., and Baker, S. 2001. "Teaching Reading Comprehension Strategies to Students with Learning Disabilities: A Review of Research." *Review of Educational Research* 71:279–320.

Gunning, T. 2001. *Building Words: A Resource Manual for Teaching Word Analysis and Spelling Strategies.* Boston, MA: Allyn and Bacon.

Hargreaves, A. 1995. "Development and Desire: A Postmodern Perspective." In *Professional Development in Education: New Paradigms & Practices,* ed. T. Guskey and M. Huberman. New York: Teachers College Press.

Healy, J. M. 1990. *Endangered Minds: Why Children Don't Think and What We Can Do About It.* New York: Touchstone.

Heenman, J. 1985. *Product and Process.* Auckland, New Zealand: Longman Paul.

Henderson, S. H., and L. J. Dorn. 2011. "Supporting Students Who Struggle with Comprehension of Text During Literature Discussion Groups in Grades 3–6." In *After Early Intervention, Then What? Teaching Struggling Readers in Grades 3 and Beyond,* ed. R. L. McCormack and J. R. Paratore. Newark, DE: International Reading Association.

Hernandez, D. J. 2011. *Double Jeopardy; How Third Grade Reading Skills and Poverty Influence High School Graduation.* Annie Casey Foundation. http://fcd-us.org/sites/default/files/DoubleJeopardy Report.pdf.

Holdaway, D. 1979. *Foundations of Literacy.* Sydney: Ashton Scholastic.

Holman, L. 2010. "The Effects of an Intervention Coach on the Implementation of Writing Workshop in a First Grade Classroom." Educational specialist thesis, University of Arkansas at Little Rock.

Holmelund, E. 1959. "Little Bear and Owl." In *Father Bear Comes Home.* New York: HarperCollins.

Humphrey, A. 1997. "Effects of an Early Literacy Group on the Writing Development of At-Risk First Graders." Educational specialist thesis, University of Arkansas at Little Rock.

Hutchins, P. 1971. *Rosie's Walk.* New York: Aladdin.

———. 1986. *The Doorbell Rang.* New York: Scholastic.

Johnston, P. 1992. *Constructive Evaluation of Literate Activity.* White Plains, NY: Longman.

———. 2004. *Choice Words.* Portland, ME: Stenhouse.

———. 2012. *Opening Minds.* Portland, ME: Stenhouse.

Juel, C. 1988. "Learning to Read and Write: A Longitudinal Study of Fifty-Four Children from First Through Fourth Grade." *Journal of Educational Psychology* 80: 437–447.

Karpov, Y. V. 2003. "Development Through the Lifespan: A Neo-Vygotskian Approach." In *Vygotsky's Educational Theory in Cultural Context,* ed. A. Kozulin, B. Gindis, V. S. Ageyev, and S. M. Miller. New York: Cambridge University Press.

Kimbrell, J. 2009. "A Study of the Model of Mastery as a Theoretical Framework for Coaching Teachers' Writing." Educational specialist's thesis, University of Arkansas at Little Rock.

Lesnick, J., R. M. Goerge, C. Smithgall, and J. Gwynne. 2010. *Reading on Grade Level in Third Grade: How Is It Related to High School Performance and College Enrollment?* http://www.chapinhall.org/research/report/reading-grade-level-third-grade-how-it-related-high-school-performance-and-college-e.

Lobel, A. 1970. *Frog and Toad Are Friends.* New York: Harper & Row.

Loughran, J.J. 2002. "Effective Reflective Practice: In Search of Meaning in Learning About Teaching." *Journal of Teacher Education* 53 (1): 33–43.

Lupart, J. 1996. "Exceptional Learners and Teaching for Transfer." In *Teaching for Transfer: Fostering Generalization in Learning,* ed. A. McKeough, J. Lupart, and A. Marini. Hillsdale, NJ: Lawrence Erlbaum.

Luria, A. R. 1973. *The Working Brain: An Introduction to Neuropsychology.* New York: HarperCollins.

———. 1982. *Language and Cognition.* New York: Wiley.

McCormick, S. 1977. "Should You Read Aloud to Your Children?" *Language Arts* 54: 139–143.

McNamara, D. 1990. "Research on Teachers' Thinking: Its Contribution to Educating Student Teachers to Think Critically." *Journal of Education for Teaching* 16 (2): 147–160.

McNamara, M. 2009. *The Life Cycle of a Butterfly.* Pelham, NY: Benchmark Education.

Meichenbaum, D., and A. Biemiller. 1998. *Nurturing Independent Learners: Helping Students Take Charge of their Learning.* Cambridge, MA: Brookline Books.

Melser, J. 1990. *The Chocolate Cake.* Bothell, WA: Wright Group.

Mertler, C. 2006. *Action Research.* Thousand Oaks, CA: Sage.

National Governors Association for Best Practices (NGA Center) and Council of Chief State School Officers (CCSSO). 2010. Common Core State Standards for English Language Arts and Literacy in History/Social Studies, Science, and Technical Subjects. Washington, DC: NGA Center and CCSSO.

National Research Council. 1998. *Preventing Reading Difficulties in Young Children,* ed. C. Snow, S. Burns, and P. Griffin. Committee on the Prevention of Reading Difficulties in Young Children. Washington, DC: National Academy Press.

Palincsar, A. S. 1986. "The Role of Dialogue in Providing Scaffolded Instruction." *Educational Psychologist* 21: 73–98.

Paris, S., M. Y. Lipson, and K. Wixson. 1994. "Becoming a Strategic Reader." In *Theoretical Models and Processes of Reading, 4th ed.,* ed. R. D. Ruddell, M. R. Ruddell, and H. Singer. Newark, DE: International Reading Association.

Parkes, B. 1989. *Goodnight, Goodnight.* Crystal Lake, IL: Rigby.

———. 1997. *At the Beach.* New York: Newbridge Discovery Links.

———. 2009. *The Great Enormous Watermelon.* Pelham, NY: Benchmark Education.

Phillips, G., and P. Smith. 1997. *A Third Chance to Learn*. Wellington: New Zealand Council for Educational Research.

Pinnell, G. S., and A. McCarrier. 1994. "Interactive Writing: A Transition Tool for Assisting Children in Learning to Read and Write." In *Getting Reading Right from the Start: Effective Early Literacy Interventions,* ed. B. E. Hiebert and B. Taylor. Needham Heights, MA: Allyn and Bacon.

Potter, B. 2002. *The Tale of Peter Rabbit*. London: Penguin.

Presley, D. 2007. "Study of the Influence of Contextual Conditions on the Development of Self-Reflective Teachers." Educational specialist thesis, University of Arkansas at Little Rock.

Randell, B. 1996a. *Late for Soccer*. Crystal Lake, IL: Rigby.

———. 1996b. *Tabby in the Tree*. Crystal Lake, IL: Rigby.

Robart, R. 1986. *The Cake That Mack Ate*. Boston: Little, Brown.

Rogoff, B. 1990. *Apprenticeship in Thinking: Cognitive Development in Social Contexts*. New York: Oxford University Press.

Short, D., and Fitzsimmons, S. 2007. *Double the Work: Challenges and Solutions to Acquiring Language and Academic Literacy for Adolescent English Language Learners*. A report to Carnegie Corporation of New York. Washington, DC: Alliance for Excellent Education.

Smith, F. 1994. *Understanding Reading*. Hillsdale, NJ: Lawrence Erlbaum.

Snow, C., W. Barnes, J. Chandler, I. Goodman, and L. Hemphill. 1991. *Unfilled Expectations: Home and School Influences on Literacy*. Cambridge, MA: Harvard University Press.

Snow, C. E., M. S. Burns, and P. Griffin, eds. 1998. *Preventing Reading Difficulties in Young Children*. Washington, DC. National Academy Press.

Sylwester, R. 1995. *A Celebration of Neurons: An Educator's Guide to the Human Brain*. Alexandria, VA: Association for Supervision and Curriculum Development.

Teale, W. H. 1984. "Reading to Young Children: Its Significance for Literacy Development." In *Awakening to Literacy*, ed. H. Goelman, A. Oberg, and F. Smith. Portsmouth, NH: Heinemann.

———. 2003. "Reading Aloud to Young Children as a Classroom Instructional Activity: Insights from Research and Practice." In *On Reading Books to Children; Parents and Teachers*, ed. S. A. Stahl, A. Van Kleeck, and E. B. Bauer. Mahwah, NJ: Erlbaum.

Tharp, R., and R. Gallimore. 1988. *Rousing Minds to Life: Teaching, Learning, and School in Social Context*. Cambridge, UK: Cambridge University Press.

Titherington, J. 1986. *Pumpkin, Pumpkin*. New York: Greenwillow.

Vygotsky, L. 1978. *Mind in Society*. Cambridge, MA: Harvard University Press.

Wadsworth, R., and L. Laminack. 2006. *Reading Aloud Across the Curriculum: How to Build Bridges in Language Arts, Math, Science, and Social Studies*. Portsmouth, NH: Heinemann.

Waterland, L. 1985. *Read with Me: An Apprenticeship Approach to Reading*. Stroud, UK: Thimble Press.

Wells, G., and G. Chang-Wells. 1992. *Constructing Knowledge Together*. Portsmouth, NH: Heinemann.

Wertsch, J. V. 1984. "The Zone of Proximal Development: Some Conceptual Issues." In *Children's Learning in the Zone of Proximal Development*, ed. B. Rogoff and J. V. Wertsch. San Francisco: Jossey-Bass.

———. 1985. *Culture, Communication, and Cognition: Vygotskian Perspectives.* Cambridge, UK: Cambridge University Press.

Wiggins, G. and J. McTighe. 2005. *Understanding by Design.* 2nd ed. Alexandria, VA: Association for Supervision and Curriculum.

Williams, R. L. 1994. *Where Do Monsters Live?* Cypress, CA: Celebration Teaching Press.

Williams, S. 1989. *I Went Walking.* New York: Harcourt Brace.

Wood, D. 1980. "Teaching the Young Child: Some Relationships Between Social Interaction, Language, and Thought." In *The Social Foundations of Language and Thought,* ed. D. Olson. New York: W. W. Norton.

———. 1988. *How Children Think and Learn.* Cambridge, UK: Basil Blackwell.

———. 2002. "The Why? What? When? And How? of Tutoring: The Development of Helping and Tutoring Skills in Children." *Literacy, Teaching, and Learning* 7 (1, 2): 2–30.

Wood, D., J. Bruner, and G. Ross. 1976. "The Role of Tutoring in Problem Solving." *Journal of Child Psychology and Psychiatry* 17 (2): 89–100.

Wylie, R. E., and D. D. Durrell. 1970. "Teaching Vowels Through Phonographs." *Elementary English* 47: 787–791.

York-Barr, J., W. A. Sommers, G. S. Ghere, and J. Montie. 2006. *Reflective Practice to Improve Schools: An Action Guide for Educators.* 2nd ed. Thousand Oaks, CA: Corwin Press.

Zull, J. 2002. *The Art of Changing the Brain.* Sterling, VA: Stylus.

———. 2011. *From Brain to Mind: Using Neuroscience to Guide Change in Education.* Sterling, VA: Stylus.

INDEX

Page numbers followed by an *f* indicate figures.